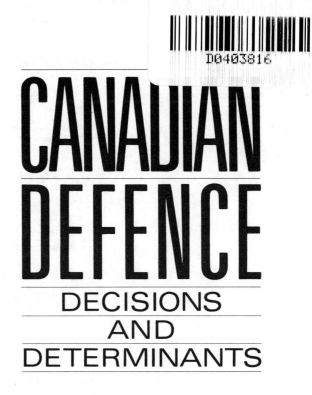

CANADIAN DEFENCE

DECISIONS
AND
DETERMINANTS

D0403816

CANADIAN

DEFENCE

DECISIONS
AND
DETERMINANTS

D. W. Middlemiss
Dalhousie University
J. J. Sokolsky
Royal Military College

Harcourt Brace Jovanovich, Canada
Toronto Orlando San Diego London Sydney

Copyright © 1989 by Harcourt Brace Jovanovich Canada Inc., 55 Horner Avenue, Toronto, Ontario M8Z 4X6

All rights reserved. No part of this publication may be reproduced or transmitted in any form or by any means, electronic or mechanical, including photocopy, recording, or any information storage and retrieval system, without permission in writing from the publisher.

Requests for permission to make copies of any part of the work should be addressed to Permissions, College Division, Harcourt Brace Jovanovich, Canada, 55 Horner Avenue, Toronto, Ontario M8Z 4X6

Canadian Cataloguing in Publication Data

Middlemiss, Danford William, 1945–
    Canadian defence : decisions and determinants

Bibliography: p.
Includes index.
ISBN 0–7747–3085–4

1. Canada – Military policy.   I. Sokolsky, Joel J., 1953– .   II. Title.

UA600.M53 1989   355'.0335'71   C88–094375–0

Publisher: David Dimmell
Acquisitions Editor: Heather McWhinney
Developmental Editor: Sandra Peltier
Publishing Services Manager: Karen Eakin
Production Editor: John Caldarone
Copy Editor: Darlene Zeleney
Typesetting: True to Type, Inc.
Interior Design: Peter Maher
Cover Design: Michael Landgraff
Printing and Binding: Webcom Limited

Printed and bound in Canada
1 2 3 4 5 93 92 91 90 89

To Bob and Crystal Middlemiss
and in memory of
Rose and Leonard Sokolsky

CONTENTS

PREFACE

The purpose of this book is to describe contemporary Canadian defence policy to students of external relations and to the wider public. The book examines and explains defence decisions in the context of various domestic and international constraints. Its central argument is that, contrary to what is usually assumed by the average Canadian and by many specialists, Canada does have a significant degree of autonomy—within the bounds faced by all states in the nuclear age—in the making of its defence policy. Whether one agrees or disagrees with the manner in which Canada has exercised that autonomy, the starting point of any informed discussion must be the recognition that our defence policy is the result of choices made by the government of Canada. To argue that Canada has choices is not to say that the decisions are obvious or easy. Sometimes they are, but most often they involve difficult trade-offs and adjustments to the realities of domestic and international constraints. To deny that choices were and are available is to doubt Canada's standing as a sovereign and independent country—a doubt that is not justified in light of the present international environment.

This book is not only the result of a co-operative effort between the two authors, but also owes much to the contributions of several other individuals and institutions. Many thanks go to Marilyn Langille, Eileen LeVine, and Paulette Chiasson of Dalhousie University, who helped in the preparation of several drafts of the manuscript. The Department of Political and Economic Science and the Art Division of the Royal Military College gave encouragement and support. We also appreciate the continuing support of the Department of National Defence through its Military and Strategic Studies Program. Paul Buteux and David Haglund also offered valuable comments and suggestions for improvement. We are especially indebted to Sharon Hobson and Brig. Gen. (Ret'd) George G. Bell for their meticulous reviews of the manuscript.

For all this invaluable assistance, we are truly grateful. For any remaining errors, omissions, or unsound analyses, we alone are responsible.

List of Abbreviations

AAW	anti-air warfare
ABC countries	United States, Britain, and Canada
ABM	antiballistic missile
ADI	Air Defense Initiative
ADM (Fin)	assistant deputy minister (finance)
ADM (Mat)	assistant deputy minister (matériel)
ADM (Per)	assistant deputy minister (personnel)
ADM (Pol)	assistant deputy minister (policy)
ADMP	Air Defence Master Plan
AIRCOM	Air Command
ALCM	air-launched cruise missile
AMF (L)	Allied Mobile Force (Land)
ASW	antisubmarine warfare
AWAC	airborne warning and control
BMD	ballistic missile defence
BMEWS	Ballistic Missile Early Warning System
C³I	command, control, communications and intelligence
CAST	Canadian Air-Sea Transportable
CDA	Conference of Defence Associations
CDI	Conventional Defence Improvements
CDS	chief of the defence staff
CF	Canadian Forces
CFB	Canadian Forces Base
CFE	Canadian Forces Europe
CINCHAN	Commander-in-Chief, Channel
CINCNORAD	Commander-in-Chief, NORAD
CPF	Canadian Patrol Frigate
CUSRPG	Canada-United States Regional Planning Group
DAD	deterrence, arms control, and disarmament
DCDS	deputy chief of the defence staff
DCINCNORAD	Deputy Commander-in-Chief, NORAD
DEA	Department of External Affairs
DEW	Distant Early Warning
DM	deputy minister
DMC	Defence Management Committee
DND	Department of National Defence
DOB	dispersed operating base
DoD	Department of Defence (U.S.)
DPFD	defence planning and force development

DPMS	Defence Program Management System
DPSA	defence production sharing arrangements
DSP	Defence Services Program
DSR	Defence Structure Review
EEC	European Economic Community
FLQ	Front de Libération du Québec
FOFA	follow-on forces attack
FOL	forward operating location
GDP	gross domestic product
GLCM	ground-launched cruise missile
GNP	gross national product
ICBM	intercontinental ballistic missile
INF	intermediate-range nuclear forces
JUSCADS	Joint United States-Canada Air-Defence Study
LRPA	long-range patrol aircraft
MAD	mutual assured destruction
MARCOM	Maritime Command
MBFR	mutual and balanced force reductions
MCC	Military Co-operation Committee
MFO	Multinational Force and Observers
MIRV	multiple independently targeted re-entry vehicle
MND	minister of national defence
MOBCOM	Mobile Command
NATO	North Atlantic Treaty Organization
NDHQ	National Defence Headquarters
NDP	New Democratic Party
NFA	new fighter aircraft
NORAD	North American Aerospace Defence Command
NWS	North Warning System
OTH-B	over-the-horizon backscatter radar
PEMS	Policy and Expenditure Management System
PGT	Planning Guidance Team
PJBD	Permanent Joint Board on Defence
POM	personnel, operations, and maintenance
PMO	Prime Minister's Office
RCAF	Royal Canadian Air Force
RCN	Royal Canadian Navy
ROCC	Region Operations Control Centre
SACEUR	Supreme Allied Commander, Europe
SACLANT	Supreme Allied Commander, Atlantic
SALT	Strategic Arms Limitation Talks

SCEAND	Standing Committee on External Affairs and National Defence
SCOND	Standing Committee on National Defence
SDA 2000	Strategic Defence Architecture 2000
SDI	Strategic Defense Initiative
SDIO	Strategic Defence Initiative Organization
SLBM	submarine-launched ballistic missile
SLCM	sea-/submarine-launched cruise missile
SLOC	sea lines of communication
SRP	ship-replacement program
SSBN	ballistic missile-firing nuclear-powered submarine
SSN	nuclear-powered attack submarine
SSW	surface-to-surface warfare
START	Strategic Arms Reduction Talks
UN	United Nations
USAF	United States Air Force
USSPACECOM	United States Space Command
VCDS	vice chief of the defence staff

1

INTRODUCTION:
APPROACHES TO THE
STUDY OF CANADIAN
DEFENCE POLICY

Many Canadians greet the assertion that their country has a defence policy with surprise and sometimes even scepticism. This reaction may be attributed, in part, to the perception of Canada as an unmilitary nation. It also reflects a general attitude that, because of the relatively small size of the Canadian Forces (CF)[1] and the proximity of the United States, the Canadian military does not really matter very much in the broader scheme of things; that, in any case, serious defence policy and, therefore, major decisions are matters best left to the larger players on the international stage.

Of course, this attitude is not shared by all, but even among the attentive public, Canadian defence policy decision making tends to be regarded almost exclusively as an exercise in adjusting to prior United States and North Atlantic Treaty Organization (NATO) decisions. In short, Canada is usually viewed as being highly constrained by external factors in making its defence policy. From this perspective, the preservation of some degree of independence of action, either inside or outside Canada's traditional military alignments, is seen as the dominant concern of Canadian defence policy. Much of the existing literature on the subject takes this condition of dependence as a given, and is replete with suggestions for redressing it.

There can be little doubt of the importance of external factors in Canadian defence policy making. Along with other non-superpowers, Canada exercises only limited influence in shaping the international security environment and must react and adjust to the world as it finds it in pursuing its own national security interests. But an excessive concentration on the external factors has lent an overly deterministic cast to some analyses of Canadian defence policy. Such discussions tend to imply that Canadian decision makers have few real choices when it comes to fashioning the country's defence policy and force posture (the current structure and capabilities of the military establishment). This approach is too simplistic and reflects a limited understanding of the way defence policy is actually made. It fails to acknowledge that while Canada, like most other countries, must make defence policy with due regard for the international environment, it is nonetheless confronted with an array of complex and difficult choices in deciding exactly how that adjustment should and can take place. In the absence of such an appreciation, Canadian defence policy making remains a largely neglected and misunderstood area of study.

It is important to note a further obstacle to the thorough understanding of defence policy decision making: perhaps more than in any other public policy field, national security calls for a degree of secrecy that hinders access to documents and to the decision makers themselves.[2] This poses a significant difficulty for the serious student or researcher. It is, however, still more significant that, as we suggested earlier, few academic (or other) writers have considered it worthwhile to address the decision-making dimension of Canadian defence policy.

One reason for this relative neglect can be found in the status of Canadian defence studies within the university community. Traditionally, academics have treated Canadian defence policy as an offshoot or a subsidiary element of Canadian foreign policy. The following passage from an article by Denis Stairs is representative of the standard view of how defence policy is made:

> Whatever their peripheral functions . . . the primary purpose of armed forces is to act, whether in the context of defence against external menace, the waging of acquisitive aggression, the pursuit of peacekeeping operations, or the general conduct of diplomacy, as an instrument of foreign policy. It follows that foreign policy decisions are prior decisions, and their relation to military decisions is as the relation between ends and means.[3]

This orientation is understandable in that it emerges from the intellectual concerns and expertise of people engaged primarily in the study of Canada's external relations; and, after all, "Canadian Foreign Policy" is in itself a subfield of international politics and a relative newcomer to most university curricula. In addition, repeated assertions by successive administrations in Ottawa to the effect that defence policy is the logical extension of Canadian foreign policy[4] have further reinforced the subordinate status of Canadian defence policy studies. Finally, it is worth noting that the academic community concerned with Canada's foreign and defence policies is a small and thinly spread one, both in Canada and abroad. This is especially true of the field of political science, where one might expect the greatest interest to be concentrated.[5]

Notwithstanding these factors inhibiting the study of Canadian defence policy, there is a small body of literature dealing with this subject. The literature can be divided into two main categories, historical and prescriptive. Scholars such as C.P. Stacey, Desmond Morton, and James Eayrs have written lengthy and detailed histories of Canadian defence policy. While invaluable as historical background, these studies do not serve well as textbooks on the defence policy decision-making process itself.[6]

Prescriptive works include somewhat journalistic and polemical treatments as well as more scholarly analyses.[7] These works do not accept the notion that Canada has little room to manoeuvre in the area of defence policy and call for changes ranging from a total withdrawal from NATO or the North American Aerospace Defence Command (NORAD) or both, to proposals for various restructurings of the armed forces' posture to enable Canada to better contribute to its alliances. These works are not intended to serve as basic texts covering the main elements of Canadian defence policy making. Moreover, because they adopt an approach that emphasizes preferred policy outcomes, they tend not to deal with the actual conditions and processes in which defence policy is formulated and implemented. This tendency is unfortunate, for in the Canadian context, process often plays a significant role in determining substance.

Despite the dearth of works on the Canadian defence policy-making process, there is still much we do know. A great deal of the information, however, is scattered, narrow in scope and approach, uneven in quality, and dated. What is required now—and what we propose to do in this book—

is to synthesize, update, and build upon this body of knowledge. We shall identify the general patterns that characterize the making of Canadian defence policy, then analyze the factors that give substance and meaning to the observed regularities of policy-making behaviour. Using such an approach, we hope to enhance the reader's understanding not only of the historical evolution of Canadian defence policy but also of the conditions and processes involved in major Canadian defence decisions.

Our task is made somewhat easier by the fact that there is much that is observable about Canadian defence policy-making behaviour. Decisions are regularly taken about the levels and allocations of defence budgets, weapons procurement programs, and the deployment and use of Canada's military forces. Furthermore, in comparison with that of other states, Canada's defence policy making involves fewer players and is more centralized and, perhaps, more bureaucratized.

It is not our intention to be comprehensive in our coverage of issues nor overly rigorous in the explication of arcane theory. Rather, our goal is to focus on the policy-making nexus of Canadian defence and to bring the various strands of existing research and insight to bear upon this often ignored subject. We employ an approach that we believe makes this undertaking manageable within the confines of a single volume and comprehensible to specialists and general readers alike.

There are many different approaches to the study of policy making. Some overlap and some present conflicting interpretations of the available data. The task of description and explanation is inherently selective; thus, "where one finishes in any analysis of a given political phenomenon depends in large part on where one starts".[8] Mindful of the wisdom of this proposition, we have tried to be explicit about those concepts, assumptions, and questions that together constitute the guiding perspective of this volume.

Policy is essentially concerned with the making of choices. These choices are shaped and constrained by many factors, including: (1) the interests, motivations, and preferences of various *actors* (individuals, organizations, and institutions); (2) the nature and interplay of the *processes* by which decisions are formulated and implemented; (3) the character of the *environments* in which these actors and processes operate. Taken together, these factors determine the policy outcomes that are of interest to Canadians.

Policy outcomes can involve non-decisions, that is, decisions to do nothing. This concept is important, for what often passes as a policy vacuum in the Canadian context—for example, the failure to produce a promised review of Canadian defence policy—may be the result of a conscious decision to take no action. Options may have been examined and proposals suggested at the bureaucratic level, but decisions may have been deferred or rejected at the higher political level of government because of their political, military, or economic ramifications. Inaction, therefore, is not necessarily synonymous with the absence of decision.

Decisions are taken on a great number of different issues. The sheer volume and variety of decision making, together with the complex interaction of actors, processes, and environments, suggests that defence policy making in Canada is not a homogeneous process lending itself to simple definition. Neither the Canadian government nor the Department of National Defence (DND) is a monolithic actor following a standard set of decision-making procedures and routines. There is much to be learned by penetrating the veil of traditional "black-box" explanations of Canadian defence policy.

The central argument of this book is that Canadian defence policy makers have considerable latitude in making decisions. Canada has confronted and made several landmark decisions—and a host of lesser ones—on matters of defence. This has certainly been the case in the post-1968 period, with the policy choices evident in the Trudeau defence and foreign policy reviews of the late 1960s and early 1970s, the major weapons-procurement decisions of the mid-to-late 1970s, and the Mulroney government's more recent decisions regarding NATO and NORAD.

This book looks at the choices made, and examines the influence of the governmental and domestic environments, as well as of the external environment, on Canadian defence policy making. It identifies and analyzes the various factors operating in these environments and explores the interrelationships among them. Its focus is on the actual problems and choices facing Canadian policy makers in the period from 1968 to the present. Our main purpose is to describe and explain Canadian defence policy rather than to speculate on what it might or ought to have been. In essence, this book explores the perennial "who, what, when, how, and why" questions of contemporary defence policy making in Canada.

The book begins with an overview of the major developments in post–World War II Canadian defence policy (Chapter 2), and pays particular attention to the decisions of the Trudeau and Mulroney governments (Chapter 3). Chapters 4, 5, and 6 examine in a general way each of the main environments—governmental, domestic, and external—that collectively make up the decision-making "landscape" of Canadian defence policy. Individually, these chapters are intended to identify the key decision makers, organizations, and processes that operate in each milieu.

Three particular cases, selected both for their topical interest and their continuing relevance to some perennial themes and issues of Canadian defence, are analyzed in some detail in Chapter 7. This chapter demonstrates the influence of particular environmental factors on specific policy options and decisions. The book concludes, in Chapter 8, with some observations on the general patterns of Canadian defence policy making and the ways in which those patterns are shaped and defined by various factors operating in and across the three environments. These factors ultimately determine the possiblities and limits of Canadian defence policy making.

Notes

1. The official name of the armed forces in Canada is the Canadian Forces (CF). Although the name Canadian Armed Forces is also commonly used, we have restricted ourselves to the use of the official name throughout this book.

2. Professor James Eayrs' account of his frustrations in this regard is instructive; see his *In Defence of Canada*, vol. 3, *Peacemaking and Deterrence* (Toronto: University of Toronto Press, 1972), pp. ix–x.

3. Denis Stairs, "The Military as an Instrument of Canadian Foreign Policy," in *The Canadian Military: A Profile*, ed. Hector J. Massey (Toronto: Copp Clark, 1972), p. 86.

4. The quintessential statement of this relationship was made by former Prime Minister Pierre Trudeau, who said, "It is a false perspective to have a military alliance determine your foreign policy. It should be your foreign policy which determines your military policy." See "The Relation of Defence Policy to Foreign Policy," *Statements and Speeches*, no. 69/8, 12 April 1969. Official statements in a similar vein can be found in the following: Canada, Department of National Defence, *Defence in the 70s, White Paper on Defence* (Ottawa: Information Canada, 1971), p. 3; *White Paper on Defence* (Ottawa: Queen's Printer, 1964), p. 5; and *Defence 1959*, White Paper on Defence (Ottawa: Queen's Printer, 1959), p. 5.

5. Joseph T. Jockel, "Defence Objectives, Commitment, and Organization" (Paper presented to the conference on the Canadian Military: Directions for Future Research, York University, Downsview, Ont., 20–21 November 1982).

6. Some of the standard historical works on Canadian defence policy include: James Eayrs, *In Defence of Canada*, 5 vols. (Toronto: University of Toronto Press, 1964–83); J.L. Granatstein, *Canada's War: The Politics of the Mackenzie King Government, 1939–1945* (Toronto: Oxford University Press, 1975); Jon B. McLin, *Canada's Changing Defense Policy, 1957–1963* (Baltimore: Johns Hopkins Press, 1967); Desmond Morton, *A Military History of Canada* (Edmonton: Hurtig Publishers, 1985); C.P. Stacey, *Arms, Men and Governments: The War Policies of Canada, 1939–1945* (Ottawa: The Queen's Printer, 1970); and George F. Stanley, *Canada's Soldiers: The Military History of an Unmilitary People*, rev. ed. (Toronto: Macmillan of Canada, 1960).

7. Examples of prescriptive treatments with a polemical flair include: Andrew Brewin, *Stand on Guard: The Search for a Canadian Defence Policy* (Toronto: McClelland and Stewart, 1965); Lewis Hertzman, John Warnock, and Thomas Hockin, *Alliances and Illusions: Canada and the NATO–NORAD Question* (Edmonton: M.G. Hurtig Ltd., Publishers, 1969); Peter C. Newman, *True North* Not *Strong and Free* (Toronto: McClelland and Stewart, 1983); Gerald Porter, *In Retreat: The Canadian Forces in the Trudeau Years* (n.p.: Deneau & Greenberg, n.d.); and John W. Warnock, *Partner to Behemoth: The Military Policy of a Satellite Canada* (Toronto: New Press, 1970).

  Other works with a decidedly scholarly cast include: Brian Cuthbertson, *Canadian Military Independence in the Age of the Superpowers* (Toronto: Fitzhenry & Whiteside, 1977); Colin S. Gray, *Canadian Defence Priorities: A Question of Relevance* (Toronto: Clarke, Irwin, 1972); Hector J. Massey, *The Canadian Military: A Profile* (Toronto: Copp Clark, 1972); and Joseph T. Jockel and Joel J. Sokolsky, *Canada and Collective Security: Odd Man Out*, The Washington Papers, no. 121 (New York: Praeger, 1986).

8. Denis Stairs, *The Diplomacy of Constraint: Canada, the Korean War, and the United States* (Toronto: University of Toronto Press, 1974), p. 299.

2

THE EVOLUTION OF CANADIAN DEFENCE POLICY FROM CONFEDERATION TO THE COLD WAR

Introduction

The major theme of this book is that Canadian defence policy, far from being simply the reflex action of a small and weak power caught in the vortex of international relations, has represented the deliberate policy choices of a sovereign and independent government. To a certain extent, the tendency to view Canadian defence policy as unimportant in either a national or international context is the result of one major feature of that policy since Confederation in 1867—that Canada has chosen to seek national security in alliance with more powerful nations. It has formed such alliances not only with stronger countries but with the most powerful nations of the past century, the British Empire and later the United States of America. Through these alliances, Canada found itself caught up in the great global struggles of the 19th and 20th centuries: its armed forces were postured to participate in these global efforts rather than to provide solely for security along its own borders and in its ocean approaches.

Given this characteristic, it is not surprising that Canadian defence policy strikes many as having no independent history worthy of study. In fact, however, decisions about the nature and extent of Canadian involvement in its alliances have been made at every stage. Sometimes Ottawa elected to limit or curtail its expenditure of resources on defence. At other times exigencies of war demanded a maximum effort, while the armed peace of the early Cold War years brought forth an expenditure on defence approaching eight percent of gross national product. The decline in the level of national resources devoted to defence since the late 1960s, while lamented by some, still represents the deliberate policy decisions of governments that have had to balance the need for armed forces against a host of competing social and economic demands. To be sure, the nature of the international political and strategic environment has greatly influenced the formulation of Canadian defence policy, but, within that broader context, there has been scope for choice.

From Alliance to Alliance: Canadian Defence Policy, 1867–1945

When Canada became a dominion of the British Empire in 1867, its international status was ambiguous. On the one hand, it had been granted nearly full internal sovereignty. On the other, in matters of foreign and defence policy, London had the final say. In subsequent years, the new country gradually developed the competence and won the right to act abroad on its own, eventually even in matters of defence. By the time the British government enacted the Statute of Westminster in 1931, conferring full sovereignty on all the dominions, Canada had achieved a distinct international character and a nationally directed foreign policy. For the most part, Canada's external relations at that time were concerned with trade as Ottawa sought to develop a solid economic base.

On strategic matters, there was an automatic alliance with Britain as part of the empire until 1931. Until the end of World War I, if the British Empire were at war, Canada would be at war. Afterwards, Canada exercised some discretion as to the degree of its involvement, if any.

In the early years of Confederation, the main direct threat to Canadian security was seen as coming from the United States. To meet this threat, Canada elected not to rely on its own resources. It devoted little to maintaining armed forces of any kind beyond a small and poorly equipped militia. Instead, like other smaller powers, Canada sought to ally itself with a larger power to protect it from an immediate threat. Continued allegiance to the British Empire, and the concomitant support of the Royal Navy, seemed to provide all the deterrence the young country needed.

Although it relied on the British connection for security in North America, Canada was aware that any Anglo–American confrontation over issues not directly related to Canada could make it hostage to, or even a target of, American actions. Thus, Ottawa largely supported the growing Anglo–American entente of the late 19th and early 20th centuries. This entente, more than British military power, was the foundation of Canadian security. It allowed Canada to spend comparatively little on defence.

In the years before World War I, Canada fought for the British Empire, but it did so in Sudan and South Africa, not in Southern Ontario or Saskatchewan. As it was not directly defending its own territory, Ottawa sought limited commitments. London could declare war on behalf of Canada, but it could not legally demand expenditures. Thus, Canada would allow volunteers to fight for Britain and would pay some of the costs (as in the South African War), but it was not about to raise and maintain standing forces to support Britain's global interests. Some efforts were made to build up independent capabilities (as, for example, with the creation of the Royal Canadian Navy (RCN) in 1910), but, with no immediate threat to Canadian security, national interest simply did not require large armed forces. The sentiment of the day was perhaps best caught by Robert L. Borden who, though a staunch imperialist, declared in 1911: "I am for the Empire against the world, but within the Empire I am for Canada first."[1]

When Britain declared war on Germany in August 1914, it did so on behalf of Canada as well. The extent of Canada's contribution, however, and the manner in which its forces were to support the British war effort, remained the prerogative of the Ottawa government. A wave of imperialist sentiment swept over English Canada and eventually some half a million troops were sent to Europe, sustaining 60 000 deaths. It was a contribution, and a price, out of all proportion to the country's size. Yet, it was a Canadian decision, or rather a series of decisions, that had determined the nature of the country's involvement.

Why had such fateful decisions been taken? The popular notion is that it had all been done out of a misguided sentimentality toward the empire. Yet, for Canada, the stakes in the war were real and immediate: with the United States maintaining neutrality (until 1917), a victory for Germany would certainly not have served Canadian interests. Victorious, Germany might have been able to dominate the European continent and then to challenge Britain for supremacy of the seas, especially in the Atlantic. This was a fundamental factor in Britain's decision to intervene on the continent, reflecting its long-standing determination to maintain a balance of power in Europe. Canada's decision to exert itself represented a similar, or at least complementary, approach to Europe, one which would form the basis of its 20th-century defence policies and postures. If the border with the United States constituted part of Canada's strategic perimeter, another part lay in Europe. And in view of the steadily declining threat from the south, the European front had become more important. Canada therefore had an interest in maintaining the balance of power in Europe and in allying itself with the country that could prevent the domination of that continent by a single power. Such considerations would also contribute to bringing the United States into war—not only in 1917, but again in 1941. After 1945, the United States replaced Britain as the balancer of power in Europe.

The decision to mount a major effort in World War I can also be seen as part of Canada's determination to assert its international independence. As the war dragged on, Ottawa demanded a greater say in overall direction. Along with other dominion governments, it pressed the British to establish the Imperial War Cabinet, composed of the dominion prime ministers and British cabinet members. In order to secure Canada's voice in this new body, Prime Minister Borden pledged to increase Canadian contributions. This promise required conscription, which proved domestically unsettling when Quebec, although supportive of the war effort, took issue with the draft. Nevertheless, Borden set a precedent that has been followed by Canadian governments to this day: that contributions of armed forces to alliances are the necessary price Canada must pay if it is to have influence in international councils as a sovereign and independent nation.

The seat in the Imperial War Cabinet was a first step toward a separate seat at the Versailles Peace Conference. There, Canada took part in the deliberations and eventually signed the treaty on its own (although as part of the British Empire delegation). Canada also became a full member of the League of Nations, using its seat to project the image of an independent nation.

But the heavy losses of World War I had left their mark on Canadian external and defence policy. While active in the League, Canada avoided making any pledges to send armed forces abroad to enforce the decisions of the world body. Similarly, it would no longer support Britain's imperial interests throughout the world. In 1922 Canada rejected a British call for forces to intervene against Turkey. As in the United States, there was a growing isolationist, almost antimilitary, sentiment in Canada. During the interwar period, Canada asserted its independence partly by choosing not to maintain armed forces of any significance. Not unlike other countries at that time, Canada put its faith in various disarmament and peacemaking efforts. During these years Canada also emphasized to Britain that it had to consider itself a North American nation and thus take into account the security considerations of the United States. Canada wanted to avoid at all cost a situation in which it might have to choose between U.S. and British interests.

William Lyon Mackenzie King, who was prime minister during most of the interwar period (as well as throughout World War II), was particularly anxious not to be drawn into another war alongside Britain. Not only was he somewhat distrustful of "old world" diplomatic machinations, he was also concerned about his domestic political situation. War meant conscription. During World War I, the country had been almost torn apart by French Canadian opposition to the draft. Furthermore, King's Liberal party was built on an alliance between English and French that allowed him to draw considerable support from Quebec.

By the late 1930s, however, war seemed imminent: Germany was on the rise and becoming threatening, Japan was waging aggressive war against China, and Italy was on the march in Africa. Canadian military links to Britain, which had never been broken off, were now intensified, and a modest rearmament program was initiated. Although King wanted to avoid war and supported the British appeasement policy of the day, he did let Hitler know that, in the event of war, Canada would side with Britain. When war did come in September 1939, Canada moved quickly to formally ally itself with Britain and France. By this time, London was no longer empowered to declare war on behalf of Canada. Hence, the Canadian declaration of war, following one week after the British and the French, represented a fully independent decision by a fully sovereign power. As in the previous war, the extent of Canada's contribution remained the prerogative of Ottawa. Even as the first Canadian troops sailed for Britain in December 1939, there was some hope that the large commitment of forces required in the previous struggle could be avoided and that Canada would be able to support Britain through its industrial capacity and by providing training facilities such as those established under the Commonwealth Air Training Program.

Ottawa's hopes for a short war of "limited liability" ended with the German sweep through Western Europe in the spring of 1940. England and the Commonwealth now stood alone against the Nazis. Britain's weakened position presented the first direct threat to Canadian security in over a century. As long as Canada remained in the war, it would be a target for German forces, especially naval forces, since the Nazis and their allies had come to dominate the European mainland. While Canada would heed Winston Churchill's call to carry on the struggle overseas, the Anglo–Canadian alliance now offered little security. Thus, Prime Minister King, who had been as uneasy about close military ties with the United States as with Britain, began to look southward for security and a new alliance.

Until the 1920s, Canadian war plans had included provisions for a possible invasion by the United States. Such plans were as unrealistic in their assessment of Canadian military capabilities as they were anachronistic in relation to the existing political-strategic situation in North America. The United States had not seriously threatened Canada since before Confederation. Nor, apart from their brief alliance during World War I, had the two countries considered themselves partners in the defence of the continent. Quite simply, there had been no external threat sufficient to compel either government to seek out closer military ties.

In the late 1930s, President Franklin D. Roosevelt, although facing a still-isolationist public and Congress, began to consider North American defence in view of the deteriorating international situation. In 1938, speaking in Kingston, Ontario, Roosevelt declared that "the Dominion of Canada is part of the sisterhood of the British Empire. I give you assurance that the people of the United States will not stand idly by if domination of Canadian soil is threatened by another Empire." Two days later, Prime Minister King replied:

> We, too, have our obligations as a good friendly neighbour, and one of these is to see that, at our own instance, our country is made as immune from attack or possible invasion as we can reasonably be expected to make it, and that, should the occasion ever arise, enemy forces should not be able to pursue their way either by land, sea or air, to the United States across Canadian territory.[2]

Although these statements did bespeak a genuinely warm sentiment between the two countries (and the two leaders), they also reflected still-divergent strategic interests. Roosevelt did not promise to aid Canada if it became involved in a European war through the Anglo–Canadian alliance. Rather, he ensured that Canadian territory (and by extension the United States itself) would be protected from the threat of invasion or occupation by European forces. In essence, Roosevelt affirmed the Monroe doctrine in the context of Canada. For his part, King recognized the American strategic interest in Canadian security, but did not pledge a joint approach to continental defence. Indeed, he suggested that Canada on its own would provide for security, as far as could "reasonably" be expected, against an attack upon itself or one directed against the United States across Canadian territory.

In September 1939 the United States did stand by while Canada exerted itself in alliance with Britain, but Roosevelt was not entirely idle. The president sought to give what aid he could to Britain and its allies, despite the isolationist leanings of Congress and the U.S. public. And, in the summer of 1940, with France and the rest of western Europe conquered, he took steps toward greater co-operation in North American defence.

On 17 August 1940, more than a year before the Japanese attack on Pearl Harbour that would bring the United States into the war, Roosevelt invited King down from Ottawa to meet him at Ogdensburg, New York. There the two leaders, by a simple exchange of notes, not only planned the co-ordination of North American defence for the duration of the war, but established the Permanent Joint Board on Defence (PJBD). This board, on which Canadian representation was to be equal to that of the United States, would oversee the combined efforts of the two countries to secure the continent. It ushered in an unprecedented integration of the strategic efforts of the two nations. As the war progressed, co-ordination expanded to encompass the economic sphere. In the Hyde Park declaration of 20 April 1941, the two governments agreed that their war economies should be meshed in order to obtain the greatest possible efficiency and productivity.

Soon after the United States entered the war (on 7 December 1941) this new Canadian–American alliance was overshadowed by the grand alliance of the United States, Britain, and the Soviet Union. Yet the Canadian decision to formalize strategic co-operation with the United States through the PJBD and a host of other bilateral institutional arrangements marked both a continuation of previous policies—the search for security through alliance—and a milestone, in that the United States had formally replaced Britain as Canada's principal ally. Important too was the fact that the bilateral defence arrangements afforded Canada a measure of equality with its more powerful ally. Despite the disparities in military might, strategic relations were far from a matter of the Americans proposing and the Canadians accepting.

During World War II Canada once again contributed out of all proportion to its size. More than in the previous war, Canada was able to exploit its contributions to play an active role in Allied diplomacy and also to reinforce the image of the country as a truly distinct and indeed major international player. With the fall of the Axis powers and the weakening of Britain and France, Canada, physically untouched by the war, had been strengthened relative to other nations by the boost it gave to the development of its industry and resources.

The Cold War Years: 1945–1968

Even before the war ended, Canada had begun to plan the shape of its postwar armed forces. The military did not want to see the country return to the position in which it had been in the late 1930s, when its armed forces were small and ill-equipped. The military staffs proposed that Canada have balanced air, sea, and land forces commensurate with its international standing and economic might. Prime Minister King, still very much in charge, was determined to return to normalcy, however, and the size of the armed forces began to decline with the war's end.

Canadian foreign policy, on the other hand, did not return to the semi-isolationism of the 1930s. Far from avoiding international involvement, Ottawa's postwar foreign policy was predicated on Canada's taking an active role in global diplomacy and adopting international stability and order as its goals. While recognizing that the United States and the USSR, along with the revived European powers, would play a leading role in international affairs, Ottawa nevertheless saw the potential to promote Canadian security through the creation of new multilateral arrangements that would enhance world peace.

Initially, Canadian hopes were centred on the United Nations (UN), where Canada quickly became active. Although the UN achieved much, it soon became mired in the growing tensions between the Soviet Union and the United States. As an instrument of collective security, its utility for Canada rapidly diminished. The advent of nuclear weapons further increased the dangers of war, especially as the world was becoming increasingly bipolar and unstable. Canada, still anxious to play an active role in global affairs, associated itself with the Western powers led by the United States, with its growing nuclear arsenal.

As John Holmes has written, a *pax Americana* was not what Canada had in mind at the end of the war. Yet Canadian leaders were becoming "concerned with the dangers of international communism largely because it posed a threat to world order." Given this view (at which Canada arrived independent of the Americans), Ottawa understood that "for the time being the United States alone could provide the sinews for a *pax* and must therefore remain strong." Thus, during this period, "Canadians saw themselves as acting collectively as loyal and responsible allies and associates in a good cause."[3] And they did so, according to Holmes, not out of some blind sense of servitude or resignation to American policy, but with a clear understanding of national interests. Canada's postwar foreign policy orientation as a Western ally was determined by a number of realities: the rigid bipolar structure of the international system, geographic fact, historical linkages, domestic political and economic structures, and public attitudes. Any other position, whether one of alliance with the Soviet Union or even one of neutrality, would have run counter to these realities. Canada's decision to conduct an active foreign policy and to ally itself with the United States were the key factors in determining defence policy during the Cold War years and beyond.

Within this general approach to security, the military co-operation with the United States that had begun during the war continued. Unlike the situation after World War I, the two countries took steps to build on their wartime collaboration. In 1946, on the recommendation of the PJBD, the Military Co-operation Committee (MCC) was established to provide for an exchange of military information between the two defence establishments on matters relating to North American defence. In February 1947 Prime Minister King and President Harry Truman issued a joint statement on defence co-operation. During these years the United States Air Force (USAF) and the Royal Canadian Air Force (RCAF) began to address jointly the problems of continental air defence in light of the Soviet potential for intercontinental delivery of nuclear weapons by bombers. Under a Basic Security Plan, air defence co-operation was supplemented by plans for the land and sea defence of North America.

Multinational arrangements also continued after the war. Canada, the United States, and Britain collaborated on maritime security in the North Atlantic and engaged in joint naval exercises. These years also saw the beginnings of intelligence co-operation among the United States, Britain, and Canada (the so-called ABC countries), as well as Australia and New Zealand, a collaboration that created a global network.

Not only was Canada willing to ally itself with the United States, it was also determined to play a leading role in the creation of a trans-Atlantic alliance that would link North American and West European security and in doing so would serve a multitude of Canadian strategic, political, and even economic interests. In 1947 Canadian Secretary of State for External Affairs Louis St. Laurent became one of the first Western leaders to call publicly for a trans-Atlantic pact. Speaking before the UN, which had become stalemated, St. Laurent served notice that Canada could no longer "accept an unaltered [Security] Council." Placing the blame squarely on the Soviet Union, he announced that, if forced to, Canadians would "seek greater safety in an association of democratic peace-loving states willing to accept more specific international obligations in return for a greater measure of national security."[4]

Canada acted as St. Laurent said it would, not only seeking membership in a trans-Atlantic alliance but helping to create NATO. It was an attractive arrangement. Canada shared the view that war could be avoided by formally linking British, American, and West European security so that, as St. Laurent said in 1948, "it would appear to any possible aggressor that he would have to be prepared to overcome us all if he attempted any aggression."[5] By maintaining the balance of power in Europe, ultimately through a reliance on the American nuclear superiority of that time, Canadian security would be assured.

Apart from its deterrent value, NATO would help to resolve a pressing Canadian foreign policy problem. With the decline of the Anglo–Canadian alliance, the rise of the United States to superpower status, and the strategic realities of the nuclear age, a multilateral security pact afforded a desirable alternative for Canada to a strictly bilateral security arrangement with the United States. Although Canada supported the continuance of the PJBD into the postwar era, and although it acknowledged the need for the United States to play an active role in the world, Ottawa was still concerned about its sovereignty and independence. However warm the bilateral relationship with the United States, and however complementary the two countries' strategic out-looks, the inevitable pressures toward integration in military matters ran counter to Canada's desire to see itself, and to be seen by other states, as a distinct international actor—even on security issues.

Thus, NATO appeared to offer Canada both security and a means of maintaining its independent status in the world. As one senior Canadian diplomat stated in a cable from London during the negotiations on the establishment of NATO:

> A situation in which our special relationship with the United Kingdom can be identified with our special relationship with the other European countries in western Europe, in which the United States will be providing a firm basis, both economically and probably militarily, for this link across the North Atlantic, seems to me such a providential solution for so many of our problems that I feel we should go to great length and even incur considerable risks in order to consolidate our good fortune and ensure our proper place in this new partnership.[6]

Beyond the desire for a "proper place" through which to influence trans-Atlantic security issues, Canada also viewed NATO as a means by which to foster greater economic co-operation among the allies. At Canada's urging, Article II of the North Atlantic Treaty was inserted, pledging the allies to "eliminate conflict in their international economic policies and . . . encourage economic collaboration."

When NATO was created in 1949, the member nations did not expect to maintain forces permanently under allied command. The alliance did set up regional planning groups to co-ordinate defence co-operation. One of these was the Canada–U.S. Regional Planning Group (CUSRPG), which joined the MCC and the PJBD as the third bilateral Canadian–U.S. strategic institution (but the only one formally under NATO's governing body, the North Atlantic Council). Canada also participated in allied planning for the defence of the Atlantic Ocean.

It was not until the outbreak of the Korean conflict in June 1950 that Canada, along with the United States and other allies, really began an accelerated rearmament program. While Canada did participate in the fighting in Korea, its efforts were primarily directed toward supporting NATO. With the exception of CUSRPG, the regional planning groups were replaced by an integrated multilateral command structure with three major commanders: Supreme Allied Commander, Europe (SACEUR), Supreme Allied Commander, Atlantic (SACLANT), and Commander-in-Chief, Channel

(CINCHAN). The alliance sought to maintain standing forces under these commanders and Canada, still relatively stronger economically than most NATO nations, was asked to contribute. During the early 1950s, Canada postured its armed forces to meet the NATO needs. The army commitment was for an infantry division, with one brigade group (approximately 7000 men) stationed in West Germany and the balance in Canada ready to reinforce upon mobilization. The air force had an air division stationed at various bases in France and West Germany. Naval and naval air forces in the Atlantic were almost entirely earmarked for SACLANT as Canada had assumed responsibility for a large area of the North Atlantic.

As in the two world wars, Canada's front line was in Europe. Its contributions were intended to promote international stability by providing the European allies with a measure of military and political confidence, thereby making Western Europe less vulnerable to Soviet influence. Behind all allied military contributions lay the strategic nuclear arsenal of the United States. Although NATO attempted, with some success, to augment its own conventional forces, the allied deterrent posture ultimately rested on the nuclear forces of the United States. The Canadian defence contribution was part of a larger context wherein nuclear weapons were the dominant factor in the balance of power between East and West. Reliance on nuclear weapons reduced the need for larger conventional forces.

Active participation in NATO, while undertaken by Canada's political leadership for a number of reasons, also provided the armed forces with a credible role in the nuclear age. Having watched the political leadership sign the NATO treaty and then agree to contribute standing forces, Canada's military could reasonably turn to the government for the funds needed to fulfil those commitments. Without NATO, it would have been difficult at best to justify the maintenance of modern conventional armed forces, equipped with tanks, artillery, fighter aircraft, and a wide range of anti-submarine warfare (ASW) forces. The need for Canada to live up to its obligations would become one of the most potent arguments the military could use in requesting increased funds.

As the Canadian government was making major decisions and commitments regarding support for NATO, its strictly bilateral security relations with the United States in North America were becoming increasingly co-operative. Under the MCC and the PJBD, the two countries jointly developed a series of plans for the land, sea, and air defence of the continent. In the new age of atomic weapons and intercontinental bombers, it was the air threat that most concerned the United States. While Canada's political leaders may not have shared the urgency with which the military on both sides of the border viewed the potential Soviet air threat to the continent, they appreciated that the United States would want to take measures to meet such a threat and that these measures would inevitably involve Canadian territory. A study by the Department of External Affairs noted that "it may be very difficult indeed for the Canadian government to reject any major defence proposals which the United States Government presents with conviction as essential for the security of North America."[7]

In the late 1940s and early 1950s, neither the U.S. government nor the USAF was advocating strategic defence against Soviet attack with much conviction. Instead, the American government was emphasizing deterrence, based on the threat to potential aggressors of massive retaliation by its own strategic bombers. But gradually the United States started to pay some attention to the possibility of Soviet bomber attack, not from the perspective of its threat to the population of the two countries as much as to the deterrent itself; that is, the USAF bombers could be vulnerable to a surprise Soviet first strike. The RCAF increased its co-operation with the USAF. A series of radar lines was constructed in Canada, with the Cadin-Pinetree line in the south, the Mid-Canada line further north, and the Distant Early Warning (DEW) line in the high Arctic. The United States paid for, built, and initially manned the DEW line, while the Cadin-Pinetree line was a co-operative effort, and the Mid-Canada line an entirely Canadian undertaking.

In 1958, the North American Air Defence Command (NORAD)[8] was established by a simple exchange of notes between the two countries. Although there has been some controversy as to the role the RCAF played in getting the newly elected Conservative government of Prime Minister John G. Diefenbaker to agree to NORAD, its creation was the logical next step in an increasingly integrative and co-operative approach to air defence. NORAD was simply a joint command, headed by a USAF general with a Canadian deputy; it was jointly responsible to both governments for the air defence of the continent. Its headquarters were eventually located at the Cheyenne Mountain complex in Colorado Springs, Colorado.

Although it was not created by treaty, NORAD can be viewed as an alliance similar to NATO. As is characteristic of alliances, NORAD entailed an agreement between two sovereign countries to collaborate militarily against a perceived common enemy. It also involved a *de facto* pooling of defence resources. Like NATO, NORAD was a "latent war community" that rested on definite understandings and expectations "about the purposes and circumstances of the specified military operations in times of war".[9] And as with NATO, these expectations were bolstered by close peacetime integration of defence efforts.

But NORAD was not a NATO command subordinate to the North Atlantic Council, even though North America fell within the geographic region protected by NATO. To be sure, NORAD supported NATO to the extent that it helped defend Canada and the United States (and especially U.S. deterrent weaponry). Canada–U.S. air defence co-operation in NORAD was fully compatible with NATO membership and obligations. But there was no formal link between the two save for reporting on general North American defence efforts through the CUSRPG. Canada would have preferred a closer link between NORAD and NATO's multilateral institutions, but the United States did not share this view. Thus, although Canadian leaders sometimes made reference to NORAD as a NATO command, the two were in fact separate military commitments.[10]

Despite some misgivings, NORAD was still viewed as the best means by which to assure military effectiveness and a clear Canadian role in air defence. In addition, because the United States assumed the bulk of NORAD's financing, the arrangement provided Canada with a measure of air sovereignty at an acceptable cost. This arrangement also freed Canadian defence resources for European commitments. While it might seem anomalous for Canada to have agreed to American funding and manning of air-defence facilities in Canada while Canadian air forces were stationed in Europe, the decision reflected Ottawa's assessment of the importance of Europe in maintaining overall allied security and of the need to maintain a visible Canadian military presence in Europe for political purposes.

Despite American subsidization, the Canadian defence effort during the Cold War years did become financially difficult to maintain given the other spending priorities the government faced. In particular, as the 1959 cancellation of the Arrow aircraft project demonstrated, Canada could not economically develop and manufacture major weapons systems for its own armed forces. This meant that such equipment had to be bought off-shore—mainly in the United States—which in turn represented a further drain.

The U.S. government recognized the problems Canada was having in keeping up with the demands of collective defence, and in 1959 the two countries entered into a series of Defence Production Sharing Arrangements (DPSA).[11] The arrangements involved a partial free-trade regime in defence products, giving Canadian industry access to a large defence market and the armed forces the benefit of lower prices (because of longer production runs) on the larger items produced in the United States. As a result of DPSA, and subsequent agreements covering development, Canada's defence industry abandoned the goal of producing a complete range of defence equipment for the armed forces and instead concentrated on producing specialized, internationally competitive products for export, mainly to the United States. This led to the situation wherein the United States became the largest market for Canadian defence products, while the Canadian armed forces purchased most of their equipment from U.S. manufacturers.

Thus, the 1950s saw Canadian defence policy—in its political, strategic, and even economic dimensions—becoming increasingly meshed with Western collective-defence efforts, dominated by the United States. But the decade also saw Canada assume a defence role that would distinguish it from other Western nations. Under UN auspices, Canadians had served in a number of peacekeeping and peace observation capacities in the Middle East. Canadian troops had also been involved in Vietnam after the 1954 accords had divided the country between the Communist North and the Western-oriented South. In 1956, as a result of the Suez crisis, Canada's external affairs minister, Lester B. Pearson, took peacekeeping much further by proposing a large-scale international force to be deployed between Israel and Egypt. Several hundred Canadian soldiers joined the force, which remained in place until war broke out again in 1967. The initiative, which earned Pearson the Nobel Peace Prize, inaugurated a major Canadian world role as a supplier of peacekeeping forces. Subsequent years would see Canadians in the Congo, Cyprus, Yemen, and Vietnam, as well as continuing their involvement in the Arab–Israeli dispute. At their highest level in 1964, Canadians serving under the UN flag numbered over 2000.[12]

The decision to expend defence resources on international peacekeeping was consistent with Canada's overall approach to foreign and defence policy since World War II. Canada had above all sought to promote international order and stability, seeing in the furtherance of these goals the best means of enhancing its own security. Alliance membership and peacekeeping were two of the ways in which Canada pursued these goals. If contributions of Canadian personnel and expertise could help the UN and other peacekeeping efforts to function more effectively, international conflict might be avoided or at least postponed to allow for peacemaking. Moreover, peacekeeping was consistent with Canada's standing as a strong Western ally, since the West, including the United States, often had an interest in conflict resolution as well. In the case of the Greek–Turkish dispute over Cyprus, Canada's involvement was directly related to protecting the NATO alliance from a serious rift. Although it preserved a measure of neutrality as a participant, Canada was nevertheless seen as representative of the Western powers in most peacekeeping operations.

The defence policy and postures adopted by Canada in the Cold War years were to determine the roles and tasks of the armed forces for the next 30 years and, indeed, still do so today. Since the institutional frameworks of NATO and NORAD to a large extent determined the types of forces Canada would maintain, Canadian armed forces were postured to fulfil several collective-defence roles. There was the air and sea defence of North America; for NATO, there was the concentration on ASW to protect the sea lines of communication to Europe and the deployment of air and ground forces in Europe. To these collective-defence roles was added peacekeeping, an activity to which Canada sustained a significant commitment into the 1980s.

One defence task that was not openly emphasized during the Cold War years, but that would emerge in later years as a designated task, was sovereignty protection. Although Ottawa was concerned about sovereignty during the 1950s, from a military perspective there did not appear to be any direct threat to Canadian sovereignty apart from the general threat posed by the Soviet Union to the United States and the West. The answer to this wider threat was collective defence through alliance membership, and thus the roles assumed by the armed forces implicitly addressed both international and specifically national tasks. For example, the army's Mobile-Strike Force, an airborne unit stationed in Canada, was available for territorial security, especially in the north; the navy's icebreakers and the RCAF's aircraft were also active there. In addition, there were Canada–U.S. plans for the defence of Alaska and the Yukon.

As for sovereignty protection against non-military threats such as illegal fishing, it was assumed that forces dedicated to military roles would be available to support the civil authority as necessary and that there was no need to single out non-military tasks.

In a similar vein, the question of an "independent" Canadian defence policy—one that would depart significantly from U.S. policy—did not emerge during the Cold War years in the same way as it would in later years. Here again, it was not because governments were unconcerned about Canadian independence but rather because close strategic cooperation with the United States and other allies was regarded as consistent with Canadian interests. The international institutional framework within which Canadian defence policy was conducted was viewed as the best means by which to foster Canadian independence because it involved recognition, by the United States and other allies, of Canada as a partner in collective defence. Canadian decision makers had no illusions about the disparity in military power between Canada and its allies (and adversaries). Indeed, precisely because they recognized this, they also saw that an independent defence policy would simply serve to exclude Canada from much of international politics. Canada's decision to maintain a defence policy oriented toward collective defence complemented other major decisions taken in the international economic sphere, where Canada was, by virtue of its economic strength, a major global actor. Close military ties with the United States and Western Europe proceeded in tandem with active Canadian involvement in the international economic institutions that developed during the Cold War years.

The decision to seek security through alliance and to structure the armed forces to fulfil allied commitments did not, however, automatically determine all of Canada's defence policies. Within this larger framework, other decisions had to be made as to how and at what levels Canada would contribute. As noted earlier, this involved choices between European forces and those dedicated to North American defence. It also involved decisions regarding the allocation of funds among the land, sea, and air services. In the 1950s the RCAF seemed to be the favoured service because of the obvious need for air power in North America and in Europe. Decisions had to be made about which weapons to buy and where to buy them, from U.S. suppliers or from Canadian manufacturers.

One major decision that Canada had taken early in the postwar era was to forgo the development of nuclear weapons of its own. Although a participant in the wartime research that led to the development of the atomic bomb and also possessing large uranium reserves, Canada was supportive of UN efforts to foster international control of atomic energy and was anxious to curtail proliferation of nuclear weapons, setting an example by its own decisions. This did not, however, prevent Canada from recognizing the importance of the American nuclear arsenal to Western collective defence when it became clear that international control and general disarmament were not feasible within the existing state of East–West relations. Ottawa lent its support to the deployment of American theatre and tactical nuclear weapons in Europe in order to strengthen the NATO deterrent posture.

In the late 1950s Canada itself moved to acquire a nuclear capability for its North American and European forces in order to make them more compatible with allied forces. The military ordered a number of weapons systems that required nuclear warheads to be worth their cost and to be effective. These systems included air-to-air missiles, nuclear bombs, and artillery for use in Europe. Canada would not produce the warheads, but was to acquire them from the United States. Arrangements would be made similar to those negotiated with other allies, whereby a decision by both national authorities was required to release the warheads for use.

It fell to the Conservative government of John Diefenbaker to conclude the arrangements regarding the acquisition of these weapons. Prime Minister Diefenbaker delayed the final decision for several years, touching off a major dispute with the United States. The controversy also precipitated a public split within his cabinet that contributed to the defeat of the government in the 1963 general elections.

While there was a good deal of confusion in Diefenbaker's handling of the nuclear-weapons controversy, his initial reluctance to give the armed forces a nuclear capability also reflected a new approach to defence policy. He and his secretary of state for external affairs, Howard Green, were not as convinced as the Liberals had been that Canadian prestige, independence, and influence were being well-served by close military co-operation with the United States. In particular, for Canada to acquire nuclear weapons would mean abandonment of its efforts toward arms control through the UN.

Prime Minister Diefenbaker also became sceptical about the actual extent of Canadian influence as a result of the Cuban missile crisis in the fall of 1962. When the United States discovered that the Soviet Union was placing missiles in Cuba capable of striking at targets within the United States, President John F. Kennedy demanded their immediate removal. He imposed a naval blockade around the island, prepared for invasion, and warned the Soviet Union that the United States would launch a nuclear attack on the USSR itself if any of the Cuban missiles were fired at any country in the Western Hemisphere. As the world waited for the Soviet response, U.S. forces went on alert and Washington asked for support from NATO allies. Worried that Kennedy had acted too hastily, and angered over the failure of the United States to consult before it took unilateral action, Prime Minister Diefenbaker at first refused to put Canadian forces on alert. Two days later he officially ordered an alert, although Canadian forces had in fact begun stepping up operations and preparing for war shortly after the American alert was announced.

The return of the Liberals under Lester B. Pearson in 1963 brought about a quick acceptance of the nuclear role for Canada. The new government argued that Canada had to live up to its obligations as a member of NATO: "Having accepted responsibility for membership in a nuclear armed alliance, the question of nuclear weapons for Canadian Armed Forces is a subordinate issue."[13] Pearson moved quickly to improve relations with the United States. He was also concerned about the maintenance of Canadian influence in the alliance and about allied cohesion in general. As did previous Liberal governments, Pearson's viewed participation in Western collective-defence measures as the cornerstone of Canadian defence policy.

However, alliance membership could not determine the whole spectrum of defence policy decisions and the Pearson government put in motion major changes in defence policy within the larger framework established during the Cold War years. In its 1964 White Paper on Defence, the government reaffirmed all the existing roles of the armed forces in NORAD and NATO, but sought ways in which Canada could make a more identifiable—and more economical—contribution. Peacekeeping received special emphasis in the White Paper along with the traditional alliance tasks, and protection of sovereignty was accorded separate mention. For the NATO roles, the emphasis was placed on "forces-in-being." Thus, while the brigade group and eight squadrons were to remain in Europe, less attention would be paid to the reinforcement of the central front. This in turn meant that the reserves would play a steadily decreasing role in Canada's military posture and plans.

But the major change announced in the paper was the government's intention to integrate the headquarters of the three services into a single headquarters and then to unify the services themselves by abolishing the army, the navy, and the air force as distinct entities to create a single service—the Canadian Forces (CF). These steps were taken between 1964 and 1968. This was the origin of the present-day Mobile Command (MOBCOM), Maritime Command (MARCOM), and Air Command (AIRCOM).

The government gave several reasons for implementing unification. There was the economic factor. Given the combined costs of maintaining modern armed forces and expanding domestic social programs, savings had to be made in the operation of the military—Canada could not afford three separate service organizations. Unification would also allow for a general reduction in personnel, freeing up funds for capital improvements, that is, the purchase of new equipment. From the military standpoint, the government argued that Canada needed flexible, mobile forces that integrated air and land units capable of quick deployment to Europe or to fulfil peacekeeping obligations. Overall, military and economic efficiency would be improved by dividing the forces along functional lines rather than the formal ones of the traditional service divisions.

Although unification proceeded as planned, the savings promised were largely consumed by inflation, thereby reducing the amount of new equipment that could be purchased. By 1968 personnel levels had dropped by over 20 000 to just over 100 000. Under the newly established Mobile Command, Canada did create a force dedicated to rapid movement overseas in either a NATO or peacekeeping capacity. In 1964 the government earmarked two Canadian-based battalions for participation as necessary in NATO's Allied Mobile Force (Land) (AMF(L))—one for the European northern flank and the other for the southern flank. However, since these forces were to be integrated with allied forces that had not been unified, Canada continued to offer discrete air, land, and naval units to NATO as well as to NORAD. Because of this, the armed forces never really stopped operating as an air force, an army, and a navy, although formally the RCAF, the Canadian Army, and the RCN had been abolished along with their distinctive uniforms and rank-ings. Finally, the White Paper's emphasis on peacekeeping was dramatically called into question in the spring of 1967 when the Egyptian government ordered the UN force out of the Sinai and war followed shortly thereafter. "If the as-sumption that is put forward by nations other than Cana-da is correct, namely that the UN peacekeeping role can be abandoned by any affected [host country] member," asked a Conservative critic, "what will happen to this government's defence policy?"[14]

Whatever its difficulties and unfulfilled promises, unifi-cation of the Canadian Forces indicated that Canadian gov-ernments did have room to manoeuvre in the formulation of defence policy. It was possible for Canada both to remain within the larger framework of Western collective defence and to implement changes in the nature of its contributions and the structure of its forces. It was also possible to reduce both the size of the armed forces and the level of real de-fence expenditure (particularly on new equipment), without adversely affecting Canada's political relations with allies. The Diefenbaker government had run into trouble with the allies because it had procrastinated on accepting nuclear weapons and chafed under close military ties with the United States. The Pearson government of 1963-68 declared its acceptance of the nuclear role and the need for Cana-da to contribute to allied solidarity. But under both govern-ments, real expenditures on defence declined.

In part this room to manoeuvre was made possible by changes in the broader international environment. The Cold War was coming to an end. In the wake of the Cuban missile crisis, American–Soviet relations slowly improved and the persistently high levels of tension that had characterized previous years gave way to a still uneasy, but nevertheless markedly more stable, relationship. Throughout the West-ern alliance, governments were reducing levels of military expenditure. These were also the years of American involve-ment in Vietnam. Not only did the war consume U.S. en-ergies, it raised questions about the wisdom of the need to "contain" perceived Soviet and communist expansionism.

In Canada the mid-1960s were years of rising nationalist sentiment. To a certain extent this was a reaction to the growth of the separatist movement in Quebec. But it also reflected a growing pride among Canadians in their country as its Centennial of Confederation approached. There were calls for a more independent foreign policy commensurate with Canada's distinctiveness and respected standing in the

world. Often these calls manifested themselves in suggestions for a defence policy oriented less toward collective-
defence obligations, which entailed close military ties with
the United States, and more toward exclusively Canadian
interests, such as sovereignty protection. Combined with the
easing of Cold War tensions and public reaction against
American involvement in Vietnam, this rising public support
for an identifiably Canadian foreign policy introduced a new
set of domestic determinants into the formulation of defence
policy.

Notes

1. John English and Norman Hillmer, "Canada's Alliances," *Revue inter-
   nationale d'histoire militaire* (Édition Canadienne) 51 (1981), p. 34.

2. James Eayrs, *In Defence of Canada*, vol. 2, *Appeasement and Rearmament* (Toronto: University of Toronto Press, 1965), p. 183.

3. John W. Holmes, *The Shaping of Peace* vol. 2, *Canada and the Search
   for World Order 1943–1957* (Toronto: University of Toronto Press,
   1982), p. 10.

4. Robert Mckay, ed., *Canadian Foreign Policy 1945–1954: Selected
   Speeches and Documents* (Toronto: McClelland and Stewart, 1971),
   p. 97.

5. Escott Reid, "The Birth of the North Atlantic Alliance", *International
   Journal* 22 no. 3 (Summer 1967): p. 431.

6. Escott Reid, *Time of Fear and Hope: The Making of the North Atlantic
   Treaty 1947–1949* (Toronto: McClelland and Stewart, 1977), p. 132.

7. Canada, Department of External Affairs, "Continental Radar Defence,"
   confidential study, 3 October 1953, Brooke Claxton Papers, vol. 102,
   Public Archives of Canada, Ottawa.

8. The acronym NORAD now stands for North American *Aerospace* Defence Command. The command was renamed in 1981 to reflect a significant shift in its role. This development is discussed in Chapter 3.

9. Robert E. Osgood, *Alliances and American Foreign Policy* (Baltimore:
   Johns Hopkins University Press, 1968), p. 19.

10. Joseph T. Jockel, *No Boundaries Upstairs: Canada, the United States
    and the Origins of North American Air Defence, 1945–1958* (Vancouver:
    University of British Columbia Press, 1987), pp. 96–97.

11. See Danford W. Middlemiss, "Economic Defence Co-operation with
    the United States, 1940–63," in *An Acceptance of Paradox: Essays on
    Canadian Diplomacy in Honour of John W. Holmes*, ed. Kim Richard
    Nossal (Toronto: Canadian Institute of International Affairs, 1982), pp.
    86–114.

12. Peyton V. Lyon, Introduction to *Canada and the Third World*, eds. Pey-
    ton V. Lyon and Tareq Y. Ismael (Toronto: Macmillan of Canada, Ltd.,
    1976), p. xxii.

13. Canada, Department of National Defence, *White Paper on Defence* (Ot-
    tawa: Queen's Printer, 1964), p. 13.

14. Canada, House of Commons, *Debates*, 19 May 1967, p. 419.

3

FROM WHITE PAPER

TO WHITE PAPER

The 1971 White Paper and the Trudeau Years

Upon coming into office at the head of a majority Liberal government in the spring of 1968, Prime Minister Pierre Elliott Trudeau initiated a major review of both foreign and defence policy. The spirit of both reviews reflected changing sentiments toward East–West relations, relations with the United States, and Canada's external relations. According to Trudeau, defence policy had for too long determined foreign policy and not the reverse, as should be the case. And foreign policy had been determined on the basis of a liberal-internationalist tradition that defined Canadian interest in terms of the search for global economic, political, and military stability. This had led Canada to its support for NATO and bilateral Canada–U.S. arrangements, including NORAD, as the best available means of assuring stability in light of the nature of East–West relations. Although he did not question Canadian membership in either NATO or NORAD, Trudeau set out to formulate defence and foreign policies with greater regard to specific Canadian national interests. Indeed, external policy would reflect domestic priorities rather than those of the international system in which Canada operated. Again, the Trudeau government, like previous Liberal governments, recognized that Canada had options in the area of defence policy and that it could make decisions about defence that furthered national priorities. Accordingly, the Canadian Forces could be made to serve as a symbol of independence, not simply as the measure of Canada's contribution to collective defence.

Even before the foreign policy and defence reviews were completed, Trudeau made a major decision regarding the disposition of the armed forces: he reduced Canada's forces in Germany by half. Since the early 1950s, these forces had represented, both substantively and symbolically, Canada's strong support for NATO and collective defence. Trudeau defended his actions on the simple grounds that the essential nuclear deterrent rested with the United States. With regard to conventional forces, he argued that the "magnificent recovery" of Western Europe had given those countries the ability to provide for their own defence. Although consideration had been given to a complete withdrawal from Europe, the prime minister had been persuaded that it was necessary to maintain some forces there as "visible evidence of Canada's commitment to the Alliance." With regard to NATO itself, Trudeau recognized its importance to the maintenance of peace and rejected a Canadian withdrawal on the grounds that only by remaining within allied councils could Canada play a role in the promotion of détente and arms reduction. At the same time, despite recommendations to the contrary by an interdepartmental Special Task Force on Relations with Europe, he did not consider the decision to reduce the size of Canadian forces in Europe as detrimental to either the alliance as a whole or to Canadian political influence.[1]

In addition to reducing the size of Canada's European forces, the Trudeau government was also determined to change their roles. Both the land and air elements were to shed their nuclear weapons and assume more reserve functions away from the front lines. The 2800-man ground force would also switch from its mechanized heavy-armour role to become a light "air-mobile" force, while the three remaining air squadrons would abandon the nuclear-strike role and assume ground support or reconnaissance tasks.

Even before these changes were announced, the government, in late 1968, decided to terminate the Canadian commitment to send a reinforcement brigade to Germany by sea in the event of war. Instead, a brigade-strength unit called the Canadian Air–Sea Transportable (CAST) combat group would be available for deployment to either Norway or Denmark. The CAST group would include the air-transportable battalion earmarked for the AMF(L) in the north of Europe. The other Canadian AMF(L) commitment to the south was ended. Subsequently, the CAST and AMF(L) north reinforcement commitments were backed up by a pledge to send two squadrons (20 aircraft) of Canada-based CF-5 fighters to northern Europe.[2]

Canada retained all its NATO maritime-defence commitments, still designating most of its Atlantic forces for SACLANT.

However, here as well there would be cutbacks. The single aircraft carrier was decommissioned and eventually scrapped; its Tracker ASW aircraft were deployed to land bases and plans were made to dispose of them. Building would continue on four helicopter-destroyers, but no new ASW surface forces were planned. The long-range ASW Argus aircraft was to be replaced by a new aircraft with capabilities geared more toward non-military sovereignty surveillance—particularly in the Arctic—than to the traditional, NATO-oriented missions.

The major changes initiated during the first two years of the Trudeau government were reflected, and explained further, in the 1971 White Paper on Defence entitled *Defence in the 70s.* The basic roles for the armed forces had already been announced on April 3, 1969:

- the surveillance of our own territory and coastlines, i.e. the protection of our sovereignty;
- the defence of North America in co-operation with United States forces;
- the fulfilment of such NATO commitments as may be agreed upon; and
- the performance of such international peacekeeping roles as we may, from time to time, assume.[3]

Even though the White Paper did not specifically give priority to any of these roles and stressed Canada's continued adherence to its alliances, the emphasis was clearly on sovereignty protection. Thus, the decision to reduce the size of the forces in Europe was explained in the White Paper by the fact that "other national aims—fostering economic growth and safeguarding sovereignty and independence—dictated increased emphasis on the protection of Canadian interests at home." Also mentioned were the financial constraints faced by the government and the need to ensure a greater compatibility between overseas and Canadian-based forces. Decisions on new equipment were to be based more on considerations of sovereignty protection than on the need to contribute to collective defence.

The Trudeau government believed it could approach defence policy in this way because of its assessment of the nature of the threat to Canadian security and of what Canada could reasonably be expected to do in response. Basically, the White Paper held that the strategic nuclear balance was stable and, while arms control and détente should be fostered, Canadian security would rest primarily upon nuclear deterrence. Conventional forces, whether at sea or along the central front in Germany, were needed, but since it was unlikely that a protracted conventional struggle would develop between East and West, their importance was limited. All the more limited, therefore, were Canadian contributions to the allied conventional posture.

This approach was applied not only to NATO but to NORAD as well. When the joint command had been established, it was directed against possible bomber attack. During the 1960s, however, both the Soviets and the Americans deployed land-based intercontinental ballistic missiles (ICBMs) and submarine-launched ballistic missiles (SLBMs). Although NORAD adopted a missile surveillance and attack-warning role, there was no defence against a ballistic missile attack and, given the magnitude of the missile threat relative to that of the bomber, there appeared to be no reason to maintain substantial bomber-defence forces of the kind Canada had contributed to NORAD. Thus, the White Paper told Canadians that: "There is, unfortunately, not much Canada herself can do by way of effective direct defence that is of relevance against massive nuclear attack." The government was not "prepared to devote substantial sums to new equipment or facilities for use only for active anti-bomber defences." Rather, contributions would be updated "only to the extent that this is required for general control of Canadian airspace."[4]

It should be noted that the Trudeau policies' lesser emphasis on North American air and sea defence was in line with trends in U.S. strategy. The United States was not then devoting major resources to strategic defence, particularly not against bombers. And indeed under the Antiballistic Missile (ABM) Treaty signed with the Soviets in 1972, the United States would essentially abandon efforts to provide for ballistic-missile defence.

Trends in international relations also influenced the Trudeau approach to peacekeeping. In the 1964 White Paper, this role had been highlighted and was used as a partial justification for the unification of the services. But in May 1967, UN peacekeeping suffered a serious blow when tensions rose between Israel and the Arab states. President Nasser of Egypt ordered the United Nations Emergency Force out of the Sinai and the UN secretary-general complied. War followed within a few days. With the efforts of the International Commission for Supervision and Control in Indochina also falling victim to the expanding war in Vietnam, previous high hopes for peacekeeping and for Canada's role in it were fading. The 1971 White Paper noted that "the scope for useful and effective peacekeeping activities now appears more modest than it did earlier, despite the persistence of widespread violence in many parts of the world." Canada would not automatically reject any request, but in the future the government would only send troops when there were "realistic terms of reference" reflecting "a consensus by all parties on the purpose which the operation was intended to serve and the manner in which it was to discharge its responsibilities." In its foreign policy White Paper, the Trudeau government drew particular attention to the possibility of peacekeeping in Vietnam should that conflict not be settled. "It would be unwise," the government cautioned, "for Canada to go any distance in advance toward undertaking a new obligation to supervise a political settlement until it has been fully defined."[5]

Going the extra distance in an attempt to secure peace had been one of the hallmarks of the Pearsonian liberal-internationalist tradition. De-emphasizing peacekeeping together with collective defence signalled turning away from this tradition in favour of more Canadian-centred foreign and defence policies wherein the "national interest," broadly defined, was the key determinant in policy choices.

Given the vast extent of Canadian territory, airspace, coastline, and ocean area over which some kind of jurisdiction was asserted, a sovereignty-protection emphasis in defence policy should have demanded increases in defence expenditure. But accompanying the de-emphasis on collective-defence roles—which in the past had really driven Canadian defence spending—was a major real reduction in national resources devoted to defence. Between the 1968–69 and 1972–73 fiscal years, defence spending rose by less than $200 million dollars, from $1.761 billion to $1.932 billion. Taking inflation into account, this represented a real decrease. Capital expenditures fell to an all-time low of eight percent of the defence budget, while personnel levels declined from 98 473 in 1968 to 81 626 in 1972 (and down to 77 929 by 1976).[6] With such cutbacks in the regular forces, it was not surprising that the reserves suffered even more. There were no mobilization plans. Indeed, even the permanent force lacked adequate personnel (for example, the brigade group in Germany was operating with only 58 percent of its authorized peacetime establishment).

Despite the Trudeau government's declarations about sovereignty protection and its public statements about the need to fashion a more distinct and independent defence posture reflecting national priorities, not a single major allied commitment had been abandoned. Indeed, with the creation of the CAST combat group, Canada had actually increased its commitments. Even peacekeeping, which the White Paper had seriously questioned, continued to draw resources as Canadian soldiers served in Cyprus, the Middle East, and, for a short time, in Vietnam. In 1975 Canada was still supplying the largest national component of UN peacekeeping forces.

Canada had retained all its allied commitments, especially the central front role, because it feared that a complete withdrawal from any one of them would adversely affect relations with allies. The Trudeau government did not want to strain its external relations further and, by maintaining its existing land, sea, and air commitments, believed it was showing ample evidence of its continued commitment to collective defence. To be sure, the NATO allies were not happy with the Canadian reductions of the early 1970s and they let Ottawa know. By honouring all of its commitments, however, Canada avoided jeopardizing its valued seat in allied councils and continued to participate in important deliberations relating to East–West security issues. The 1970s were active years for Canada on the NATO diplomatic front. It was represented on the Nuclear Planning Group and took part in the discussions that led to the two-track decision on intermediate-range nuclear forces in 1979 in which NATO would plan for the deployment, but also stated that it was willing to negotiate the reduction, of these forces. Canada was also a participant in the Mutual and Balanced Force Reduction (MBFR) talks and the Conference on Security and Co-operation in Europe that involved nearly all the European states and the two superpowers.

The 1970s, however, were also years during which NATO sought to improve its conventional force posture as dictated by its strategy of "flexible response," which had been accepted by all alliance members in 1967:

> This concept, which adapts NATO's strategy to current political, military, and technological developments, is based upon a flexible and balanced range of appropriate responses, conventional and nuclear, to all levels of aggression. These responses, subject to appropriate political control, are designed, first to deter aggression and thus preserve the peace; but should aggression unhappily occur, to maintain the security and integrity of the North Atlantic Treaty area within the concept of forward defence.[7]

With this strategy, NATO retained its reliance on nuclear weapons and on the threat of first use should conventional defence against a Soviet conventional attack fail. But the goal of the strategy was to widen the spectrum of deterrence to include a more credible conventional component. Although the central front in Germany remained focal, flexible response also extended to the northern and southern flanks. The strategy implied, as well, that protection of the sea lines of communication would be crucial, since NATO's ability to sustain conventional resistance in Germany and to defend the flanks depended on sea-borne reinforcement and re-supply. Thus, part of NATO's efforts in the 1970s to improve its conventional posture included strengthening forces and allied co-operation at sea.

Canada was certainly aware of the changes in NATO strategy toward an emphasis on conventional deterrence; indeed, Ottawa was on record as supporting flexible response. It could be argued that the decisions of the Pearson government during the period from 1964 to 1968 giving the forces more mobility were in line with the basic idea of more flexibility in the allied posture. The same cannot be said, however, for the policies of the Trudeau government in the 1968–73 period. Decisions to reduce the forces in Europe by half and cut back on defence spending were at odds with the NATO policy of the day since the alliance was looking for more of the types of conventional forces that Canada had been contributing.

The Trudeau government was able to weather allied objections to its initial defence policies. These were the years of détente between the United States and the Soviet Union, when European governments were seeking better relations with the USSR as well. For its part, the Nixon administration was not putting direct pressure on Canada despite the provisions of the "Nixon Doctrine," whereby the United States was looking to allies to carry more of the conventional defence burden. "We were not made to feel," Trudeau reported of his talks with presidential advisor Henry Kissinger, "that if we were nice on the military strategic problems they would be nice on the bilateral problems."[8]

Later in the 1970s, as détente waned and NATO continued its conventional-force improvements, Canada found that its decision to reduce forces without abandoning commitments placed a serious constraint on the policy approach of the 1971 White Paper. As long as the CF remained committed to multiple allied roles, it would have to maintain capabilities compatible with those of its allies' forces. That is, collective-defence obligations would continue to dictate the kind of equipment Canada needed. It was not so much a question of the allies telling Canada what to do with its defence spending as of Canada having to live up to the commitments it had independently decided to retain.

There was a related aspect to this situation. As part of its new thrust in foreign policy, especially foreign economic policy, the Trudeau government sought to increase ties with areas of the world beyond the United States. This was in line with a long-standing tradition in Canadian foreign policy to seek "counterweights." In the immediate post-Confederation period, Canada had used its ties to Britain to counter the continental pull of the United States. During the first half of the 20th century, Canada had often emphasized its ties to the United States to counter imperial ties. After World War II, Canada had sought out membership in international organizations partly as a counter to the United States, which had become its largest trading partner and with which it had developed close military relations. One reason why Canada had so vigorously promoted NATO was that it viewed multilateral security as a preferable arrangement to strictly bilateral security with the United States. Although NORAD was eventually established, Canada always viewed North American defence efforts as part of its NATO obligations (a view that was not shared by Washington).

The North Atlantic Alliance had not had any appreciable impact on Canada's trading relations or other non-military policies, which were heavily oriented towards the United States. The Trudeau government wished to redress this imbalance with its 1972 "Third Option" policy, which called for expansion of other bilateral relations. Because of its wealth and size, Europe appeared to be the prime area for expansion. In the early 1970s the Canadian government sought to conclude a contractual link with the European Economic Community (EEC) that would provide the basis for an expansion of economic ties. When it came to negotiating the link, however, Ottawa found that the Europeans were still unhappy about Canada's defence reductions. Germany in particular wanted some evidence that Canada was prepared to improve its allied contributions.

By 1975 the United States had joined the European allies in urging Canada to upgrade its forces committed to NATO. Speaking in Ottawa, U.S. Secretary of Defense James Schlesinger said: "The basic premise, I believe, is that unless we are prepared to defend parts of the world other than the North American continent, we will soon have nothing more than the North American continent to defend, and that would be a calamity from the standpoint of both our nations."[9] This was in line with the long-held U.S. view that Canadian contributions to North American defence (which were not being upgraded in any case) did not offset its obligations in Europe. Moreover, by the mid-1970s, as the rate of growth in the U.S. defence expenditures declined in reaction to Vietnam, Washington was increasingly looking to allies to assume more of the burden for conventional defence.

European and American concerns about security in Europe, and hence about the future of Canada's contributions there, together with other domestic and foreign factors— the decision to retain all commitments, the overall foreign policy of strengthening ties with Europe, and the sheer physical necessity of replacing aging equipment—had already compelled the Trudeau government to reassess its defence policy within three years of releasing the 1971 White Paper. In December 1974, under the direction of the cabinet, a Defence Structure Review (DSR) was initiated. The review was led by a steering committee chaired by the secretary to the cabinet and comprising the deputy minister of defence, the under-secretary of state for external affairs, the secretary of the Treasury Board, and the chief of the defence staff (CDS), General J.A. Dextraze.

The DSR was carried out in three phases. First, the tasks of the armed forces as set forth in the White Paper were reviewed and reaffirmed. Second, the DSR examined "optional force structures which provided various levels of effort in meeting" these tasks. Significantly, the options were structured according to "combat capability" rather than sovereignty or peacekeeping tasks. The "residual capability" to perform these tasks was identified so that "later 'add-ons' could be made to the option selected to ensure the Forces could undertake all . . . [their] assigned tasks." As Dextraze put it, "hard operational needs" would determine the basic structuring of the forces.[10] The third phase of the DSR involved an examination of the specific weapons systems and funds needed to achieve sufficient capability for the identified tasks.

Phase two, completed in late 1975, also resulted in a revised and more realistic funding formula for defence. All components of the defence budget were to be indexed to inflation, and spending on capital equipment was to increase by an additional 12 percent annually until it reached at least 20 percent of the total defence budget.[11]

Even before the full review was completed, there was a distinct change in the Trudeau approach to defence, one in which NATO re-emerged as the *de facto* top defence priority. In June 1974, the NATO Council met in Ottawa for the first time in over a decade. Out of this meeting emerged the "Declaration on Atlantic Relations," which not only reaffirmed all members' support for the basic purpose and unity of the alliance, but also specifically drew attention to the importance of having Canadian forces stationed in Europe: "All members agree that the continued presence of Canadian and substantial numbers of U.S. forces in Europe plays an irreplaceable role in the defence of North America as well as Europe."[12] A year later, in May 1975, Prime Minister Trudeau assured the NATO allies that Canada would not again reduce its contribution. But, if Canadian forces were to remain in Europe, then decisions would have to be made about their roles and equipment. This was being undertaken as part of the DSR, and in November 1975 the minister of national defence announced that Canada would retain the current posture in Europe with an armoured brigade and an air group, and that both would be re-equipped.

Out of the DSR and the general reaffirmation of the importance of NATO emerged a series of decisions on weapons purchases in the late 1970s that would continue until the late 1980s. Under pressure from Germany, which was explicitly linking the status of Canada's NATO commitments with the chances of a contractual link with the EEC, Ottawa purchased 128 German-built Leopard C1 tanks for its ground forces in Europe. This meant that the forces in Europe (CFE) would retain a heavy-armour role and would not, as had been planned, become more lightly armed. In a similar fashion, the Argus long-range maritime patrol aircraft was replaced by the Aurora, whose sophisticated ASW capabilities were geared primarily to allied roles. The Trudeau government decided to build a new class of patrol frigates and to give them advanced ASW and anti-aircraft capabilities, again reflecting their role in support of NATO at sea. For both the NATO and NORAD air commitments, Canada bought the CF-18 fighter. At the time that the Liberal government was voted out of office in September 1984, it had been planning purchases of new jeep-type vehicles, heavy trucks, and a low-level air defence system for the forces in Europe.

Some steps had been taken to improve the CAST reinforcement commitment to NATO's northern flank. In 1976 the option of going to Denmark was dropped and Norway became CAST's sole deployment area. Agreements were made with Norway to allow some pre-positioning of equipment and to arrange for Norwegian ships to transport the rest of the CAST equipment in the event of a crisis.

By the end of its term in office in 1984, the Trudeau government had also reversed its earlier approach to NORAD. At the time of the 1971 White Paper, it seemed that the bomber threat to North America would continue to diminish. Both Canada and the United States had reduced the level of forces and facilities devoted to air defence: radar stations were closed and interceptor squadrons were cut back. NORAD's emphasis had shifted from active defence against the bomber to surveillance and warning of missile attack. (In 1981 the command was renamed the North American Aerospace Defence Command to reflect this shift.) For the missile warning and surveillance task, Canadian territory and airspace were not important and no U.S. Ballistic Missile Early Warning System (BMEWS) stations were built in Canada. NORAD's regions had been reorganized so that no region straddled the border and all Canadian airspace was under the command of two regional control centres located in Canada. During the 1970s it seemed that the Trudeau government's primary aim was to enhance Canadian sovereignty within NORAD.

Toward the end of the decade, however, new concern arose in the United States over the bomber threat and over a new potential threat—Soviet long-range cruise missiles. These low-flying, air-breathing missiles could be fired from bombers (air-launched cruise missiles [ALCM]) or from submarines (sea-/submarine-launched cruise missiles [SLCM]). Although it did not consider the new missiles to be a major threat, the United States did conclude that existing NORAD radars had deteriorated to the point that too many Soviet bombers and cruise missiles could enter North American airspace undetected. The U.S. Department of Defense (DOD) consequently drew up an Air Defense Master Plan (ADMP) that served as the basis for negotiations between Canada and the United States for the joint modernization of NORAD. Substantial agreement had been reached before the Conservatives took office in 1984.

Not only did the Trudeau government reverse the thrust of its 1971 White Paper with regard to NATO and NORAD, it did so with respect to peacekeeping as well. The turnabout came quickly. Despite its own warnings against involvement in a Vietnam settlement, the government agreed to send peacekeeping forces there following the January 1973 peace accords between the United States and North Vietnam. Within six months Canada withdrew in frustration as the accords began to unravel. In October of the same year, war broke out again between Israel and the Arabs. In the wake of various interim agreements brokered by Washington, Canada again dispatched peacekeeping troops under United Nations auspices. During the summer of 1974 unrest increased in Cyprus, and Turkey invaded the island despite the presence of UN peacekeeping forces. Although condemned by most members of the international community, Turkey maintained over 25 000 troops on the island and Cyprus became even more divided than before. UN forces, including a large Canadian contingent, continued to be deployed between the Greek and Turkish sectors.

The sustained support that the Trudeau government gave to peacekeeping was, as in the past, fully consistent with, and indeed supportive of, American and other allied interests. And it did not require spending increases, new equipment, or changes in the posture of the armed forces.

Judged on the basis of major spending decisions, there was clear continuity between the defence policy of the Trudeau government and previous governments. Alliance-oriented, collective-defence roles rather than non-military sovereignty-protection tasks continued to drive procurement. This was because Canada had decided to retain all its alliance commitments. The Department of National Defence explained to a Senate committee in 1984 that, while sovereignty was the "ultimate priority,"

> this does not necessarily imply that the first role [sovereignty] need have the highest priority in terms of force structure design, readiness, manning, or resource allocation. Indeed, distinction must be made between the priorities established by government for Canadian Defence Policy, and the appropriate priorities which must be established to ensure the optimum allocation of limited resources to support that policy.
>
> This distinction is necessary because the more military demanding roles usually subsume the capabilities for less demanding activities and commitments. It follows that the purpose of developing an appropriate force posture, priority must be given to the roles of defending North America in conjunction with U.S. forces, and the collective defence of the NATO area. Thus, although other roles may well determine the nature of the activities in peacetime, the fundamental purpose of force structure development must be to meet the demands of collective defence and deterrence . . . [13]

The defence policies of the Trudeau era were directed toward meeting "the demands of collective defence and deterrence." But the cumulative impact of defence-budget restraints that dated back to the early sixties and became more pronounced in the Pearson and Trudeau years created a gap between the capabilities and the commitments of the armed forces. Between 1968 and 1984 overall federal expenditures increased almost tenfold, from about $11 billion to nearly $110 billion. This dramatic rise was the result of both inflation and the expansion of government services, particularly in the area of social-welfare programs, including education and health care. During that same period, defence spending increased by just over a factor of five, from $1.7 billion in 1968 to about $9 billion in 1984. The difference reflects decisions about the relative priority of defence in national policy, or, specifically, the decision to favour domestic programs over those in the foreign and defence policy fields.

As indicated above, however, once Canada decided to maintain modern armed forces and to commit them to collective-defence roles, increases in defence spending could not be avoided. Out of the DSR had come a pledge to raise spending, and increases in the late 1970s did sometimes exceed 15 percent per year. But these years also experienced the highest sustained inflation levels of the postwar period; thus, real increases in defence spending often fell below three percent. Emphasis was placed on capital-equipment improvements, and the percentage of the defence budget allocated for this purpose rose to 20 percent by 1977–78, and higher in later years.[14] Although the Trudeau government agreed in 1978 to implement the NATO target of three-percent annual real increases, these increases were being made on a reduced base because of the cutbacks of the early 1970s. Moreover, regular force levels were to rise very slowly: the CF was limited to increases of only 400 positions annually from 1978 forward.

During the 1979 election campaign, the Conservatives under Joe Clark pledged to improve Canada's performance in defence. On coming into office at the head of a minority government in May, Prime Minister Clark promised reviews of both foreign policy and defence policy. He instituted a Policy and Expenditure Management System (PEMS) to improve decisionmaking, and set up a task force to review unification. The Clark government, defeated in the February 1980 election, was not in power long enough to have any significant impact on defence policy.

Trudeau returned to power and essentially picked up where he had left off. During his last years in office, his government steadily increased defence spending, sometimes exceeding NATO's three-percent goal, while other allies were failing to meet it.

Yet by most other NATO countries' standards, Canada was not perceived as pulling its weight. A standard measure of defence spending is the percentage of gross domestic product (GDP) devoted to it. In 1984, of 16 allied nations, Canada, at 2.1 percent, ranked only above Luxembourg and Iceland (the latter having no armed forces at all). According to a U.S. Department of Defense analysis, in 1985, with Canada's relative prosperity, it should have been spending twice what it was spending on defence.[15]

Such measurements are somewhat simplistic and do not accurately gauge the relative importance of allied contributions. For example, while some countries, such as Turkey and France, devote more of their national resources to defence, not all of that spending is directed toward NATO, whereas nearly everything Canada spends on defence, in Europe and in North America, is for collective defence. And, as the Trudeau government argued, in absolute terms, Canada was the sixth largest spender within the alliance and was meeting the three-percent goal.

Nevertheless, despite the major re-equipment program, the Trudeau government seemed unable to reverse the decline in capabilities. The new weapons were better than the ones they replaced, but there were fewer of them. For example, only 18 Auroras were bought to replace 33 Argus long-range patrol aircraft, and 128 Leopards replaced 300 Centurion tanks. Decisions on major purchases were often delayed and then acquisition had to be spread out over a number of years, as in the case of the CF-18 and the new patrol frigate. For the maritime forces, a series of refurbishing programs were undertaken in order to keep older ships at sea longer. Manpower levels, which first plunged to 77 703 in 1975, rose slightly to 83 630 by the end of 1984, but were still nearly 40 000 less than in 1964.

The commitment–capability gap has been identified as the major problem in Canadian defence policy. In his 1985 study for the Macdonald Royal Commission on the economy, R.B. Byers concluded that "Canadian commitments to NATO and Western security are excessive and unrealistic given the current size and capabilities of the Canadian Forces."[16] In 1986 the special joint committee of the House of Commons and the Senate reviewing Canada's international relations referred to the commitment–capability gap as "the fundamental issue in defence policy" and warned of "grave dangers in leaving the gap unattended."[17] Similar warnings had been sounded by an earlier committee of the Senate that issued several reports chronicling a wide range of deficiencies. These deficiencies were most notable with regard to Canada's allied commitments, but because the forces used to fulfil collective-defence roles were also tasked with sovereignty obligations, even this function could not be assured. Thus, as the Senate committee observed in the case of maritime forces "MARCOM, which is responsible for the country's seaward defences, cannot meet its commitments to the protection of Canadian sovereignty, to the defence of North America—much less to NATO."[18]

The Mulroney Government

During the federal election campaign in the summer of 1984, the Progressive Conservative party, led by Brian Mulroney, charged the Liberals with doing the "ultimate disservice to Canada by running down our armed forces." This "unacceptable" situation would be corrected under a new Conservative government. Defence spending was to be increased and Canada was to pull its weight in its alliances.

On coming into office that September, the Mulroney government initiated a review of both foreign policy and defence policy. The foreign policy review process moved much faster than the defence review, producing a discussion paper in the spring of 1985. Following this, a special joint committee conducted wide-ranging public hearings across the country and issued its report in June 1986. The report, entitled *Independence and Internationalism*, contained over one hundred recommendations, including important defence-related ones, such as the need to enhance Arctic sovereignty. Rather than producing a formal White Paper on foreign policy, in December 1986 the Department of External Affairs (DEA) issued a point-by-point response to the joint committee report, which then served as the Mulroney government's statement on foreign policy.

The department's response accepted most of the recommendations of the committee and also agreed with the general thrust of the report, which was that Canada's welfare depended heavily on the broader international political, economic, and strategic situation and that active involvement in international affairs was therefore a necessity. The tone was decidedly Pearsonian in that it called for increased Canadian involvement in all aspects of international politics, from trade to development to arms control. In the area of national security, the DEA response reaffirmed the fundamental approach that had been taken since the Cold War years. Noting that national defence was the "foundation of a country's security" and that the government was "determined to ensure that Canada's military capabilities are appropriate for the tasks required of them," it stressed that

> Canada's security rests, first and foremost, on the maintenance of the strategic balance between East and West. In this endeavour, Canada has stood and will continue to stand alongside its Western partners. It could not be otherwise; our values and our determination to defend freedom and democracy against an undiminished political and military challenge align us in the most fundamental way with other Western industrialized countries.[19]

The importance of NATO was particularly emphasized because of the opportunity it afforded Canada to maximize its security and influence. Europe remained the most critical military region, and the inner-German border the "security fault-line in East–West relations." Mention was also made of the "renewed importance" of NORAD. In addition, sovereignty protection was stressed along with the need to maintain allied commitments. This was especially evident in the stated intention to establish a new "northern" dimension for foreign policy, with greater emphasis on Arctic sovereignty. As for peacekeeping, it would continue in accordance with the internationalist spirit that would guide foreign policy under the Conservative government.

Despite the early drafting of a Green (or discussion) Paper, the defence White Paper did not emerge until June 1987. In the meantime, however, the policy decisions and in particular the defence-spending priorities of the Mulroney government gave a rather clear indication that collective-defence roles would continue to determine the posture of the CF in that it was making an effort to close the commitment–capability gap with regard to NATO.

One of the government's first decisions was to augment the forces in Europe by 1200, bringing them closer, although not up to, war strength. The double-tasking of the Canadian reinforcement to NATO's AMF(L), whereby the battalion constituting Canada's commitment would eventually have to join up with the CAST group in Norway, was ended. Henceforth, each commitment would stand alone, in effect increasing the Canadian reinforcement pledge by one battalion. In the autumn of 1986, the CAST commitment was exercised in full scale for the first time.

When the Mulroney government came into office, negotiations with the United States on the modernization of NORAD were close to conclusion. In March 1985, at a summit meeting between the prime minister and President Reagan, an agreement was signed to upgrade NORAD's capabilities. The bulk of the new facilities would be located in the United States, but a new North Warning System (NWS) would replace the DEW line. Also, new forward operating locations (FOLs) for interceptors and dispersed operating bases (DOBs) for airborne warning and control (AWAC) aircraft, were to be constructed in the Canadian north. The total cost of the modernization was set at $7 billion. The Canadian portion would be about 12 percent, although Canada agreed to assume 40 percent of the specific cost of the NWS.

In addition to reaffirming the NATO and NORAD roles, the Conservative government also continued Canada's contribution to international peacekeeping efforts. Forces were maintained on Cyprus, along the Israeli–Syrian border, and in the Sinai, as part of the Multinational Force and Observers (MFO) established under the 1979 Camp David agreement between Israel and Egypt.

The Conservative government proceeded with the re-equipment programs that had been initiated by the Liberal government, including a new low-level air defence system for the forces committed to Europe. The government also announced that it would be examining replacements for the Seaking ASW helicopters and the three submarines. Personnel levels were to be increased and new uniforms were ordered, restoring the traditional colours associated with the army, navy, and air force. Unification was not to be undone, but it would now be possible to distinguish sailors from pilots and tank commanders.

But all this—including the new uniforms— would take longer than the Conservatives had anticipated. The reason was money. Faced with a large federal deficit (which in proportion to the populations was nearly twice as large as that of the United States) and continuing public demand for social services and other government support for individuals, businesses, and regions, the Mulroney government was unable to increase the defence budget significantly. Although DND was spared the spending cuts that were applied elsewhere in the federal government, real growth would be held to under three percent and indeed was projected to fall to just two percent per year through to 1990–91, that is, less than it had been during the last years of the Trudeau government.

As the Mulroney government was attempting to cope with the serious commitment–capability gap it had inherited, particularly with regard to allied obligations, the sovereignty issue re-emerged. The focus was on the Arctic, where an increase in American and Soviet naval activity was viewed as raising new challenges to Canada's claims, and served to highlight the lack of military capabilities in the region. This was compounded by the continuing dispute between Ottawa and Washington over the status of the Northwest Passage. DEA's call for a northern foreign policy addressed these concerns, as did the decision to build a $500–$750 million Class 8 icebreaker with some of the funds coming from DND.

In recent years, new concerns over arms control and Canada's relations with the United States have been closely associated with calls for greater protection of Canadian sovereignty. President Reagan's Strategic Defense Initiative (SDI) was the target of much public criticism and there were charges in the press and before parliamentary committees that Canada would become involved in SDI through its participation in NORAD and the defence production-sharing arrangements it had with the United States. In 1986 the Mulroney government turned down an American request to enter into SDI co-operation on a government-to-government basis, but did not rule out involvement by private Canadian firms. In general, a rising public interest in arms-control and security issues focussed more attention on defence policy and the White Paper.

The 1987 White Paper on Defence

While the Mulroney government was making a series of decisions on defence policy, it was also conducting a review in preparation for the release of a new White Paper. The review was hampered by the frequent turnover of individuals in the position of minister of national defence. When he assumed the post in June 1986, Perrin Beatty initiated a new review. He consulted widely within government and with allies, and also conducted a series of discussions with individuals outside government. The final decisions were made by cabinet, and the White Paper, entitled *Challenge and Commitment: A Defence Policy for Canada*, was tabled in the House of Commons on 5 June 1987. Mr. Beatty declared that it represented a "made-in-Canada" defence policy. And indeed, its content reaffirmed that while Canada's security must be pursued within the constraints imposed by the international environment, Canadian governments do have a measure of choice.

The White Paper attempted to distinguish the policies of the Mulroney Conservative government from those of the preceding Trudeau government, and hence to put some distance between the two. It described the 1971 White Paper as overly optimistic in its assessment of the future course of international relations. Imbued with the spirit of détente and the hope for arms control, the document had "looked forward to a world in which military forces would be less relevant in their traditional roles." While the nuclear balance had remained stable and some progress was recorded in arms control, "the great hopes of the early seventies [had] not been realized." Détente waned and nuclear and conventional arsenals continued to grow. "The realities of the present," the White Paper observed, "call for a more sober approach to international relations and the needs of security." From the Canadian standpoint, part of sobriety meant recognition of a "significant commitment–capability gap," the result of "decades of neglect." "Much of the equipment of most elements of the Canadian forces is in an advanced state of obsolescence or is already obsolete." The White Paper's intention was to provide a defence policy to meet the realities of international relations and to set forth a rebuilding plan for the armed forces.

In explaining their plans, the Conservatives adopted, as they had done in the foreign policy review, an approach consistent with the overall thrust of Canadian security policy since the Cold War years. Echoing a familiar theme, the White Paper declared that "the first objective of Canadian security" was the promotion of "a stronger and more stable international environment in which our values and interests can flourish." Canada would pursue this objective "within the framework of collective security":

Like each of its predecessors, this Government believes wholeheartedly that there is no acceptable alternative and rejects as

naive or self-serving the arguments of those who promote neutrality or unilateral disarmament. Canada has never been neutral. We have always sought our security in a larger family of
like-minded nations. In light of our position in the world, the
values and traditions which have been defended steadfastly by
previous generations of Canadians, and our political and economic interests, neutrality would be hypocrisy. Our security
would continue to depend on the deterrence provided by our
former allies, but we would have opted out of any contribution
to and, equally significantly, any say in the management of that
deterrent. We could turn our backs on the obligation to work
for a stable world order; technology and geography would not,
however, allow us to escape the consequences should that
order collapse.[20]

Working for a more stable world order included supporting arms control and the peaceful settlement of international disputes. Canada would continue to encourage superpower negotiations on the limitation of nuclear weapons
and would remain a contributor to peacekeeping operations. However, the emphasis in the White Paper was clearly
on the military aspects of collective defence and the government was straightforward in identifying where the military threat to Canada and its allies originated:

While the conflict between East and West is not intrinsically
military, it could lead to a clash of arms. For its part, the West
would resort to armed force only in its own defence. Although
some would say that the same is true of the East, can Western
governments responsibly base the well-being and future of
their own people on expressions of goodwill and on the most
optimistic interpretation of the intentions of others? It is a fact,
not a matter of interpretation, that the West is faced with an
ideological, political and economic adversary whose explicit
long-term aim is to mould the world in its own image. That
adversary has at its disposal massive military forces and a
proven willingness to use force, both at home and abroad, to
achieve political objectives. Perhaps this is a reflection of a
deep-rooted obsession with security, well-founded on the bitter
lessons of Russian history. It cannot but make everyone else
feel decidedly insecure. This does not mean that war with the
Soviet Union is inevitable or that mutually beneficial arrangements should not be pursued. It does mean that unless and
until there is concrete progress, the West has no choice but to
rely for its security on the maintenance of a rough balance of
forces, backed up by nuclear deterrence.[21]

In accordance with this perspective, the White Paper
stressed Canada's commitment to both NATO and NORAD. In

the case of NATO, it also reiterated the long-held Canadian view of central Europe as the "geographic focus of the wider conflict between East and West." "A free and secure western Europe" was important to Canada because, if it were to be "subverted, overrun or destroyed, what remained of the West would face a bleak future." "It is difficult to imagine," the White Paper observed, "what place Canada would have in such a world, the context in which this nation seeks its destiny would be diminished in every respect and the most profound concerns about Canada's future as an independent nation would arise."

The 1987 White Paper was not, however, simply a reaffirmation of past themes and commitments. In his speech to the House of Commons, Beatty noted that defence policy had failed "to take into account the significant geo-political and geo-strategic changes affecting Canadian security since the last White Paper was tabled in 1971." The first of these changes was the growing importance of the Pacific Ocean in international political, economic, and strategic relations. Soviet naval power had also expanded, particularly in the North Pacific. Canada's economic, cultural, and strategic interests in the Pacific had likewise increased and this had to be reflected in defence policy. The second change was the emergence of the Arctic as a region of strategic importance, especially as it was becoming an operating area for foreign submarines and was hence raising security and sovereignty concerns for Canada: "Technology . . . is making the Arctic more accessible. Canadians cannot ignore that what was once a buffer [between the two superpowers] could become a battleground." A third trend the White Paper identified was the development by the Soviets of ALCMs and SLCMs "and Canada's vulnerability to attack by these weapons systems from our three ocean approaches." The fourth change that previously had not been taken sufficiently into account was the "requirement for sustainable, supportable ground, and air forces in Europe." This requirement would become even more pressing should agreements be reached to eliminate or reduce intermediate-range nuclear forces in Europe, "where the Warsaw Pact has a preponderance of the conventional forces."

The major policy proposals contained in the White Paper dealt with the equipment that the armed forces would have to procure to properly address these changes in the international security environment. As three of the changes were related to maritime security, it was not surprising that the centrepiece of the White Paper's proposals was the creation of a balanced "three ocean Navy." Such a navy would be able to provide surveillance and assert Canadian sovereignty. It would also be available to sustain Canada's ASW commitment to NATO. The White Paper proposed:

- an additional six frigates (beyond the six under construction);
- a fleet of ten to twelve nuclear-powered attack submarines;
- installation of a modern, fixed, under-ice surveillance system in the Arctic;
- developing new sonar systems for surface ships;
- acquisition of new shipborne ASW helicopters;
- an additional six maritime long-range patrol aircraft and modernization of the existing medium-range aircraft;
- mine countermeasures vessels (to be used by the reserves).

To meet the bomber, ALCM and SLCM threats, the White Paper stated that Canada would continue with NORAD modernization under the 1985 agreement. This entailed construction of the North Warning System (NWS) and the upgrading of northern airfields as forward operating locations (FOLs) and dispersed operating bases (DOBs). But the White Paper stressed that the government would be promoting Canadian research into new space-based and airborne air surveillance systems. It would also be seeking to co-operate with the United States in that country's air-defence research projects, such as the Teal Ruby surveillance satellite and the USAF's Air Defense Initiative (ADI).

Canada would be adjusting its forces to meet NATO's requirement for sustainability on the central front. Based on the Brave Lion exercise of 1986 and other analyses, the government concluded that the CAST commitment to Norway was a hollow one and that Canada could not effect a timely reinforcement in the event of a crisis or hostilities or sustain those forces if they managed to arrive in time. Since the government of Norway does not allow the stationing of foreign forces in peacetime and since Canada could not both improve CAST and maintain a presence in Germany, Ottawa decided to drop the CAST commitment altogether. The brigade group and two air squadrons would be redirected to a German reinforcement effort. The former CAST brigade group, when combined with the 4 Canadian Mechanized Brigade Group and additional troops, would form a mechanized division on the central front with the objective of providing NATO with a stronger reserve for counterattack. The current Canadian Air Group in Germany was to be reinforced with two Canada-based squadrons and would be redesignated as an air division.

Without making specific pledges, the White Paper noted that new tanks and other equipment would be purchased for the two brigades dedicated to Germany. Other improvements would be made to improve the sustainability of these forces. Canada would also retain its commitment to the AMF(L) for use in either Norway (where existing pre-positioned stocks would be left) or Denmark. To provide additional personnel for the European commitments, the White Paper proposed an expansion and upgrading of the reserves, as well as their integration into regular force units, especially in MOBCOM.

Reserve units would also become more important in the territorial defence of Canada, another role slated for improvement. In the event of a reinforcement of the European forces, Canada would have few land units available "to protect military vital points and to deploy rapidly to deal with threats in any part of the country." To correct this, the White Paper proposed the creation of additional brigades, mainly from the reserves, "organized for the purposes of command, control and support into a task force structure and provided with modern equipment." The White Paper also proposed the establishment of a northern training centre to prepare the regular and reserve forces for the territorial defence of the country. Still another role for the reserves was the operation of the new mine-countermeasures vessels.

To pay for all the new equipment, the White Paper proposed a funding formula that involved annual real increases in defence spending of at least two percent per year, with major capital acquisitions being funded above this level in the years in which the procurements were made. The government would work with a "rolling" five-year plan and cabinet would conduct an annual review of defence spending for the following five-year period.

Overall then, the 1987 White Paper on defence promised to rebuild the CF in accordance with a traditional Canadian approach whereby Canadian security was predicated on that of the United States and the West European allies. Within these parameters, however, there was an unmistakable shift of emphasis from the primarily European orientation of the Cold War years to North American roles. Of the four changes identified by the minister, three of them—the importance of the Pacific and of the Arctic and the growing ALCM/SLCM threat—necessitated more attention to the

direct defence of Canada. In closing the commitment–capability gap, it is noteworthy that the one commitment cut was in Europe. While Canada would attempt to
improve its posture in Germany and while the new navy
would be available for NATO roles, the bulk of the capital
acquisitions was clearly related to the air and sea defence
of North America.

The government shifted emphasis because it saw an increased Soviet threat to the United States and Canada. Yet
it was also evident that Prime Minister Mulroney and his
cabinet were responding to growing public concern over
sovereignty protection, particularly in the Arctic. This had
been reflected in the foreign policy review with its call for
a more northern orientation. In this sense, the 1987 White
Paper was actually consistent with the thrust of the 1971
White Paper in that it proposed the acquisition of equipment
that would help Canada patrol its own maritime approaches
and assert its sovereignty.

There was, though, a key difference in the approach that
the two White Papers took to the sovereignty problem. In
1971 sovereignty protection was seen in the context of a
declining direct military threat to North America from Soviet air forces and general-purpose maritime forces. Ballistic
missiles constituted the only major threat, and there was
no defence against them save deterrence. Thus the emphasis
in 1971 was on sovereignty protection from non-military
threats, such as fishing violations or pollution.

The 1987 White Paper was based on the premise that North
American defence would become more important in the
broader strategic context as the Soviets developed new
generations of cruise missiles and bombers and increased
their activity in the Arctic. Theoretically, this would bring
about a heightened concern on the part of the United States
for continental defence, consistent with its general trend toward strategic defence. Thus, the Mulroney government saw
a threat to sovereignty in the existing lack of Canadian capabilities: if not rectified, it would in time result in an overwhelming dependence on the United States for the defence
of Canada at sea and in the air.

The need to do more for North American defence as a
means of protecting Canadian sovereignty put the 1987
White Paper somewhat at odds with the views of some arms-
control groups in Canada. This was so because in order
to maintain its contribution to the joint defence of the continent, Canada would have to acquire the kinds of forces
that would allow it to participate with the United States in

maritime and air defence. With regard to maritime and Arctic defence, the minister observed that

> some people would suggest that we contract out the defence of Canada to others. The Government is prepared to discuss co-operation in all aspects of the defence of North America, but we will not allow Canada's sovereignty to be compromised. We will be a partner with our allies and not a dependent.[22]

On the decision to proceed with investigation of space-based air surveillance research, the White Paper stated:

> Should the results of our studies and those of the United States show that space-based radar is feasible, practical and affordable, the Department will have to devote, over the next 15 years, significant resources to the establishment of a space-based surveillance system for North American air defence. Decisions regarding our contribution to a joint space-based radar system, or the development of a national system, if a co-operative endeavour is not possible, will have to be taken in the course of the next 5 to 10 years. Failure to meet this challenge could mean forfeiting the responsibility for surveillance of Canadian airspace to the United States.[23]

At the time of writing this book, it remains to be seen whether the policies set forth in the 1987 White Paper (especially the spending proposals) will be fully implemented. There are questions about the cost and necessity of certain weapons, particularly the nuclear-powered submarines. Any new non–Progressive Conservative government in Ottawa will not be bound by this document. Both the Liberal and New Democratic parties have criticized the White Paper and have indicated changes they would make if elected to office. The NDP, whose standing in public opinion polls reached historic heights in 1987, has adopted a platform calling for withdrawal from both NATO and NORAD. Simultaneously, the party's official response to the White Paper suggested major increases in defence spending, particularly in the area of maritime forces and North American air defence. Thus, while the NDP opposes nuclear submarines and has called for the withdrawal of Canadian forces from Europe, it also advocates a balanced maritime force with more surface ships, long-range patrol aircraft, and conventionally powered submarines. And although it would dismantle NORAD, the NDP would have Canada continuing to work closely with the United States in the air defence of the continent, operating the NWS, deploying more CF-18 interceptors, and even acquiring AWAC aircraft.[24] For their part, the

Liberals, while also criticizing the nuclear-submarine decision, appeared to support the other procurement proposals contained in the White Paper.

Whatever the outcome of the next federal election, it is unlikely that the major thrust of the 1987 White Paper—that is, to shift the emphasis of Canada's defence efforts toward North America and toward maritime tasks—will be abandoned even if Canada continues to identify its security closely with that of the Western allies.

That this shift is a reaction to broader strategic trends brought about by the decisions of other countries—adversaries as well as allies—is not new to Canadian defence policy. Since 1867 Canada has had to seek its security in reference to the actions and policies of the great powers. Nevertheless, now, as in the past, options and choices are available within the larger strategic and political environment. The constraints are ever-present, but so is the capacity to make decisions that reflect Canada's independence and sovereignty.

Notes

1. Larry R. Stewart, ed., *Canadian Defence Policy: Selected Speeches and Documents 1964–1981* (Kingston: Centre for International Relations, Queens University, 1982), pp. 10–21. On the NATO decision, see Bruce Thordarson, *Trudeau and Foreign Policy: A Study in Decision-Making* (Toronto: Oxford University Press, 1972).

2. Joseph T. Jockel, *Canada and NATO's Northern Flank* (Toronto: York Centre for International and Strategic Studies, York University, 1986), p. 22.

3. Canada, Department of National Defence, *Defence in the 70s* (Ottawa: Information Canada, 1971), p. 16.

4. Canada, *Defence in the 70s*, p. 30.

5. Canada, Department of External Affairs, *Foreign Policy for Canadians*, booklet on the Pacific (Ottawa: The Queen's Printer, 1970), p. 24.

6. Danford W. Middlemiss, "Department of National Defence," in *Spending Tax Dollars: Federal Expenditures 1980–1981*, ed. G. Bruce Doern, (Ottawa: School of Public Administration, Carleton University, 1980), pp. 82–85.

7. *NATO Final Communiqués* (Brussels: NATO Information Service, n.d.), p. 197.

8. Thordarson, *Trudeau and Foreign Policy*, p. 141.

9. United States, Department of Defense, Transcript of Joint Press Conference of U.S. Secretary of Defense, James R. Schlesinger, and Canadian Minister of National Defence, James Richardson, September 1975.

10. General J.A. Dextraze, "A New Era for Canada's Armed Forces," *Statements and Speeches*, no. 76/3, 16 January 1976. See also C.J. Marshall, "Canada's forces take stock in Defence Structure Review," *International Perspectives* (January/February 1976), pp. 26–30.

11. Dan Middlemiss, "Paying for National Defence: The Pitfalls of Formula Funding," *Canadian Defence Quarterly* 12, no. 3 (Winter 1982/3): 24–29.

12. Cited in Stewart, *Canadian Defence Policy*, p. 41.

13. Canada, Senate, Special Committee on National Defence, *Proceedings*, Issue no. 8, 17 April 1984, p. 8A:6.

14. R.B. Byers, "Canadian Security and Defence: The Legacy and the Challenges," *Adelphi Papers* 214 (Winter 1986), pp. 33–34.

15. United States, Department of Defense, *Report on Allied Contributions to the Common Defense* (Washington, D.C., 1986), p. 20.

16. R.B. Byers, "Canadian Defence and Defence Procurement: Implications for Economic Policy," in *Selected Problems in Formulating Foreign Economic Policy*, research coordinators Denis Stairs and Gilbert R. Winham (Toronto: University of Toronto Press, 1985), p. 138.

17. Canada, Special Joint Committee of the Senate and the House of Commons on Canada's International Relations, *Independence and Internationalism* (Ottawa: Supply and Services Canada, 1986), pp. 48, 50.

18. Canada, Senate, Subcommittee on National Defence of the Standing Committee on Foreign Affairs, *Canada's Maritime Defence* (Ottawa: Supply and Services Canada, 1983), p. 2.

19. Canada, Department of External Affairs, *Canada's International Relations* (Ottawa: Supply and Services Canada, 1986), p. 11.

20. Canada, Department of National Defence, *Challenge and Commitment: A Defence Policy For Canada*, 1987 White Paper (Ottawa: Supply and Services Canada, 1987), p. 3.

21. Canada, *Challenge and Commitment*, p. 5.

22. The Honourable Perrin Beatty, Minister of National Defence, "Address upon the Tabling of the Defence White Paper in the House of Commons," 5 June 1987.

23. Canada, *Challenge and Commitment*, p. 59.

24. Derek Blackburn, "Canadian Sovereignty, Security and Defence: A New Democratic Response to the Defence White Paper," Ottawa, 30 July 1987.

4

THE FEDERAL GOVERNMENT

POLICY-MAKING

ENVIRONMENT

Introduction

As discussed in Chapter 1, Canadian policy making occurs within three environments—the governmental, the domestic, and the external. Of these three, the governmental environment, embracing the political executive, the legislature, and the bureaucracy, is the most crucial to an understanding of where and how the key decisions regarding the formulation and implementation of Canadian defence policy are made. The federal government is the paramount institution with respect to national-security issues: it filters the interests, demands, and pressures emanating from Canadian domestic society and from the broader reaches of the international system. Here, competing and often contradictory influences on defence policy are brought together and assessed, and authoritative decisions are rendered regarding their relative priority. Here, too, broad decisions on policy substance are translated into their budgetary and resource components and are then transformed into the particulars of military posture and deployment through the process of policy implementation. In short, the federal government is the focal point for the creation of Canadian defence policy.

The pre-eminence of the federal government in the making of Canadian defence policy is constitutionally sanctioned. Section 15 of the British North America Act of 1867 (now the Constitution Act, 1867) states: "The Command-in-Chief of the Land and Naval Militia, and of all Naval and Military Forces, of and in Canada, is hereby declared to continue and be vested in the Queen."[1] Furthermore, Section 91(7) designates the "Militia, Military and Naval Service, and

Defence" as one of the enumerated classes of subjects falling under the exclusive legislative authority of the Parliament of Canada.[2]

While the BNA Act unambiguously vests the Queen and Parliament with formal legal authority over matters pertaining to the defence of Canada, it does not specify how or by whom this responsibility is to be exercised on a day-to-day basis. As might be expected, the sovereign's actual powers with respect to defence policy have been clarified and modified over time through the passage of legislation and by the evolution of parliamentary practice.

In the course of the historical development of cabinet government in Canada and the "fusion" of powers that now characterizes this form of government, three main sets of decision makers have come to dominate the making and administration of Canadian defence policy: the political executive, the legislature, and the civil service.[3] Because legal and *de facto* power is not equally distributed among these actors, each has acquired a different role in, and has exerted a different type and degree of influence on, the formulation and implementation of Canadian defence policy. This chapter will seek to establish what these differences of power, role, and influence are by identifying the main sets of federal government defence decision makers and by examining and explaining their individual roles and influence in the policy-making process.

Of course, the phrase *policy-making process* is in itself somewhat misleading in that there are several different processes through which defence decisions are generated in Canada. For example, we frequently find references to the strategic-policy planning process, the budgetary process, the personnel-management process, and the weapons-acquisition process. Each deals with its own particular set of issues and generates its own decisions. Collectively these decisions comprise what we commonly refer to as Canadian defence policy.

Nevertheless, these process-derived differences can have a significant bearing on which sets of actors play what roles in exerting their particular influence on different types of defence issues. For example, it is reasonable to expect that high-level decision makers in the executive and legislative branches of government—those who possess the formal authority and power to decide—will address themselves to different types of policy decisions and with a different frequency than the lower-level officials in the bureaucracy, who are mainly responsible for marshalling the information and options on which higher-level decisions are based and for carrying out those decisions once they are made.

It is equally reasonable, however, to expect some blurring of these distinctions and some overlapping in interest, role and influence among these groups of actors. Policy making is not always a neatly compartmentalized activity. Therefore, a second concern of this chapter will be to identify the points of both differentiation and overlap, to explain why they exist, and then to suggest what their implications might be for policy. Which actors examine what issues? What is the relative salience of these issues to the different actors? What are their interests and what considerations are uppermost in their assessments? What constituencies do they serve? Where and how do they act in the policy-making processes? Who sets the agenda of defence policy? What accounts for their relative success or failure in achieving their desired objectives?

In seeking to answer these and related questions, we shall examine the general patterns and methods of interaction both within each group of government decision makers and among the different types and levels of actors. An appreciation of these different relationships and modes of interaction is crucial to an understanding of the dynamics and rationality of the Canadian defence policy-making process as a whole.

The Political Executive

As noted earlier, the important principle of civilian control of Canadian defence policy is rooted in the Constitution. As the sovereign's representative, the Governor General has been the commander-in-chief of Canada's armed forces since the earliest colonial days. With the development of the Canadian system of parliamentary government, however, the actual locus of political–legal authority over defence policy has changed, as have the formal mechanisms by which this control is exercised. Thus, while the Governor General remains the titular head of the Canadian Forces, Parliament, and more specifically, the cabinet, has become the dominant defence policy-making agency in Canada.

But the cabinet itself is not monolithic, and there has emerged within this pre-eminent executive body a wide constellation of actors, each having a particular role in the defence decision-making process. The most important of these decision makers are the prime minister and the minister of national defence. Other potential sources of cabinet influence on defence policy include the following: the ministers of other portfolios; various cabinet committees (the Priorities and Planning Committee, the Committee on Foreign and Defence Policy, the Treasury Board)[4]; various parliamentary secretaries and assistants; and the bureaucracies of the Privy Council Office and the Prime Minister's Office (PMO). By virtue of their legal responsibilities, expertise, administrative services, and access to decision makers, each of these actors provides information, advice, and recommendations that help to shape the form and content of contemporary Canadian defence policy.

The Prime Minister Given the recognized primacy of the prime minister within the cabinet,[5] and his historical preeminence in the making of Canadian foreign policy generally,[6] it might be expected that the prime minister would act as the dominant decision maker in the field of defence policy. This is only partly true.

Beginning with Mackenzie King, Canadian prime ministers and their cabinets have been confronted by the military establishment's aspirations for a higher position among competing national priorities. During the early post-World War II years, the government tended to view the military as a necessary evil in the context of the new postwar system of order based on collective security. The military was not to be trusted, in that it harboured parochial, self-aggrandizing notions of its role and was uneducated—literally and figuratively—in the niceties of domestic political intercourse.[7] Its voice was demanding and occasionally shrill (often manifesting itself in unpardonable public displays) and its advice regarding the necessity of peacetime national preparedness was both unwelcome—in that it meant a drain on funds required for social welfare and national development—and, for the most part, unheeded, at least until external military crises made it impossible to ignore.

Since 1945 the conduct of Canadian foreign policy has generally been viewed as a political-diplomatic preserve, not a military one. The defence portfolio has not been regarded as a promising avenue for political career advancement. Not a single minister of national defence (MND) has ever been elevated to the position of *primus inter pares* within cabinet, and no serving prime minister has ever headed the defence portfolio—in marked contrast to the situation with the more prestigious senior ministry of external affairs.[8]

Prime-ministerial interest in national-defence issues has been sporadic and, when (even if infrequently) manifested, has tended to be constraining. From the standpoint of DND and the military, these occasional sallies of higher-level interest have been viewed as disruptive at best and debilitating at worst. Diefenbaker's abrupt cancellation in February 1959 of the procurement program for the CF-105 Arrow jet interceptor was a blow to the pride of the RCAF insofar as it deprived that service of a state-of-the-art aircraft.[9] Moreover, his dilatory and indecisive handling of the delicate issue of the acquisition of nuclear warheads for Canadian delivery systems in the early 1960s not only led to the resignation of Douglas Harkness as MND, but also called into question Canada's reliability in carrying out what the military perceived as clear-cut defence obligations to its allies.[10] Finally, Trudeau's review of Canadian defence policy in the late 1960s, which contributed to the decision to halve Canada's forces in NATO Europe in 1969 and culminated in the new statement of defence policy priorities in the White Paper of 1971, was viewed with considerable dismay by DND and the military. Not only was DND's policy advice not accepted by the prime minister, but the military also had its budget frozen for a three-year period and its primary mandate revised from the traditional NATO orientation to the less glamorous, quasi-military one of "sovereignty protection."[11]

Prime ministers have tended to restrict more than to stimulate Canadian defence policy. For the most part, they have not been greatly interested in the details of policy decisions. Their main, and certainly not inconsequential, role has been to set the broad parameters of policy, and to ensure that defence has not exacted an undue drain on federal finances. They have tended to avoid making defence a prominent and therefore potentially contentious issue of national policy. With the exception of Trudeau, none has used his power and prestige to make sweeping changes in defence policy.

Moreover, to the extent that they have been interested in defence matters, most prime ministers have been attracted by the political benefits to be derived from promoting defence either as a protection against foreign (usually U.S.) encroachments on Canadian sovereignty or as the legitimate "political dues" required for Canada to purchase diplomatic, and possibly economic, influence within NATO.

Most Canadian leaders have shared Trudeau's reluctance to "put a lot of dough into armaments,"[12] and they have been largely successful in resisting DND's requests for a substantially greater share of federal expenditures.

If the prime minister's direct personal role in defence policy making has been limited, his indirect role has been more substantial. A chief source of prime-ministerial power in Canadian politics derives from his prerogative to appoint his own cabinet and to structure it to his own design and purposes.[13] Thus, the prime minister, in choosing his minister of national defence and in deciding whether to place him within his circle of closest advisers on the so-called inner cabinet, exercises considerable influence in determining the prestige and importance of the position of senior political defence-policy adviser.

The Minister of National Defence In practice, the holder of the defence portfolio has been selected more for his past political service or for the geographical areas he represents than for his (there have been no female MNDs to date) expertise or interest in defence matters.[14] In general, and in marked contrast to the external affairs portfolio, the defence portfolio has not been a prestige appointment for its ministerial incumbent (arguably, only Paul Hellyer viewed the post as a potential stepping-stone for his party leadership and prime-ministerial ambitions).[15] Moreover, the modest prestige of the office is reflected in the relatively high turnover of its holders: since Trudeau came to office in 1968, there have been fourteen different ministers to date, making the position a veritable "revolving door." Finally, only two defence ministers have ever been appointed to the important Priorities and Planning Committee of cabinet: Robert Coates for a brief five-month period in the Mulroney government, and more recently, Perrin Beatty.[16]

Despite the low political stature of the office, the MND remains the key cabinet executive official and spokesman for Canadian defence policy. The process of drawing together the formal control of defence administration into the hands of a single cabinet minister began in the interwar period. Prompted by the allure of both greater economy and efficiency in managing the armed forces, in 1922 Parliament passed the National Defence Act, which combined the existing departments of Militia and Defence and of the Naval Service, as well as the Air Board, into one Department of National Defence.[17] In announcing the bill, George P. Graham, heir apparent to the new position of minister of national defence, stated that he hoped to achieve "a well organized, snappy, defence force that will be a credit to Canada without being too expensive."[18] This emphasis on economy was to become the leitmotif of virtually every succeeding MND. The rigours of administering Canada's war effort forced Mackenzie King to create, in addition to the MND, separate ministries responsible for each of the military services. However, by discontinuing the ministries of National Defence for Air and also for Naval Services on 11 December 1946, the prime minister reverted to the prewar—and now standard—practice of a single minister of national defence.

The MND has broad legal authority to administer his department. For example, under Section 3 of the National Defence Act of 1950, the minister was responsible to Parliament "for the control and management of the Canadian Forces" and "all matters relating to national defence including preparation for civil defence against enemy action."[19] An amendment to this section of the act in 1976–1977 clarified the minister's responsibilities for "construction and maintenance of defence establishments and all works for the defence of Canada" and for defence-related research.[20]

As in the case of different prime ministers, some MNDs have taken a greater interest in, and have more zealously carried out their legal responsibilities for, Canadian defence policy. Indeed, one analyst has recently concluded that the influence of the MND "has almost no boundaries."[21] While this may be true in principle, in practice few MNDs can be said to have exerted a significant influence on Canadian defence policy. This suggests the existence of a number of constraints on the defence minister's power.

Brooke Claxton has become the standard against which the power and influence of MNDs can be judged. He clearly suited the job. Through a combination of stamina, resolute will, collegiality, and a "healthy scepticism" of military advice, he proved to be the longest tenured of Canada's peacetime defence ministers, holding office from 12 December 1946 to 30 June 1954, a tenacity unheard of among subsequent MNDs. Since then, few MNDs have held office for more than three years, and since Prime Minister Mulroney's victory in 1984, there have been four different MNDs. Such short terms in office can be a serious handicap to those MNDs seeking to play a greater role in the shaping of Canadian defence policy.

In large measure, Claxton owed his remarkable longevity as MND to the fact that he got along well with his cabinet colleagues. As Eayrs notes, Prime Minister Louis St. Laurent valued Claxton as "a loyal and diligent colleague," and was content to leave the complexities of defence in his capable hands. Claxton also enjoyed good working relations with L.B. Pearson in External Affairs, C.D. Howe in Defence Production, and Douglas Abbott in Finance.[22]

Other MNDs have not been so fortunate in this regard. For example, George R. Pearkes (MND, 1957-59) found it difficult to discuss the issue of nuclear warheads for Canadian weapons systems with Prime Minister John Diefenbaker and was dismayed by the continual wrangling over it in cabinet (as well as by the anti-American tone such debates often took). He also suspected that the cabinet was losing confidence in him on the Bomarc missile question.[23]

Part of Pearkes' problem involved his displeasure with cabinet committee meetings in which defence matters were discussed. He felt that other ministers were simply too busy to devote the proper time and attention to defence issues and he believed that Diefenbaker himself disliked discussing defence policy in front of the chiefs of staff. In addition, he did not hold a very high opinion of the knowledge—and meddling—of his cabinet colleagues. As a self-confessed "man of action," Pearkes admitted that "this idea of having to go and postpone [a military decision] so a lot of people can talk about it infuriated me." As he later explained,

> I wasn't too enthusiastic about them [the cabinet ministers] because I didn't think they knew a damn thing about [the problems] . . . . Fleming was always helpful . . . ; he was always realistic but some of the others who attended occasionally [were not]. And it always meant arguments with Howard Green.[24]

Howard Green, secretary of state for external affairs from June 1959 to April 1963, was indeed a powerful cabinet foe. Green harboured a deep moral revulsion against Canada joining the nuclear club, whatever the military merits of the case. He was a senior cabinet minister with ready access to Diefenbaker, who shared Green's suspicion of the Pentagon's influence. Green also had an able bureaucratic ally in Norman Robertson, who, as under-secretary of state for external affairs, had become a late convert to the camp that doubted the wisdom of Canada's increasingly pro-nuclear-weapons policy.[25] In the end, faced with such powerful opposition, Pearkes resigned. A similar fate, albeit in much more acrimonious circumstances, befell his successor as MND, Douglas Harkness, over the same nuclear-warhead issue.

To succeed, MNDs also require the support of their key departmental advisers. Claxton's experience is again instructive in this regard. On the civilian side, he clearly considered himself fortunate to have his former parliamentary assistant, Ralph O. Campney, as his associate minister of national defence, as well as C.M. Drury as his deputy minister. On the military side, too, Claxton enjoyed generally good relations. He admired Air Marshall Robert Leckie, chief of the air staff, for his loyalty in carrying out policies with which he disagreed, and he stood by the flamboyant and outspoken Lieutenant-General Guy Simonds over the objections of his cabinet colleagues. Nevertheless, preferring "silent soldiers as well as sailors," on 1 February 1951 Claxton appointed General Charles Foulkes as Canada's first chairman of the Chiefs of Staff Committee, where he remained as Canada's principal military adviser until his retirement in 1960. Claxton clearly believed Foulkes possessed the requisite diplomatic traits, both military and political, for this new and demanding job. The minister also admired Foulkes for protecting Canadian interests, and for his conciliatory dexterity—as well as for his ability to cope with mountains of paperwork.[26]

Other MNDs have held a more circumspect, and less trusting, view of the advice they received from their senior military advisers. Paul Hellyer (MND, 1963–67), in his drive to implement his plan for the unification of the armed forces, became so exasperated with the lack of co-operation he felt he was receiving from his senior military advisers that he not only sought to appoint a CDS amenable to his views, but also made it clear that those who opposed his ideas would either be fired or asked to take early retirement. Hellyer ultimately got his way, but not without a breakdown in confidence between himself and the military.[27] As we shall see later, Allan McKinnon (MND, 1979–1980) suspected that he was not receiving full and accurate information from his CDS regarding the operational needs of his field commanders and therefore established a task force to review the results of unification.

There is one final constraint on the freedom of action of all MNDs. No defence minister ever inherits a clean slate for policy making. Upon assuming office, a new MND immediately encounters the policy legacies of his predecessor; sometimes these are inherited from an administration of a different political stripe. In either case, it is often very difficult for a new defence minister to alter such policies in a significant way, especially if they involve bilateral or multilateral commitments or if they deal with well-entrenched weapons-procurement programs. The Diefenbaker government faced both types of impediments when it took office in 1957.

The new administration had inherited problems from previous Liberal decisions relating to Canada's participation in continental air defence and to the acquisition and arming of several new weapons systems for the military's NORAD and NATO commitments. The government was also quickly "caught in the whirl of rapidly changing weapons systems . . . [and] conflicting intelligence coming in about Russian intentions and American technological advances."[28] In the end, Pearkes, Harkness, and their cabinet colleagues were unable to resolve the difficulties that were created when they tried to escape the policy agenda they had inherited from the Liberals.

The Cabinet While there is no formal reference to a "cabinet" in the Canadian constitution, Section 11 of the BNA Act provides for a Queen's Privy Council for Canada and Section 13 construes the Governor General in Council as "the Governor General acting by and with the Advice of the Queen's Privy Council for Canada." The modern Canadian cabinet has since come to be recognized "as a committee of Privy Councillors whose members have seats in Parliament."[29] Collectively, this body is responsible for making the final decisions on matters relating to Canadian defence policy.

In practice, however, cabinet as a whole seldom deals with broad defence policy questions. Apart from the MND, individual ministers, burdened with the pressing issues of their own particular departments, rarely have the time to involve themselves in defence policy. (Although, as we will see later, this situation may be changing as a result of the post-1980 changes in the Policy and Expenditure Management System). Indeed, cabinet members have often displayed little inclination to become involved in defence policy, partly because the issues frequently revolve around arcane matters of strategic doctrine and sophisticated technology of which the average cabinet minister may understand very little. Ministers may also feel at a disadvantage compared to the defence minister, who can draw freely on the expertise of his staff and bureaucratic advisers. The secrecy surrounding many issues of national security undoubtedly contributes to a degree of compartmentalization of defence policy issues and to their insulation from the day-to-day concerns of most cabinet members who are not privy to all defence issues.

There are other reasons for the relative inattentiveness of cabinet to defence policy. Canada remains a small player, militarily, on the global stage and thus there are relatively few major or momentous defence policy decisions to be made in the normal course of events. Defence, therefore, is not of critical concern for most ministers. Moreover, since the late 1940s, the central tenets and organizational structures of Canadian defence policy have remained stable and, while cabinet may occasionally debate the relative priority of certain commitments, there has been little practical scope for a fundamental restructuring of these policies.

Furthermore, on a more mundane level, it must be noted that defence policy commands a very limited constituency within the Canadian body politic. Since defence policy is seldom, if ever, a central or even significant issue during elections, politicians in general, and ministers in particular, stand to win or lose very few votes by taking firm positions on such issues. Having little fear of the discipline of the ballot box over their views on defence, ministers have understandably tended to concern themselves less with defence policy than with other domestic issues.

This general pattern of relative disinterest in defence policy has held sway during much of the post-World War II era. But with Trudeau's unprecedented public questioning of Canada's NATO and peacekeeping commitments in the late 1960s, cabinet began to take a greater collective interest in certain national-security issues, albeit on a highly selective basis. After the Department of National Defence embarked on its re-equipment program in the mid-1970s, and as its weapons expenditures began to absorb a major portion of total federal capital outlays, cabinet ministers, with an eye on their regional and provincial industrial clients, began to take more interest in the allocation of DND's large procurement contracts. In many instances, the distribution of "industrial benefits" and support contracts spawned open conflicts among cabinet ministers.

Furthermore, the Canada–United States cruise missile testing agreement of July 1983 provided the focal point for the emergence of various Canadian anti-nuclear groups as an active political force.[30] This in turn had the effect of sensitizing the cabinet to nuclear-arms-control issues in general and to Canada's relationship to the United States'—and NATO's—nuclear doctrine in particular. This sensitivity was most evident in the Mulroney government's cautious approach to the questions of the future of NORAD and of Canada's participation in the U.S. SDI, both issues that received public airings in the course of several parliamentary committee hearings. In many respects, therefore, defence policy issues have been elevated to a more prominent place than they held before on the cabinet's agenda.

Notwithstanding these exceptions, defence policy remains an infrequent topic for full cabinet deliberation. The more usual locus of defence discussion lies within the cabinet committee structure. Canada has had a long history (predating Confederation) of employing smaller committees of the political executive to accelerate decision making that might otherwise lag because of increasingly congested cabinet schedules. Such committees have been used to permit more detailed examination of special problems, to facilitate policy co-ordination by involving ministers with a specific interest in certain issues, and to spread the workload more equitably among ministers.

The earliest cabinet committees—with the exception of the Treasury Board— were ad hoc, created to deal with particular problems and dissolved once these problems were taken care of. The quantity, complexity, and urgency of wartime policy-making gave rise to further experimentation with cabinet committees.[31] Following the creation of a new Cabinet Defence Committee in August 1945, the practice of employing cabinet committees to consider defence policy questions has continued up to the present, although the precise designation of, and degree of reliance upon, such committees has varied over time.

Just how much these committees are used depends a great deal on the prime minister's and, to a lesser extent, the MND's personal predilections regarding collective decision making. For example, in contrast to the St. Laurent government, in which the Cabinet Defence Committee met at least once a month, under the administration of John Diefenbaker, this committee met about once every four months.[32] As MND Pearkes noted, "Diefenbaker didn't want these committee meetings; there is no question about that. He didn't want to discuss in front of the Chiefs of Staff all the various problems. He hated talking in front of generals and he had never been a strong committee man."[33] Of course, Pearkes himself shared Diefenbaker's aversion to cabinet defence committee meetings.

In the case of the Diefenbaker government, this preference for ad hoc and individual (as opposed to collegial) defence decision making produced some unfortunate results. Diefenbaker approved the NORAD agreement without reference to any cabinet defence committee, an action later deemed to be precipitous by some critics. Similarly, Diefenbaker acted unilaterally, at times over the objections of his cabinet colleagues, in initially refusing to support the United States during the 1962 Cuban missile crisis, then later abruptly ordering Canadian forces to a higher state of alert. Finally, MND Douglas Harkness believed Diefenbaker's political difficulties with the nuclear-warheads issue could be traced in part to the prime minister's failure to involve cabinet fully in the decision-making process.

From 1964 to 1968, Prime Minister Pearson revamped the cabinet committee system extensively. Eventually 11 standing committees oriented toward defined policy areas were established in addition to numerous ad hoc committees. In a departure from past procedure, these standing committees were now to consider their specialized policy matters before referring them to the full cabinet for final decisions. One of the new committees was that of External Affairs and Defence, chaired by the prime minister. Although this committee, like the others, met more frequently than under the Diefenbaker regime, the new committee system itself was not altogether successful. Forced to cope with a minority government and a proliferation of cabinet committees, individual ministers served on an average of seven committees and were simply overworked (as was Pearson himself, who chaired no less than six). Adequate preparation, regular attendance, and proper co-ordination were difficult to achieve, and, because in a minority situation every agenda item tended to assume greater importance than usual, decisions tended to be deferred to the meetings of the full cabinet.[34] This did not, however, prevent a determined MND from successfully pressing his views on his ministerial colleagues: Hellyer's efforts with respect to his unification plan were a case in point.[35]

Pierre Trudeau revised both the structure and procedure of Pearson's cabinet standing-committee system. Five "subject" committees (including external policy and defence) and four co-ordinating committees were created. These not only met much more often than in the past, thereby reducing the workload of the cabinet as a whole, but they were also given the power to make certain decisions without reference to the full cabinet. Under Trudeau's reforms, the Committee on Priorities and Planning established by Pearson was given the pre-eminent role in developing and co-ordinating the broad policy objectives of government.

Because of the deliberately secretive nature of the Trudeau committee system, few details are known about the inner workings of the Committee on External Policy and Defence. Nevertheless, a few broad observations can be made. First, as its title implied, this committee dealt with both foreign policy and defence policy. Second, its chairmanship was transferred from the prime minister to the secretary of state for external affairs, with the MND serving as vice-chairman. Third, during the Trudeau era, no MND was ever appointed to the important Priorities and Planning Committee of cabinet. All of this tends to support the view that defence was not a high-priority concern for the Trudeau cabinet.

During the brief term of the Clark government, a new Policy and Expenditure Management System was introduced.[36] This "top-down" planning process was intended to ensure greater political control over and accountability for federal expenditures by establishing a closer link between policy objectives on the one hand and spending plans and revenue expectations on the other. The system continued the post-Diefenbaker trend toward the centralization of political decision making from the departments to the cabinet and its central agencies (via the Priorities and Planning Committee), and the decentralization of executive decision making within the cabinet (via the cabinet committees).

Under the new PEMS approach, the cabinet committees were to be delegated greater control and responsibility for the expenditures and financial consequences of their policy and program decisions. Budgetary resource "envelopes," determined by the inner cabinet (the Priorities and Planning Committee), established the upper limits of expenditure for each of nine defined policy areas, with the cabinet committee responsible for that sector directing how those resources would be used. Planning was to be given a longer-term horizon through a "rolling," five-year, annually updated financial framework. The nine envelopes were controlled by five cabinet committees, with the defence envelope being the responsibility of the Foreign Policy and Defence Committee. Significantly, unlike the other envelopes, the one for defence was not shared with any other policy sector or department.

Subsequent governments have retained PEMS and, in general, it has been received favourably both by ministers and by DND. The system has rationalized and improved the relationship between cabinet and DND. Defence policy planning is now a joint process in which regular consultation and co-operation is necessary to both the executive and the department. From the standpoint of cabinet, DND's plans and programs have taken on added significance as they comprise the overwhelming majority of the government's "major Crown projects" (i.e., capital projects valued over $100 million). For DND, the cabinet is now better informed about defence problems and must discuss and agree to DND's planning priorities on a continuing basis. With such agreement, DND believes that the aggregate size of its single-sector resource envelope will be less subject to partisan political tampering than in the past.

Nevertheless, under the new funding approach adopted in the 1987 White Paper, each of DND's major defence acquisition programs that requires incremental funding—that is, extra capital funds over and above the annual two percent real-growth floor promised by the Mulroney government—is guaranteed highly intensive scrutiny by the annual cabinet review (known as the "affordability" sessions of cabinet). Because the contracts and the regional distribution of industrial benefits are so large, the procurement program outlined in the White Paper will likely increase the politicization of defence decision making in both the Committee on Foreign and Defence Policy and the cabinet as a whole.

Executive Roles, Relationships, Influence The political executive plays a significant part in the making of Canadian defence policy. As a collectivity, the executive possesses the authority to render final judgment on the "high politics" of defence policy. Questions about the overall purposes, objectives, and commitments of the armed forces are ultimately decided at this level of defence decision making. Moreover, the executive wields the single most effective instrument of civilian control over the military—the budget. Thus, while the political executive is only rarely concerned with altering the basic objectives and direction of Canadian defence policy, its presence is always felt, if only indirectly, through the mechanism of the annual resource-allocation process. In the absence of constant or direct executive control, therefore, the defence budget becomes the *de facto* expression of broad political preferences with respect to defence policy.

But the political executive is itself fragmented into several loci of power and authority. Depending on the particular circumstances, issues, and personalities involved, its constituent actors have developed different formal and informal working relationships over time and exercised varying degrees of influence over defence policy making in Canada.

In analytical terms, it is possible to discern five general roles that characterize the policy-making behaviour of these sets of executive actors. First, there are the *initiators*, who, like Trudeau (with the decision to reduce forces in NATO and the 1971 White Paper), Beatty (with the 1987 White Paper), and Hellyer (with the 1964 White Paper and unification), have sought to make sweeping changes in policy. The impetus for change in these cases is derived from personality factors relating to ambition, the desire to "leave a mark," interest, and sheer force of personal will. Second, there are the *brokers*, who seek to establish the necessary consensus to carry out already mandated policies, or to rationalize and implement decisions dictated by the prime minister and cabinet collectively. Such a role was assumed by MNDs like Claxton, Harkness, Richardson, Danson, and Lamontagne, although Pearson as prime minister would also fall into this category. Third, there are the *arbiters* who, by virtue of time and budgetary pressures, are denied the comparative luxury of the broker's role and are forced to resolve conflicts of interest that emanate from the lower echelons of decision makers. Pearkes (the CF-105 cancellation) is a prime representative of this category. Fourth, there are the *inhibitors* who, using delaying and obstructionist tactics, become outright opponents of change in defence policy. Diefenbaker (with the nuclear-warheads issue) is perhaps the most significant example here. Finally, there is a loosely defined group of *caretakers* who, because of the brevity of their appointments, show little interest in, or exert minimal influence on, defence policy. Joe Clark had no time to develop an understanding of defence issues, although his committee and budgeting reforms have had a lasting impact in this area. Abbott and Churchill were obviously temporary appointees, as were Campney, Benson, Dubé, Drury, and Nielsen. It has been suggested that Leo Cadieux was given the defence post because he was no threat to Trudeau's authority, while Donald Macdonald was brought in to write the 1971 White Paper because he had been a strong advocate of withdrawing Canadian troops from Europe and was thus in tune with Trudeau's own desire for some reduction in the NATO contribution.[37]

While defence policy may be shaped by the interests and preferences of key individuals in the political executive, for the most part personalities have exerted only an occasional, albeit sometimes dramatic, influence on the wide range of issues that dominate the defence policy agenda. A far more important factor is the pattern of relationships, both personal and institutional, among these executive actors. For the MND, the most crucial of these relationships is, first, that between himself and the prime minister, and, second, that between himself and the rest of his cabinet colleagues.

With respect to the first, prime ministers normally have been content to exercise only a "passive oversight role" with regard to foreign policy in general and defence policy in particular. This tendency toward prime ministerial detachment has created a fairly permissive environment for MNDs in the day-to-day execution of their departmental responsibilities. On the whole, and unlike the American experience, Canadian prime ministers have not displayed a keen interest in security matters. They have been content to delegate responsibility for defence policy to their MNDs so long as the basic tenets of policy are not tampered with, and always with the understanding that defence expenditures are to be held in check. In this tacit division of labour, prime ministers have preferred that defence issues not be allowed to become matters of high domestic policy; in the minds of prime ministers, apparently, "no news is good news" as far as defence is concerned.

In the absence of direct and continuing interest "at the top," the relationship between the MND and his ministerial counterparts has taken on special importance in Canadian defence policy making. Here, while the pattern has fluctuated somewhat, MNDs have generally been successful in insulating the affairs of their department from outside scrutiny and interference. Historically, the main challenge to DND's pre-eminence in the defence sphere has emanated from the Department of External Affairs. The locus of interdepartmental infighting was initially the Cabinet Defence Committee, although Claxton and later Campney were able to capitalize on St. Laurent's propensity to delegate and defer to those ministers charged with functional responsibilities, and thereby to safeguard DND's primacy at least on continental and home defence issues, at the expense of concessions on NATO and other extra-European questions.[38] Pearkes experienced increasing frustrations in dealing with his cabinet confreres on equipment procurement and nuclear issues, although he did manage to work out a *modus vivendi* with Finance Minister Donald Fleming. Harkness,

on the other hand, found it impossible to deal with the pow-
erfully intransigent combination of Diefenbaker and Green,
aided and abetted by the shrewd bureaucratic wiles of Robertson, on the nuclear-warheads issue.

Under the restructured cabinet committee system begun
by Pearson in 1964, the potential for interdepartmental rivalry became institutionally entrenched. Nevertheless, in
practice, DND and DEA ministers have tended to respect each
other's spheres of legislative and administrative jurisdiction.
True, there have been instances of friction, as when Secretary of State for External Affairs Paul Martin objected to
MND Hellyer's haste in soliciting DEA's views on the 1964
White Paper on Defence and succeeded in having the Cabinet Committee on External Affairs and Defence, which Martin chaired, refer the draft to an officials' committee for
scrutiny against "oversimplification."[39] Similar instances of
DEA's concern with DND's inadequate attention to the pro-
prieties of interdepartmental consultation had arisen in the
past, especially over the informality with which the NORAD
agreement was made in 1958 and the infelicitous timing of
Operation "Skyhawk" in 1959.[40] Under the new Trudeau administration, however, MND Cadieux and Sharp, secretary
of state for external affairs, found themselves allied in cabinet in an unsuccessful attempt to protect the traditional
NATO-first orientation of Canadian defence policy against the
reformist aspirations of Trudeau and his closest political
advisers.

But while DND and DEA were able to agree on the importance of NORAD and NATO to Canadian defence policy, by the
mid-1970s the sharp increases in equipment spending necessary to support these roles attracted an increasing
amount of attention from other interested cabinet members.
The lure of getting a "piece of the action" in the major
weapons-acquisition programs approved in the 1970s and
1980s proved irresistible to politicians anxious to ensure economic gains for their respective local and regional constituencies. With the advent of cabinet-mandated industrial benefits in the CP-140 Aurora contract, Canada's defence
procurement decisions became highly politicized, perhaps
irreversibly so. From DND's perspective, such political–economic considerations complicate the implementation of defence policy, but are recognized as a necessary
price for regular infusions of badly needed capital funds.[41]

The defence policy-making role and influence of different
actors or sets of actors within the political executive has
varied widely over time. No single component has emerged

as dominant over the entire post-World War II period. Prime ministers generally prefer to leave decision making to their MNDs and the experiences of Diefenbaker and Trudeau suggest that excessive personal involvement from above can produce unexpected and politically costly repercussions. Past structural and procedural reforms now offer the prime minister the comparative safety of the Priorities and Planning Committee as a vantage point from which to oversee the broad outlines of defence planning, budgeting, and programming.

For defence ministers, even initiators like Perrin Beatty, the regularization and streamlining of decision-making procedures and the stabilization of defence commitments and roles after the upheavals of the Diefenbaker and early Trudeau years have ultimately left their jobs with a more managerial, brokerage orientation. Their primary task now is to ensure continued cabinet support for funding stability and programmatic continuity to bridge the commitment-capability gap inherited from the neglect and uncertainty of the past. MNDs recognize the necessity of securing cabinet allies; the problem now is finding the right allies and warding off excessive predations on, and interference in, the use of DND's discretionary funds.

Cabinet now exercises its control over defence policy more continuously and directly than in the pre-Trudeau years. The Cabinet Committee on Foreign and Defence Policy plays a major role today, although its focus has shifted from influencing DND's objectives and roles to overseeing the forces' major re-equipment and modernization programs and controlling the defence-funding envelope. Cabinet plays an increasingly active role in allocating large-scale defence contracts and in monitoring, through the Treasury Board, the progress of, and economic return on, DND's long-term major Crown projects. This is a marked departure from the comparatively desultory or indifferent manner in which cabinets in earlier governments handled defence procurement decisions. For the political executive today, defence policy has indeed become "big business."

The Bureaucracy

Bureaucracies have become indispensable components of nearly all large government organizations. By virtue of their specialized expertise and duties, bureaucratic officials play an important role in the administration and smooth operation of government departments. DND is no exception in this regard. But what is the precise nature of this role? As noted earlier, the political executive in Canada has tended to confine its attention to shaping the fundamental long-range objectives and broad contours of Canadian defence policy. Within this context, the bureaucracy has acquired considerable latitude in determining the general strategies and specific tactics for achieving these fundamental objectives.[42] The bureaucracy's influence has been evident in matters pertaining to where and how DND spends its annual appropriations, especially in the area of weapons-acquisition decisions. In practice, therefore, the bureaucracy's role goes beyond that suggested by the simple homily "politicians propose and bureaucrats dispose."

But the Department of National Defence is an institution with a difference. Unlike other government departments, DND possesses two parallel and separate, yet intertwined, bureaucratic hierarchies, one civilian and the other military. Each has a distinct role, set of interests, and organizational ethos.

These differences tend to blur our usual understanding of the federal public service and give rise to questions concerning the nature of civil–military relations in Canada. Who comprises the civilian and military bureaucracies? How do their interests, and the processes by which these are articulated, differ? How do these bureaucracies interact? How, and to what extent, do the requirements of civilian control of the Canadian Forces conflict with the demands and standards of military professionalism in the CF? Are the forces becoming "over-civilianized," and are they being threatened by a "crisis of the military ethos"? Finally, what are the consequences of this civil–military relationship for Canadian defence policy?

To determine the impact of the bureaucracy in general, and the relative influence of civilians and soldiers in particular, we will begin by identifying the major actors and processes involved in Canadian defence policy making.[43]

Bureaucratic Actors and Processes For the fiscal year 1987–88, DND had an authorized level of 34 026 civilians to support an authorized regular military force of 85 627. This comparatively large civilian administrative body behind the CF reflects the enormity and complexity of the task of organizing, equipping, training, and otherwise sustaining a modern military establishment.

Nevertheless, the actual number of people involved in providing Policy Direction and Management Services for DND is relatively small: 1745 civilian and 2526 military personnel or about three percent of the total defence establishment of nearly 120 000.[44] This general management activity is now tightly centralized within National Defence Headquarters (NDHQ) in Ottawa and is led by a surprisingly small number of civilian and military bureaucrats.

On the civilian side, the key actors are the deputy minister (DM); the assistant deputy minister, policy (ADM[Pol]); the assistant deputy minister, matériel (ADM[Mat]); and the assistant deputy minister, finance (ADM[Fin]). On the military side, the key actors are the chief of the defence staff (CDS); the vice chief of the defence staff (VCDS); the deputy chief of the defence staff (DCDS); and the assistant deputy minister, personnel (ADM[Per]).

To achieve Canada's defence policy objectives, the government as a whole, and DND in particular, has developed complex and interrelated defence-resources planning and management processes. As we noted earlier, the government instituted PEMS in an effort to relate its policy goals to its expenditure plans over a multi-year period. PEMS provides the umbrella framework that links cabinet-approved policy objectives and funding decisions to DND's own internal resource decision-making processes.

Between 1964 and 1973, DND developed a formal process for making and carrying out the many decisions required to give substance to the broad defence policy objectives established by cabinet. DND was compelled to create this formal process because it was increasingly called to account— by ministers, government officials, and interest groups—for the decisions it was making, especially when these entailed large expenditures on individual weapons-procurement programs. As described by Colonel W.N. Russell, this formalized process provided a rational, stepped frame of reference against which defence decisions could be evaluated.[45] This "capabilities planning process" (to use Russell's terminology) involved two separate phases—planning and programming.

In the planning phase, DND systematically identified, considered, and selected alternate courses of action for achieving the goals set by cabinet and for responding to future requirements of the CF. This phase began with a "strategic assessment" document that sought to establish an appreciation of Canada's security requirements for the next 15 years, based on analyses of current trends and future projections. Following this initial stage, DND's Defence Posture

Review attempted to reconcile the CF's existing capabilities with those that the strategic assessment identified as necessary over the 15-year planning period to meet departmental objectives, roles, and missions as determined by cabinet. At this stage DND was expected to identify and examine different force-posture models and recommend to cabinet the one best suited to meet Canada's future defence needs. Coinciding with this step, DND was required to produce a "strategic overview" as dictated by PEMS. Serving as a "mini defence-posture review," the strategic overview satisfied the Treasury Board's requirement that DND annually review its objectives, its alternative strategies for meeting those objectives, and its proposed changes to approved policies and programs and that it report the result of its program evaluations. The overview was to be a key document in two respects: first, its strategies and proposed changes had to be costed; second, along with strategic overviews from other departments, it was to be submitted to Treasury Board by March 31 each year, considered by the cabinet policy committees in the summer, and then used as the basis for establishing DND's 5-year funding envelope each October. In this respect, the strategic overview provided the link between the policy planning process within DND and the policy planning process between DND and the cabinet.

Following these evaluation stages, DND would produce a document called a "capabilities planning guidance." This document sought to indicate the general direction along which the structure of the CF should evolve over the next 15 years. It was also meant to summarize government policy and other planning considerations in one authoritative publication, as well as to assign priorities and to amplify and, if necessary, reconcile the factors that would be involved in achieving the desired capabilities. The capabilities planning guidance analyzed the military capabilities and political intentions of potential enemies, present and future; estimated future governmental policies and funding imperatives; and identified the types (quality) and levels (quantity) of military capabilities required to fulfil the future roles and missions of the CF. In short, it was to guide senior staff officers in linking future defence needs to future force-development proposals. All planning inputs—including the strategic assessment, parliamentary reports, DND studies, and MND statements and directives—were to be collected and analyzed by the ADM(Pol) Planning Guidance Team (PGT), who would then translate them into statements of capability requirements to fulfil both peacetime and wartime defence tasks.

Based on the forecasts and general force-development directions established in the capabilities planning guidance for the CF as a whole, the military environmental staffs (the three major commands) would then prepare separate "force development guides" for the air, land, and maritime elements of the CF. These guides would provide the conceptual frameworks to allow staff officers to prepare and initiate personnel and equipment programs for their own particular service environments.

At this point in the formal process, the crucial programming phase would begin. The "program proposals/force proposals" stage would draw together the various proposals for altering or expanding the CF's capabilities into a single resource-allocation-and-management process called the Defence Program Management System (DPMS).[46]

Essentially, the DPMS is the management tool whereby DND translates the broad political objectives and resource parameters established by cabinet through its Priorities and Planning Committee into concrete military capabilities and activities for the Canadian Forces.

The DPMS is a repetitive, sequential process of planning, programming, and evaluation through which DND implements its own departmental plan, the Defence Services Program (DSP). The DSP is a detailed, flexible, and continuously updated plan for the allocation and use of resources over roughly a 15-year period. It contains those activities and projects that DND has decided are necessary to achieve the government's defence policy objectives. As such it specifies exactly how the department intends to implement the cabinet's defence policy goals within the funding limits set by PEMS, and it also outlines the goals, capabilities, and funding that may be required in the longer term in response to future political, military, technological, and socio-economic developments in both the domestic and international environments.

The DSP outlines the military activities required to meet government objectives; the capabilities required by the CF to fulfil Canada's defence policy objectives, commitments, roles, and tasks; the planned changes needed to improve the capabilities of the forces in order to carry out their activities effectively; and the allocation of DND's total resources in money, manpower, and matériel required to achieve the program activities. The DSP is the basis for the preparation and justification of DND's Multi-Year Operational Plan as required by PEMS, its annual Main Estimates, and its expenditure submissions to the Treasury Board. Thus the DSP, with its supporting documentation, is one of the chief means by which DND is held accountable for its program decisions.

Basically then, the DPMS is the sequential management process that provides the framework within which DND formulates, implements, evaluates, and modifies its departmental plan, as expressed in the DSP, in an orderly and logical manner. It is the process of planning resource allocation within DND to meet present and future requirements in accordance with government policy.

Within the DPMS there are various screening processes and decision-approval authorities. All resource decision-making authority within DND is vested in, and is delegated by, the MND. The DND decision structure is based on a hierarchy of committees that exercise their authority either as corporate consensual bodies or as advisers to their respective chairmen in whom the actual decision-making authority is vested. The four main committees that deal with defence policy, planning, and resource allocation and management within DND are:

(a) *Defence Council* The senior departmental committee, chaired by the MND with the MND parliamentary secretary, DM, CDS, VCDS, ADM(Pol), DCDS, and the commanders of the commands as members. It has no decision-making authority other than that exercised by its chairman. It meets only at the call of the MND and is not normally involved in the day-to-day management of the department.

(b) *Defence Management Committee* The senior management board within DND, co-chaired by the DM and CDS with the VCDS, group principals,[47] DCDS, and the commanders of the commands. Formed at the direction of the MND, it considers on a weekly basis all major policy, plans, programs, and administrative matters that require the approval or direction of the MND, DM, or CDS. It is responsible for all major policy decisions, such as those relating to the capabilities planning guidance, and it considers all major proposed changes to the DSP. As such it is the formal focus of all resource-allocation decisions within NDHQ.

(c) *Program Control Board* Chaired by the VCDS, with the group principals, DCDS, and other senior officials as members, it meets regularly (generally biweekly) to consider all aspects of the programming and allocation of departmental resources as reflected in the DSP. Within established financial approval thresholds, it has the authority to approve all program change and development proposals, but is obligated to pass on to the Defence Management Committee all matters that merit consideration by the senior committee.

(d) *Program Control Board Subcommittee*   Chaired by the DCDS, it has its membership and responsibilities delegated to it by its parent Program Control Board. Membership therefore may vary but usually includes representatives from the group principals, the service environments, branch chiefs, and others with responsibilities for the definition and implementation of projects. It supports its parent body by reviewing and screening all operational equipment proposals developed by the environmental-requirements staff, by developing a resource-allocation priority list for the existing DSP, and by sponsoring items for consideration by the Program Control Board.

In practice, much of DND's resource decision-making activity is centred on the planning and programming of new capital projects, and in particular on the acquisition of major new weapons systems. Since the capital portion of DND's annual budget constitutes about 26 percent of the overall defence budget, while approximately 64 percent is designated for personnel, operations, and maintenance (POM), this focus on new capital projects may seem surprising. Capital expenditures, however, represent the largest component of discretionary expenditure under DND's control; the POM component largely pays for salaries, equipment, and facilities already in the forces' inventory. As a result, weapons procurement has become a central concern of defence resources decision making both for cabinet and DND.

The end result of this elaborate formal planning and programming process was to be the acquisition of new or improved defence capabilities in the form of new equipment, infrastructure and logistical systems, and personnel. Regular feedback was to be provided through DND's Defence Performance Measurement System and the program evaluation mechanism. By comparing current defence capabilities with government objectives, evaluations of this type would ensure that the entire capabilities planning process was producing the desired results in an appropriate, cost-effective manner.

Formal decision making and management systems of the type depicted above have great appeal to those seeking rationality, coherence, and accountability in defence policy. The formal system does help to regulate the day-to-day business of DND by providing "chains of command, staff duties, ritualized paper flows and formats and committees to discipline reality," and it also "provides a measurable trail of decision taking" to help satisfy the cabinet and the public that policy is being rationally and responsibly, rather than arbitrarily, decided.[48]

In practice, however, these systems and the processes associated with them do not reflect the way in which defence decisions are actually made in Canada. The formal model exaggerates the extent to which decision making follows a sequential path wherein each stage in the planning and programming process comes to bear on the particular issue under consideration and in which clear, final decisions are made every step of the way. In reality, many stages are omitted or bypassed and decisions are often of the "maybe" rather than the "yes" or "no" variety in order to delay or block final decisions later in the process.

The fundamental point is that decisions are made by people, not by systems, organizational tables, or flow charts. Thus, to understand how defence decisions are made in Canada, it is important to identify the people who are involved and the processes that are actually used.

Bureaucratic Roles, Relationships, Influence While Canadian defence policy has always been formulated and administered by a mixed civilian–military establishment, Hellyer's efforts to integrate and unify the armed forces in the 1964–68 period initiated a dramatic change in the responsibilities and relative influence of the main sets of civilian and military policy-making actors. The impetus for this change emanated from the issue of the nature and extent of civilian direction (as opposed to civilian control) of Canadian defence policy.[49] Put simply, who is to be chiefly responsible for advising politicians on Canadian defence matters: civilian bureaucrats or military officers?

From 1946 to 1964 there was little contention on this issue. The lines of demarcation between the civilians within DND and the military in the CF were generally well understood and respected. There was (and still is) a clear basis in law for the differentiation between the Department of National Defence and the Canadian Forces and their civilian and military administrative bureaucracies, respectively. Under the

National Defence Act, the minister of national defence has overall authority for the control and management of the department. By the same act, the chief of the defence staff is responsible for the "control and administration of the Canadian Forces."[50] The essential distinction here is between a civilian-run *department* and a military-administered *force*.

Thus, contrary to the popular notion, DND and the CF are not organized and controlled as a single entity. Members of the CF are not part of the federal civil service and should not be considered public servants in the same sense as postal workers. Nevertheless, in practice, some ambiguity has developed concerning the precise administrative authority of the minister's chief civilian adviser, the deputy minister, and his chief military adviser, the chief of the defence staff.[51]

The effects of this confusion have been far-reaching. As Douglas Bland notes:

> Until 1972 the administration of defence policy in Canada was considered to have two aspects; that is, it was viewed as a command problem to be addressed by military concepts, and as a public administration problem amenable to theories of public management. Two distinct power centres, the CDS and the DM, approached these problems with organizations and processes particular to their aspect of the problem. In this context it was a political responsibility to reconcile differences and risks. After 1972, the administration of defence policy became defined as a managerial problem *alone*, with the expectation that better management practices could make the 'sharp end sharper'. This new definition of the defence problem promoted managerial skills over command experience and allowed officials to structure DND and the CF as though they were a single entity.[52]

The ultimate consequences of this transition from what Bland has called the 1946–64 "Command Era" to the current "Management Era" of Canadian defence policy have been, first, to undercut the military's role in policy making and, second, to turn the exercise of civilian control of the military over to public servants rather than to Parliament. In effect, the MND's senior military advisers have become "marginal men" with little real influence on major policy decisions, and parliamentary control over the military establishment has been seriously eroded.

The Canadian military was unable to alter the pace and direction of the organizational changes it perceived as detrimental to its interests and responsibilities during the 1964–68 unification debate. It did not play a significant role in the defence review leading to the 1969 NATO cutback decision and then to the 1971 White Paper. And finally, it has not been very successful in acquiring the funding it regarded as necessary to carry out the tasks assigned to it. These examples attest to the sharply diminished influence of the military in tendering its professional advice to its political masters.

This situation had become so serious during the 1970s that Allan McKinnon, MND under the short-lived Tory government that came to power in 1979, created a special task force to investigate the impact of unification on Canadian defence policy. In particular, McKinnon suspected he was not receiving a true picture of the operational interests and needs of the military environmental "field" commanders (the air, land, and sea commanders not stationed at NDHQ), who, with the restructuring of NDHQ in the early 1970s, had been excluded from the topmost echelons of defence policy making in Ottawa.

In its final report, the task force confirmed McKinnon's apprehension and noted that many witnesses had expressed concern over the apparent "civilianization" of NDHQ. Quite simply, the perception was that too many civilians in senior positions were involved in decision making of a purely military nature. This resulted in an excessively civilianized approach to military problems, one that led to a loss of focus on the military's "sharp end" requirements. To rectify this, the task force recommended "as an urgent priority" that the commanders of the commands be made members of the Defence Council and the Defence Management Committee, and that their influence be "fully recognized in matters pertaining to operations, training, personnel administration, and support to the operational forces."[53]

Although the government was defeated before it could act on these and other recommendations, a subsequent DND internal review of the task force's report reaffirmed the concern about "the gradual imposition, upon the Department as a whole including military members, of civilian standards and values in managing the Forces and in assessing their needs and goals," and concluded that the forces were facing "a crisis of military ethos." This was recognized as a serious "weakening" of the military profession in Canada.[54]

In response to these findings, the commanders of the three major commands—the Mobile Command, the Maritime Command, and the Air Command—were made regular members of the Defence Management Committee and the

Defence Council. While it is perhaps too early to determine whether this action has strengthened the policy-making role of the military (Bland is in fact quite sceptical in this regard[55]), it can be said that, in contrast to the 1971 White Paper, the 1987 document showed evidence of much greater military input.[56]

In the absence of sustained top-level debate over Canadian defence policy objectives, the resource-allocation process has become the focal point for civilian–military infighting within the defence bureaucracy. And it is here that Bland's two defence-management philosophies have been at loggerheads in recent years. The civilian bureaucrats, taking their cues from their budget-sensitive political masters, are more concerned with the overall efficiency and cost-effectiveness of the DSP, while the military bureaucrats, conditioned by their training and experience, are more concerned with the operational requirements of the forces. The essential distinction, then, is between a civilian approach stressing program affordability and a military approach emphasizing operational needs.

Bland argues that, in the post-1964 atmosphere of ongoing defence-expenditure constraint, this perennial affordability–needs conflict has been resolved by the politicians in favour of the civilians and against the professional advice of the military. This has been done by (1) restructuring the bureaucracy in a way that places the real decision-making power in the hands of the civilians and (2) redefining Canada's defence problem in terms of managerial rather than military effectiveness. The politicians have thus avoided, though largely by default, the necessity of making difficult (and expensive) choices on the basis of unwelcome and unpalatable military advice. Here then is the root cause of the present commitment–capability gap.

Instead of following the highly structured, sequential steps of the formal model, the process in reality was often subject to arbitrary political intervention from the top. For example, in 1984 and 1985 DND was directed to purchase six Dash-8 aircraft as navigator trainers and transports and 12 Challenger aircraft as electronic warfare trainers. These decisions were taken without much consultation with the military on the operational requirements for such equipment; furthermore, most of the aircraft were "bought contrary to the Department's planned priorities" for equipment acquisition.[57] Similarly, military officers complained that the ADM(Pol) Planning Guidance Team frequently drew up very detailed proposals for new equipment purchases and other force-development matters without any military contribution to the planning phase. These proposals were geared to available funds rather than to military assessments of operational needs. In the prevailing atmosphere, the military was expected to accept what was given and to avoid making waves. This approach not only upset the military, but also short-circuited the sequential planning–programming process within NDHQ.

The most damning evidence that the formal decision-making process bore little resemblance to the actual one was provided by the 1983–84 *Report of the Auditor General of Canada*.[58] The report indicated, for example, that there was no formally approved amendment to the strategic assessment undertaken during the 1974–75 DSR. Moreover, no formal defence posture assessment had been produced, and while updates to the 1978 Capabilities Planning Guidance had been initiated in 1982 and 1983, neither had been given departmental approval. Also, no force development guide had been produced for support services, and, in the case of the Air Development Guide and the Maritime Force Development Guide, confusion and inconsistencies had resulted concerning the total number of long-range patrol aircraft required by the different service environments. Finally, the auditor general criticized the omissions and shortcomings of DND's feedback mechanisms.

This disjointed and somewhat arbitrary process of defence resource allocation within DND has had serious consequences for Canada's defence posture. As the 1984 auditor general's report noted:

> Given the absence of a clearly defined and approved long-term force structure as a planning target, expenditures on equipment acquisitions and capital construction projects, systems development, personnel and operations have not always produced the overall capability levels that would be consistent with such a structure and with approved funding levels . . . .
> Given current perceptions of defence requirements and existing funding levels, senior management must continually compromise one or more of the major attributes of defence effectiveness, defined by DND as force structure, readiness, sustainability and combat capability.[59]

Bland notes another consequence of this weak conceptual framework and poor policy guidance: defence decision making has tended to respond to political demands and to parochial service or task-oriented pressures, without reference to more comprehensive military assessments and needs.[60]

Aware of these weaknesses, DND has tried to rectify some of the deficiencies in its decision-making processes. For instance, as Russell notes, because of continuing competition for scarce funds among the air, land, and maritime environments, in April 1983 DND instituted a capital-equipment screening process between the program proposal and DSP stages. Rather than simply satisfying the organizational needs of the individual commands and service environments, this screening process, based on "capability components,"[61] sought to ensure that the most cost-effective means of accomplishing CF missions would be achieved. Late in 1983 DND initiated a normative planning process which, by 1985, was expanded into the Defence Policy Implementation Process. The object here was to produce alternative costed force-structure options that would ultimately lead to a force-structure model adequate to the level of military capability needed for existing defence commitments. This process was eventually subsumed under the review that led to the 1987 White Paper.

More recently, DND has begun to implement a new Defence Planning and Force Development (DPFD) process to rectify some of the more obvious deficiencies of the formal process discussed earlier. This is intended to be a NDHQ-wide process of cyclical review and adjustment. It will include a review of policy and planning objectives, adjust force plans and programs to those objectives, and will try to produce greater congruence between policy goals, allocated resources, and force structure. It will include two main phases; conceptualization and implementation. The conceptualization phase will deal with government policy objectives, strategic assessments, military assessments, and other defence issues. The main change here will be to provide a much earlier and more concrete military input (via a military assessment of strategy, capabilities, and force design) into the planning–conceptualization process. The implementation phase will involve two main subprocesses: one focussing on the CDS Development Guidance, which will lead ultimately to a comprehensive Canadian Forces Total Force Development Plan, which will become the primary guidance document for acquiring, organizing, and maintaining the military capabilities required to fulfil the 1987 defence policy; the other will concentrate on programming, which, as before, will involve the DPMS–DSP process.

The new DPFD process will be characterized by two iterative, dynamic feedback loops to which access can be gained at any time and place in the system. It is intended to be a flexible and realistic management tool, one in which procedure does not dominate substance. Another key departure from the former process is that the minister, via his MND Guidance, will be positioned at the pivotal point between the cyclical conceptualization and implementation phases. Thus, a strong, activist MND such as Perrin Beatty will henceforth be in a better position to give direction and input to both cyclical phases.

In summary, after 1980 the government attempted to impose greater political control over the defence policy-making process by establishing clear links between overall policy goals and specific expenditure plans through the top-down PEMS process and through the self-contained, micromanagement rationality of DND's own DPMS. However, in the vacuum that was created by the absence of clear and continuing policy direction from the top, defence policy making in Canada has in practice been a much more "random" process than the one depicted in Russell's formal model. It has also been characterized by a continuing civilian–military struggle over needs–affordability questions relating to a series of resource-allocation and weapons-procurement issues. In this context, Colin Gray's dictum that "equipment really maketh defence policy"[62] gains added relevance as an explanation of a fundamental determinant of Canadian defence policy. It also suggests that more research into the phenomenon of defence "bureaucratic politics" might prove to be a fruitful avenue of exploration for analysts of Canadian defence policy.

Parliament

Parliament and Defence Policy During the years between Confederation and World War II, when Canada sometimes sought to disengage itself from British imperial defence commitments, prime ministers were heard to declare that "Parliament will decide" on matters concerning national defence, war, and peace. Strictly speaking, this was true. Parliament, and specifically the House of Commons, had approved the furnishing of equipment for the Canadian contingent sent into the Boer War; Parliament had voted the vast sums that were necessary during World War I; and Parliament had also approved the meagre military budgets of the interwar period. Acting under the authority granted it by the Statute of Westminster, Parliament had declared war on Germany on 10 September 1939. In the post-1945 period, Parliament had approved and funded the commitments and roles undertaken by the armed forces as part of Canada's contributions to collective defence. To the extent that a legislative body gives legitimacy to defence policy decisions in a democracy, the Parliament of Canada is part of the governmental process.

But in a practical sense, Parliament has not made the decisions, or at least has not been an active and influential participant in defence decisions. Nor has Parliament, in marked contrast to the United States Congress, exercised a vigorous oversight function of defence decisions and the military establishment. Within the federal government, Parliament has more often than not lagged far behind the political executive and the bureaucracy and has "decided" only in the sense that it has ratified what these other two branches have already decided to do. This may be changing. Yet, overall, as R.B. Byers has observed, "the role and influence of Parliament on Canadian security and defence has been minimal."[63]

There are a number of reasons for this which may be grouped into four sets of factors, relating to (1) the nature of parliamentary government; (2) parliamentary government as it has evolved in Canada; (3) the handling of defence issues in democracies; and (4) the handling of Canadian defence policy in particular.

In most parliamentary systems the political executive— the prime minister and his cabinet— are also elected members of the legislature. The executive remains in office between elections as long as it retains the confidence of the legislature. This confidence may be expressed by specific votes of confidence, but is usually manifest in the support that the legislature gives to the policies of the executive, especially its spending policies. It is the executive that sets the legislative agenda, asking for the legislature's support of its policies, usually expressed in terms of new laws or changes to existing laws, and for the authority to raise and spend tax revenue.

Members of the legislature are usually grouped together in political parties and the political executive is drawn from among the members of the party that either holds a majority in the legislature or has the greatest number of seats compared to other parties. In cases where there are many parties and where no one party has sufficient strength, a coalition executive or cabinet will be formed comprising members of several parties. It may remain in office only as long as it retains the confidence of the legislature.

When a single party forms the executive, the other parties form the opposition, with the second largest party becoming the official Opposition. In the British tradition to which Canada is heir, members of the legislature will vote strictly along party lines. Thus, a prime minister whose party commands a majority of seats is almost assured of getting his policies and programs approved by the legislature. Under the parliamentary system, therefore, there is a fusion of the executive and legislative branches of government, with the executive, particularly if it is in a majority situation, having great control over the legislative branch.

This situation may be contrasted to that which has evolved by constitutional authority and by tradition in the United States. There the president is elected separately from the houses of Congress and may in fact be of a different party than the majorities in the House of Representatives or the Senate or both. Cabinet members are appointed by the president, but are not drawn from the legislative branch (although they must be approved by Congress). Traditionally, the president has not been able to exercise strict authority over fellow members of his party sitting in Congress. Party discipline is weak and affiliation is not always an exact guide to voting behaviour. Thus, presidents may find their policies and programs challenged, changed, or rejected. In contrast to the parliamentary system, a president will remain in office until the next election no matter how much of his legislative agenda is rejected by Congress.

Because of the fusion of legislative and executive branches in a parliamentary system, the legislative branch has less independence and acts less as a check on the executive. It does not set the legislative agenda, participates less in the policy-making process, and exercises less of an oversight function over the executive and the bureaucracy. This is not to say that legislatures perform no function or that they can be ignored. Even where the political executive commands a majority and tight party discipline is practised, the prime minister and his cabinet must guide legislation through and face questions on their handling of public policy. Combined with a free and open press reporting on the views of opposition members, a legislature can exercise some influence on policy formulation and exercise some overseeing of government operations. Individuals and groups outside Parliament may find champions for their causes among individual legislators.

In addition to their legislative and oversight roles, legislatures can also serve the interest of public education on important issues. Investigations, hearings, and reports of legislative committees often serve as sources of information that complement or compete with the statements and explanations of the executive branch and the bureaucracy. On balance, though, despite wide variations among parliamentary systems, legislatures (and individual legislators) have limited influence over the governmental decision-making process.

This has certainly come to be the case in Canada. In the Canadian parliamentary process, parties have always played a major role and party discipline is tight even in comparison to the British experience. It is rare for individual members of Parliament to vote outside party lines. In addition, although Canada has a bicameral legislative system, with a Senate constituting the "upper chamber," this body has long since ceased to exercise any major influence over the political executive, which is, with rare exceptions, drawn from the House of Commons. Because it is an appointed rather than an elected body, the legitimacy of the Senate has also, at times, come into question.

The dominance of the political executive in Canada has been reinforced by the frequency and long duration of majority governments. In the 121 years since Confederation, there has been only one coalition government and eight minority governments. Six of these eight have occurred since 1957. But in the 43 years since 1945, minority governments have been in office for only eight years, with Liberal majority governments holding power for 26 years. (And, as indicated in Chapters 2 and 3, the Liberals have made most of the major defence policy decisions during those years.)

In the conduct of foreign policy and defence policy, as in other areas of government activity, political executives in democracies are responsible to legislatures. Since foreign relations sometimes affect the very security of the country, it is only proper that decisions in this area are subject to popular control through elective bodies. Yet foreign, and especially defence, policies have tended to be less amenable to legislative influence (particularly in the ongoing conduct of external relations) than are domestic policies.

In the international environment the state operates as a single unit with the political executive acting on behalf of all citizens in relations with other states. While in democratic countries the general policies and external activities of the government are known, the details of international negotiations are not wide open to public or legislative scrutiny. Moreover, in most cases, the substance of relations with foreign governments does not often require the enactment of new laws or governmental programs that would require legislative approval. Treaties are ratified by legislative bodies and this may include military treaties. But governments also tend to make agreements with each other that are not subject to legislative involvement, although the legislative branch may review such agreements and programs and may, in the course of such reviews, perform an educative role in that the substance of foreign policy is thereby brought before the public. Overall, though, political executives tend to be wary of legislative involvement in foreign policy and defence policy, and are prone to share only as much information as is politically necessary. This applies especially to defence policy, where governments can claim national-security considerations to withhold details from lawmakers. When legislatures do have some influence over defence issues, it usually stems from the traditional "power of the purse," in that political executives must obtain approval for military expenditures. This sometimes provides occasion for lawmakers to examine the conduct of security relations.[64]

If political executives are often reluctant to involve legislatures in the foreign and defence policy-making processes, individual lawmakers are often reluctant to devote much attention to external policy. On the public policy agenda of most countries, foreign and defence policies rank behind domestic issues such as taxation, unemployment, or health care. The public is more concerned about these issues, and individuals seeking election will wish to respond to these concerns. Political executives in most countries, with the possible exception of the two superpowers, also largely devote their attention to domestic issues. To be sure, matters of foreign policy and defence policy, such as the 1983–84 deployment of new intermediate-range nuclear weapons in Europe, will sometimes command the attention of the public and therefore of the legislative bodies, but, in general, lawmakers devote more of their legislative and oversight efforts to domestic matters.

Among the democratic nations, the United States is almost unique in terms of the involvement of its legislative branch, the Congress, in foreign policy and defence issues. In part, this is the result of the simple fact that the United States is a superpower and external relations rank high on the public policy agenda, particularly for the political executive. It is also the result of the American Constitution, which divides responsibility for the conduct of external relations between the president and Congress. Indeed, as one expert has noted, the U.S. constitution is an "invitation" to these two branches to "struggle over the privilege of directing foreign policy."[65] Since the beginning of the American Republic, both the House of Representatives and the Senate have played major roles in foreign and defence policy from a legislative, oversight, and public education standpoint. Being more independent and less under the control of the political executive, congressmen and senators have used the constitutional grants of power not only to challenge the policies of the executive branch, but also to initiate policies of their own. Congressional committees conduct detailed reviews of the president's policies and are assisted by large staffs and free access to information. While the president remains the single most important foreign policy actor, even he must lobby and bargain with Congress to have his programs accepted. In the defence area, senior military officials must come before Congress to defend not only their budget requests, but also their strategic assumptions. The role of Congress in defence policy has increased since the Vietnam War to the extent that much of it is now co-determined by the legislative and executive branches of government.[66]

There are a variety of reasons why the Canadian Parliament does not play a similar role in the formulation of external policies. Some of these have to do with the nature of parliamentary government as outlined above. But there are other considerations, several unique to the Canadian historical experience and the nature of Canada's defence policy.

Constitutionally, there is no inherent reason why Parliament should not be more active in defence matters. The federal government has exclusive authority in this field and hence Parliament has a legitimate claim to involvement. Historically, though, Parliament has not played a major role in either external policy or defence policy. In part this was due to the fact that for several decades after Confederation, Canada could not even conduct an independent foreign or defence policy. Nor, with its strong ties to Britain, did it need to maintain armed forces against attack. As such, it is not surprising that a tradition of legislative involvement in defence policy did not develop. There were, of course, times when Parliament witnessed intense debate and discussion on defence issues, as, for example, when Prime Minister Laurier introduced his plans for the creation of a naval service. And Parliament did have to approve the sums necessary to support forces in the two world wars. But a more continuous legislative involvement in security matters never took hold in Canada as it did in the United States. Even when Canada did begin to play a relatively important role in collective defence in the post-1945 period, Parliament was often a bystander to major policy decisions.[67]

Another factor contributing to the lack of parliamentary involvement is that for Canada, as for many other democracies, defence issues are not at the top of the public policy agenda. For the public and therefore for both the executive and legislative branches of government, domestic issues are paramount. Individual members of parliament have little to gain electorally by becoming experts on foreign policy matters.

Given this relative lack of interest, the political executive in Canada has been free to conduct foreign policy and defence policy without having constantly to refer or defer to the House of Commons (or the Senate). With their control over the legislative branch, past political executives have been markedly unwilling to share power or information on defence issues, and the military and civilian bureaucracies have not been subject to intense legislative oversight. Until 1986 committees of the House of Commons had to wait for a reference from the full House to conduct investigations of defence issues (apart from review of the budget estimates) and the decision to initiate such references very often rested with the minister in charge.

If history and Canadian parliamentary tradition have militated against a major role for Parliament in defence policy, the nature of Canadian defence policy since 1945 has also been a factor limiting legislative activity. As this book argues, Canada has made several independent and significant decisions that have shaped its defence policy and hence the posture of its armed forces. These decisions were all taken by the political executive and presented to Parliament. Sometimes, as in the case of membership in NATO, unification of the armed forces, and the dispatch of troops overseas for NATO or peacekeeping, parliamentary approval was sought. This approval served to legitimize sometimes controversial decisions. At other times, for example, when the Trudeau government decided to cut the size of the forces in Europe, no formal approval was necessary or sought. But there was rarely any major objection from members of Parliament to the broad policy decisions taken by the political executive. Since 1945 both the Liberals and Progressive Conservatives have supported Canada's involvement in Western collective defence, particularly in NATO and NORAD. There has been nearly universal support for peacekeeping.

When in Opposition, both major parties have criticized the government's handling of defence issues. Thus, during the 1970s, the Conservatives wanted more spending on defence. The Liberals, in Opposition since 1984, have alleged that the Mulroney government has been too pro-American in its defence decisions. In such cases, however, the Opposition has been "more concerned with embarrassing and attacking the government than with addressing substantive defence issues."[68] The NDP has been most critical of past Conservative and Liberal governments on defence issues. It has recently adopted strong platforms calling for withdrawal from both NORAD and NATO.

Overall, though, since 1945 the defence policies and postures adopted by the political executive have had the support of the majority of members of Parliament. With this broad support, the political executives have been relatively free to undertake specific commitments and roles for the armed forces without, again, having to refer continually to Parliament. After Canada joined NATO, forces were committed to land and air roles in Germany, naval forces were earmarked for SACLANT, and units in Canada were pledged for various reinforcement tasks such as the CAST commitment to Norway. In North America, even before NORAD was created, aircraft were dedicated to an interception role while funds were made available for radar and warning facilities. At sea, Canada's maritime forces co-operated with the U.S. navy in defending the approaches to the continent. Peacekeeping did not require force changes. Therefore, the consistency of Canada's defence commitments over the years left little scope for debate in Parliament over alternative postures. Even the early Trudeau emphasis upon sovereignty protection did not fundamentally alter the CF's posture because no major allied role was dropped. To be sure, a growing gap arose between capabilities and commitments. Yet with the exception of the Senate committee reports of the early 1980s (which we shall discuss later), Parliament did not address the commitment–capability gap seriously.

Given the consistency both of commitments and of specific armed-forces roles, the major decisions in defence policy, especially since 1968, have had to do with procurement—the purchase of new weapons systems to do the same job as the rapidly aging ones. Parliament has had little influence in the making of these decisions. They have been taken by political executives after lengthy and complicated review processes that went on for years either because the government could not agree or because it could not decide to spend the money. Involved in such decisions were not only the military and civilian bureaucracies of DND, but also representatives from other departments. The decision about the particular weapons system to be purchased often entailed much more than straightforward military analysis.[69]

Since 1968 Canada has made only a handful of these major procurement decisions—on the Leopard tanks, the Aurora long-range patrol aircraft, the CF-18, the Canadian Patrol Frigate (CPF), and the low-level air defence system. In all cases there was little direct parliamentary involvement in the final selection. Indeed, given the regional economic impact of some of these decisions, the provincial governments played a much larger role than Parliament, although Parliament did have to approve the funding. Yet because DND buys weapons in single purchases and does not have to go back to Parliament for further approval to complete a purchase that may take several years, Parliament's involvement in the procurement process largely ends once the acquisition program is approved. While the continuation of funding must be voted by Parliament in succeeding annual budgets, it is unlikely that a project, once begun, would be cancelled by the legislative branch, especially when the governing party holds a majority. (This may be contrasted to the U.S. system in which the Defense Department must get authorization each year to continue an acquisition program.)

In sum, the nature of parliamentary government as it has evolved in Canada, the way in which defence policy is handled in the Canadian governmental decision-making process, and the nature of Canadian defence policy itself have all circumscribed the role of Parliament in defence matters.

Defence and the Committees of Parliament Given the limited role that the legislative branch plays in defence policy decision making and in the oversight of the conduct of security relations, it is not surprising to find that the committees of Parliament have not been particularly important institutions in this area of public policy. Recent procedural changes and shifts in the attitude of the executive branch may change this, but in general neither the House of Commons' nor the Senate's committees that deal with defence matters have established themselves as significant actors.[70]

The House of Commons Standing Committee on External Affairs was not created until 1945. In 1968 defence was added to its mandate and it became known as the Standing Committee on External Affairs and National Defence (SCEAND). Under the changes instituted in the House committee system in 1986, SCEAND was split into two standing committees, one on external affairs and international trade and the other on national defence (SCOND).

Canadian parliamentary committees do not exercise the kind of independence that characterizes both the House of Commons and the political executive, which U.S. congressional committees do in relation to the U.S. houses of Congress and the executive branch. As in the United States, however, committee membership reflects the standing of the parties in the full assembly. Thus, if one party has a parliamentary majority, it will hold the majority of the committee seats. Given the tight party discipline found in the Canadian system, members of the majority party sitting on committees have not been prone to use the committees to challenge government policies. Nor have committees of Parliament been free to investigate any matter they choose. Until 1986 committees had to await a reference from the full House, which usually required the support of the political executive and in particular the minister in charge of the policy area for which the committee was responsible. Also limiting the role of committees is the fact that they do not have large, permanent professional staffs and are not supported by independent research organizations separate from the executive branch (the way that U.S. congressional committees are). In the areas of foreign policy and defence policy, the committees of both the House and the Senate have, since 1968, drawn on the support of a private organization, the Parliamentary Centre for Foreign Affairs and Foreign Trade, which contracts with the committees for specific enquiries. To a certain extent this arrangement has created a permanent body of expertise to assist Parliament in reviewing defence policy.

In its first 23 years the Standing Committee on External Affairs was able to review the conduct of foreign policy by examining the estimates of DEA. At the time SCEAND was created in 1968, rule changes allowed for the automatic reference of departmental estimates from both External Affairs and National Defence to this committee. In addition, specific reviews of policy were undertaken, with hearings being held and reports issued. For example, when the NORAD agreement came up for its various renewals, SCEAND received a reference to examine Canada's participation and to recommend renewal or non-renewal. Hearings have also been held on Canada's role in NATO and an examination of the 1971 White Paper was undertaken.

While SCEAND has not been inactive, it is difficult to point to any major policy changes that have emerged as a result of its deliberations and reports. In part this is because SCEAND has never questioned the broad outlines of defence policy and has generally supported the direction in which the government was already moving. For example, the 1970 report on maritime forces agreed with the thrust of the Trudeau policy changes initiated in 1969 that placed sovereignty and surveillance of Canadian waters at the head of the priority list.[71] Another reason why SCEAND has not had much impact is that the government has never been bound to accept its recommendations and, until 1986, was not even required to respond in writing. When SCEAND has expressed disagreement, the government has been free to ignore its recommendations or to proceed as if a parliamentary review was not even taking place. In 1969 a report recommended that Canada maintain its current force levels in Europe, but in April 1969 the Trudeau government announced that the forces there would be cut in half.[72]

The government has also on occasion taken policy decisions that undermined the work of the committees. For example, in the spring of 1985 SCEAND undertook a review of the NORAD agreement, which was due to expire in May 1986. But in March 1985, the Mulroney government concluded an agreement with the United States on the modernization of NORAD's facilities, making renewal of the agreement in 1986 all but certain.

There have been some cases, however, in which SCEAND did marginally influence policy. At the time of 1975 NORAD renewal, the government was considering an indefinite renewal but SCEAND was successful in persuading the minister to seek only a five-year renewal.[73]

Another function that SCEAND has performed is that of public education. Its hearings, while not greatly changing the direction of policy, have provided an open forum in which senior military and civilian officials have had to explain defence policy and provide information on the activities of the forces. They have also afforded members of the public the opportunity to make their views known. During SCEAND's 1985–86 review of the NORAD agreement, extensive testimony was heard on the possible relationship between NORAD and the American SDI.[74] To the extent that SCEAND provides a forum for the expression of public views that may differ from government policy, it can also serve to generate additional public pressure on the government to respond.

The Canadian Senate no longer plays a major role in public policy making and has become somewhat peripheral even to the Parliamentary process. Consequently, its influence on foreign and defence policy has been reduced. But in another sense, the decline of the Senate's role has freed senators from the control of the political executive and allowed it a certain independence not enjoyed by members of the House of Commons. One result of this has been a Senate committee on defence issues that has been very active in recent years.

A Senate Standing Committee on External Affairs was created in 1938, but it did not do much and considered only eight bills between the year of its creation and 1968. Between 1938 and 1963, it had only 29 enquiries, none of which dealt directly with defence or external affairs.[75] A reorganization in 1968 changed the committee's name to the Standing Committee on Foreign Affairs. In subsequent years this committee undertook a wide range of studies on external policy, from Canadian–American relations to Canadian policy in the Middle East.[76] There is little indication that the Senate committee's work has had any impact on government policy. In some instances, such as its recommendations for Canada–U.S. relations, the committee adopted positions different from the prevailing government policy.

In June 1980 the committee established its Sub-committee on National Defence, which became a special committee in 1984. This body produced four of the most comprehensive reports on Canadian defence policy ever to emerge from Parliament.[77] They dealt with manpower, maritime defence, air defence, and military air transport. In these reports the senators showed how a certain independence from the political executive could be used to advantage. Unconstrained by party discipline, they chronicled the growing gap between capabilities and commitments, highlighting deficiencies and recommending major re-equipment programs. The hearings and reports also provided the public with a great deal of material on the posture and roles of the armed forces.

As the Senate was examining defence policy, public awareness of security issues was growing in Canada. Often finding expression on the floor of the House of Commons, this concern had, however, less to do with the specifics of defence policy than with general trends in East–West relations and arms control, and the role of Canada in world affairs. Much of this concern was prompted by the deterioration in superpower relations during the early 1980s, opposition to U.S. President Reagan's SDI proposals, and the lack of progress in arms control negotiations. The decision of the Trudeau government to allow testing of the USAF's cruise missile in Canada was loudly criticized by disarmament groups outside Parliament and by the NDP within the House of Commons. Prime Minister Trudeau, while defending the decision on the cruise, was clearly sympathetic to much of this rising concern. In the winter of 1983–84 he undertook his own "peace initiative," which was widely supported in Canada. And as a measure of the government's interest in encouraging further public discussion, it created the Canadian Institute for International Peace and Security.

When the Mulroney government took office in September 1984, security issues were being debated in Canada to an extent not witnessed since the nuclear weapons debates of the early 1960s. The Conservatives had pledged to rebuild the Canadian armed forces, emphasizing alliance commitments. The new government itself became the target of NDP and now Liberal criticism because of what the Opposition viewed as its overtly pro-American stand on security issues. But the Conservatives, in particular Secretary of State for External Affairs Joe Clark, pledged to involve parliament in the foreign policy and defence policy reviews they intended to undertake.

In May 1985 the government tabled a discussion paper on external policy entitled *Competitiveness and Security: Directions for Canada's International Relations*.[78] A month later a special joint committee of the Senate and the House of Commons was created to consider the discussion paper and to "make recommendations concerning the future objectives and conduct of Canada's international relations." At this time the government was about to initiate free-trade negotiations with the United States and was also considering the U.S. invitation to become involved in SDI research.

Although the Conservatives held a commanding parliamentary majority, the government accepted the Opposition's view that the special joint committee should hold hearings and report on these two issues before the government made a final decision. Thus in the summer of 1985 the Committee held widely publicized hearings across the country soliciting the views of opponents and proponents of free trade and Canadian involvement in SDI. The committee's interim report in August 1985 supported the free-trade negotiations but did not make a specific recommendation on SDI participation on the grounds that more information was required.[79] Shortly after, the government began free-trade talks with the United States, which had become a major policy for the Conservatives. On SDI, the government decided against Canadian government participation, but was going to allow private firms and university researchers in Canada to accept SDI contracts. It was evident that opposition to Canadian participation in SDI, which the special joint committee's hearings had served to highlight, had influenced the government in its decision not to seek official involvement in SDI.

DND initiated a policy review in late 1984 with the original intention of producing a discussion paper similar to the one that had been issued by DEA, followed by parliamentary hearings. No such paper emerged, whether because of internal disagreements within the department or because of the rapid turnover in MNDs during the first two years of the Mulroney government or the experience with the public hearings on the DEA paper. When Perrin Beatty took over as MND in June 1986, he had apparently decided to go straight to a White Paper with a parliamentary review to follow.

In the meantime, the Mulroney government was making defence policy decisions without a great deal of parliamentary discussion or involvement. The government decided to increase Canadian troop strength in Europe, to modernize NORAD's facilities in conjunction with the United States, and to acquire a low-level air defence system. The 1986 renewal of NORAD was preceded by a SCEAND review, but the government did not seek, as the SCEAND report had recommended, a public assurance from the United States that it would respect the integrity of the ABM treaty.[80]

In its review, however, the special joint committee did deal with issues relating to national defence and security questions. Its report, *Independence and Internationalism*, issued in June 1986,[81] recommended continuation of Canadian participation in NATO, NORAD, and UN peacekeeping efforts, but called upon the government to address the problem of the commitment-capability gap, which it said was the fundamental issue in defence policy. The report also stressed the importance of sovereignty protection and in particular urged an enhanced Arctic defence capability as part of the "northern dimension" of Canada's external policy. Arctic sovereignty had become a public issue in the summer of 1985 when an American Coast Guard ship had transited the Northwest Passage. Thus, again, the joint committee had served to provide a forum for, and eventually an expression of, public concern.

As required by the new rules governing parliamentary committees, DEA had 120 days to respond to the recommendations contained in *Independence and Internationalism*. The department's detailed response to each recommendation and its commentary, released in December 1986, took the place of a White Paper and constituted the Mulroney government's formal statement of its foreign policy.[82] Without pre-empting the defence White Paper, but apparently co-ordinated with the still-ongoing DND review, DEA's statement supported the major recommendations and conclusions of the special joint committee on security matters. DEA welcomed the call for a northern dimension to Canadian foreign policy and stated that an element of that approach would be the modernization of the CF's Arctic capabilities. Overall, the committee's report was consistent with the views of the DEA under Joe Clark. In this case, parliamentary involvement, while it may not have dramatically altered the content of foreign policy, did serve a legitimizing function, as well as one of public education.

The committee's recommendations were also largely consistent with the White Paper on Defence that finally emerged in June 1987. The special joint committee's call for a review of the scope of Canada's commitments was nothing new to DND, but it certainly did not hurt to have parliamentary backing for a reduction in allied tasks. The parliamentary process had also highlighted public concern about the Arctic, and the White Paper went far in that direction, announcing that Canada would acquire nuclear-powered submarines. Overall, the support that the majority of the special joint committee gave to continuing Canadian membership in NATO and NORAD also provided the 1987 White Paper with additional legitimacy. Following its release, the White Paper was referred to SCOND for detailed examination.

It remains to be seen whether this new committee will take its role beyond reviewing the White Paper to vigorously overseeing its implementation. Under its new authority to investigate matters without a reference from the House, SCOND has the power to exercise more continual oversight of DND. In its report on NORAD, SCEAND recommended that not only should future reviews of the agreement begin "fully a year before [the agreement's] expiration," but that "the appropriate parliamentary committees be kept fully abreast of matters pertaining to national defence."[83] A more active parliament will not alter the dominance of the political executive and the bureaucracy in the defence policy decision-making process, but it could serve to persuade these two branches to account more completely and more openly for the decisions they make.

Notes

1. See R. MacGregor Dawson, *The Government of Canada*, 5th ed., rev. by Norman Ward (Toronto: University of Toronto Press, 1970), p. 504.

2. Dawson, *The Government of Canada*, p. 522.

3. For a discussion of the development of these different branches of the Canadian government, see Dawson, *The Government of Canada*, parts 3, 4, and 5. On the evolution of cabinet government, see W.A. Matheson, *The Prime Minister and the Cabinet* (Toronto: Methuen, 1976), chapter 1. On the fusion of powers concept, see R.M. Punnett, *The Prime Minister in Canadian Government and Politics* (Toronto: Macmillan of Canada, 1977), chapter 6.

4. The actual titles of these committees have varied over time.

5. See Matheson, *The Prime Minister and the Cabinet*, p. 4, pp. 27–28. On the sources of the prime minister's pre-eminent position, see Dawson, *The Government of Canada*, pp. 59–60, 187–92 and Punnett, *The Prime Minister in Canadian Government and Politics*, pp. 7-8.

6. See Michael Tucker, *Canadian Foreign Policy: Contemporary Issues and Themes* (Toronto: McGraw-Hill Ryerson, 1980), p. 28 and Kim Richard Nossal, *The Politics of Canadian Foreign Policy* (Scarborough, Ont.: Prentice-Hall Canada, 1985), p. 75.

7. Eayrs argues that Mackenzie King's long-standing distrust of the army was confirmed during the November 1944 conscription crisis in Canada. Eayrs further suggests that the military was ostracized by the civilian bureaucracy in the internal struggle for power within government circles, and that its members lacked the formal education of their civilian counterparts. See *In Defence of Canada*, vol. 3, *Peacemaking and Deterrence* (Toronto: University of Toronto Press, 1972), pp. 52–74.

8. Until Trudeau came to power, every Canadian prime minister had held the post of secretary of state for external affairs at one time or another in his career. Between 1912 and 1946, this portfolio was held by the prime minister by law; after that, the only prime minister to assume the position was Diefenbaker—briefly, upon taking office in 1957, and then again for a few months following the death of Sidney Smith in 1959. See James Eayrs, *The Art of the Possible: Government and Foreign Policy in Canada* (Toronto: University of Toronto Press, 1961), pp. 20–28.

9. Jon McLin claims that the cancellation statement was "disingenuous" and therefore galling to Diefenbaker's military advisers for several reasons: first, because it cited strategic rather than economic grounds for the decision; second, because it attempted to associate the government's military advisers with the strategic rationale for the cancellation; and third, because it called into question the future of the manned interceptor, which was the mainstay of the RCAF's organizational *raison d'être*. Jon McLin, *Canada's Changing Defense Policy, 1957–1963* (Baltimore: Johns Hopkins Press, 1967), pp. 75–77. For the best account of the Arrow story, see James Dow, *The Arrow* (Toronto: James Lorimer, 1979).

10. For accounts of the nuclear warheads controversy, see David Cox, *Canada and NORAD, 1958–1978: A Cautionary Retrospective*, Aurora Papers 1 (Ottawa: The Canadian Centre for Arms Control and Disarmament, 1985), pp. 22–43; John G. Diefenbaker, *One Canada: Memoirs of the Right Honourable John G. Diefenbaker*, vol. 3, *The Tumultuous Years, 1962–1967* (Toronto: Macmillan, 1977), pp. 1–16, 46–76; J.L. Granatstein, *Canada 1957–1967: The Years of Uncertainty and Innovation* (Toronto: McClelland and Stewart, 1986), pp. 101–38; J.L. Granatstein, *A Man of Influence: Norman A. Robertson and Canadian Statecraft, 1929–68* (Ottawa: Deneau Publishers, 1981), pp. 336–56; Howard H. Lentner, "Foreign Policy Decision Making: The Case of Canada and Nuclear Weapons," *World Politics* 29, no. 1 (October 1976): 29–66; Peyton V. Lyon, *Canada in World Affairs, 1961–1963* (Toronto: Oxford University Press, 1968), pp. 76–222; Jon McLin, *Canada's Changing Defense Policy, 1957–1963*, pp. 130–67; and John Warnock, *Partner to Behemoth: The Military Policy of a Satellite Canada* (Toronto: New Press, 1970), pp. 183–201.

11. Trudeau's views on the review and the new defence priorities can be found in two of his speeches: "A Defence Policy for Canada," *Statements and Speeches*, no. 69/7, 3 April 1969, and "The Relation of Defence Policy to Foreign Policy," *Statements and Speeches*, no. 69/8, 12 April 1969. For the White Paper pronouncements, see Canada, Department of National Defence, *Defence in the 70s* (Ottawa: Information Canada, 1971). For the best account of the various influences on Trudeau's NATO decision, see Bruce Thordarson, *Trudeau and Foreign Policy: A Study in Decision-Making* (Toronto: Oxford University Press, 1972), especially pp. 143–66.

12. " 'Lot of dough' for armaments kept off Trudeau's priority list," *Globe and Mail* 14 February 1980, p. A9.

13. On these twin sources of prime-ministerial power, see Matheson, *The Prime Minister and the Cabinet*, pp. 47–52, 65–68; see also Nossal, *The Politics of Canadian Foreign Policy*, pp. 74–78.

14. Vernon V. Kronenberg, *All Together Now: The Organization of the Department of National Defence in Canada 1964–1972*, Wellesley Paper 3 (Toronto: Canadian Institute of International Affairs, 1973), p. 65.

15. See J.L. Granatstein, *Canada 1957–1967: The Years of Uncertainty and Innovation* (Toronto: McClelland and Stewart, 1986), p. 233.

16. Erik Nielsen, who took over the defence portfolio in February 1985, was already a member of this committee in his other capacity as deputy prime minister.

17. The National Defence Act, *Statutes of Canada*, 1922, 12–13 George V, ch. 34. The Act was proclaimed in force on 1 January 1923. For a discussion of the origins of the department see Eayrs, *In Defence of Canada*,

vol. 1, *From the Great War to the Great Depression* (Toronto: University of Toronto Press, 1964), pp. 224–36. Interestingly enough, Eayrs notes (on p. 224) that the original amalgamation proposal was put forward in 1920 by a military officer, the Inspector-General of Militia, General Sir Arthur Currie.

18. Eayrs, *In Defence of Canada*, vol. 1, p. 236.

19. The National Defence Act, *Statutes of Canada*, 1950, ch. 34, sec. 3.

20. The National Defence Act, *Revised Statutes of Canada*, 1970, ch. N-4, sec. 4, as amended.

21. Douglas L. Bland, *The Administration of Defence Policy in Canada 1947 to 1985* (Kingston: Ronald P. Frye & Co., 1987), p. 95.

22. Eayrs, *In Defence of Canada*, vol. 3, *Peacemaking and Deterrence*, pp. 15, 25–26. In 1946 Claxton had suggested that St. Laurent accept the External Affairs portfolio as a means of keeping the latter in public office; later, Claxton spearheaded the drive to have St. Laurent run as King's successor as leader of the Liberal party. See Dale C. Thomson, *Louis St. Laurent: Canadian* (Toronto: Macmillan of Canada, 1967), pp. 210–11, 244.

23. Reginald H. Roy, *For Most Conspicuous Bravery: A Biography of Major-General George R. Pearkes, V.C., Through the Two World Wars* (Vancouver: University of British Columbia Press, 1977), p. 341.

24. Roy, *For Most Conspicuous Bravery*, pp. 340–41.

25. Robertson's influential role in opposing the acquisition of nuclear warheads by Canada is detailed in J.L. Granatstein, *A Man of Influence*, pp. 336–56.

26. Eayrs, *In Defence of Canada*, vol. 3, *Peacemaking and Deterrence*, pp. 28, 49, 59, 61–66.

27. For detailed analyses of Hellyer's role in the unification debate, see Granatstein, *Canada 1957–1967*, pp. 218–42; David P. Burke, "Hellyer and Landymore: The Unification of the Canadian Armed Forces and an Admiral's Revolt," *American Review of Canadian Studies* 8, no. 2 (Autumn 1978): 3–27; and Bland, *The Administration of Defence Policy in Canada 1947 to 1985*, pp. 33–53.

28. Roy, *For Most Conspicuous Bravery*, p. 326.

29. Matheson, *The Prime Minister and the Cabinet*, p. 7.

30. This development is discussed in more detail in Chapter 5.

31. For a discussion of the original rationale, organization, and development of the wartime cabinet committees, especially those dealing with defence matters, see C.P. Stacey, *Arms, Men and Governments: The War Policies of Canada 1939–1945* (Ottawa: The Queen's Printer, 1970), pp. 69–70, 113–19; Matheson, *The Prime Minister and the Cabinet*, pp. 83–84; and Eayrs, *The Art of the Possible*, pp. 12–14.

32. Peter C. Newman, *Renegade in Power: The Diefenbaker Years*, (Toronto: McClelland and Stewart, 1963), p. 343.

33. Roy, *For Most Conspicuous Bravery*, pp. 340–41.

34. Matheson, *The Prime Minister and the Cabinet*, pp. 86–87.

35. Judy LaMarsh, *Memoirs of a Bird in a Gilded Cage* (Toronto: Pocket Books, 1970), pp. 328–30.

36. For details of PEMS, see Richard Van Loon, "Ottawa's Expenditure Process: Four Systems in Search of Co-ordination," in *How Ottawa Spends: The Liberals, the Opposition and Federal Priorities, 1983*, ed.

Bruce Doern (Toronto: James Lorimer, 1983), pp. 93–120; and Jerry McCafferty, "Canada's Envelope Budgeting System," *American Review of Canadian Studies* 14, no. 1 (Spring 1984): 45–62.

37. Donald Ian MacLeod, "Canadian Military Participation in NATO from 1969 to 1983: An Analysis of Decision-making and Organizational Change," M.A. thesis, University of Alberta, 1983, pp. 110–11. Thordarson, *Trudeau and Foreign Policy,* suggests that Cadieux "was planning to leave political life and was not influential in the new administration" (p. 90), whereas Macdonald "was skeptical of the value of armed forces," and only accepted the defence portfolio when Cadieux retired "because it presented more prospects for advancement than did the other three cabinet posts he was offered" (p. 46).

38. David B. Dewitt and John J. Kirton, *Canada as a Principal Power: A Study in Foreign Policy and International Relations* (Toronto: John Wiley & Sons, 1983), pp. 201–202.

39. Granatstein, *Canada: 1957–1967*, pp. 223–24.

40. Granatstein, *Canada: 1957–1967*, pp. 110–11.

41. See C.R. Nixon, SCEAND, *Minutes of Proceedings and Evidence*, Issue no. 41, 20 May 1976, p. 26. Refer also to Chapters 5 and 7 for discussions of the role of industrial benefits in Canadian defence procurement.

42. Nossal, *The Politics of Canadian Foreign Policy,* p. 148.

43. The following sections draw heavily on the excellent study by Douglas L. Bland, *The Administration of Defence Policy in Canada 1947 to 1985.*

44. This Policy Direction and Management Services activity includes: the formulation and recommendation of defence objectives and policy options; the elaboration of approved policy; the overall direction of development planning; the management of the Defence Services Program; direction to the operational commands; emergency planning; and responsibility for Canadian contributions to NATO. For details, see Canada, *1987–88 Estimates*, part 3, *Expenditure Plan—National Defence* (Ottawa: Supply and Services Canada, 1987), pp. 60–62, 66.

45. For a detailed description of the formal DND decision-making process, see two articles by Colonel W.N. Russell: "The Making of Canadian Defence Policy," *Canadian Defence Quarterly,* 12, no. 4 (Spring 1983): 18–24; and "The Management of Canada's Defence Resources," *Canadian Defence Quarterly* 13, no. 4 (Spring 1984): 17–22. For a critique of this process, see Bland, *The Administration of Defence Policy in Canada 1947 to 1985*, pp. 165–84.

46. A useful description of the DPMS can be found in Chief of Program, Department of National Defence, *C Prog 55: An Introduction to the DSP and the Defence Program Management System*, 4th ed., Ottawa, 1984.

47. These are the ADM(Pol), ADM(Per), ADM(Fin), and ADM(Mat).

48. Bland, *The Administration of Defence Policy in Canada 1947 to 1985*, pp. 166–67.

49. For a discussion of the crucial distinction between civilian "direction" and "control," see R.B. Byers, "Canadian Civil–Military Relations and Reorganization of the Armed Forces: Whither Civilian Control?", in *The Canadian Military: A Profile*, ed. Hector J. Massey (Toronto: Copp Clark, 1972), p. 200.

50. The National Defence Act, *Revised Statutes of Canada*, 1970, ch. N-4, sec. 18(1).

51. Lieutenant-Colonel Douglas L. Bland, *Institutionalizing Ambiguity: The Management Review Group and the Reshaping of the Defence Policy Process in Canada*, Occasional Paper (Kingston: Centre for International Relations, Queen's University, July 1986).

52. Bland, *The Administration of Defence Policy in Canada 1947 to 1985*, p. 84.

53. Canada, Task Force on Review of Unification of the Canadian Forces, *Final Report* (Ottawa: Minister of National Defence, DND, 15 March 1980), pp. 39–41, 75–77.

54. Canada, Review Group on the Report of the Task Force on Unification of the Armed Forces, *Report* (Ottawa: Chief of the Defence Staff, DND, 31 August 1980), pp. 18–21.

55. Bland, *The Administration of Defence Policy in Canada 1947 to 1985*, pp. 123–24.

56. Douglas L. Bland, *Controlling the Defence Policy Process in Canada: White Papers on Defence and Bureaucratic Politics in the Department of National Defence*, Occasional Paper (Kingston: Centre for International Relations, Queen's University, March 1988), pp. 18, 24.

57. A report also suggests that the motivation behind the Challenger purchase was related to the troubled financial status of the aircraft manufacturer: Canada, Auditor General, *Report of the Auditor General of Canada to the House of Commons, Fiscal Year ended 31 March 1987* (Ottawa: Supply and Services Canada, 1987), sec. 9.138, 9.153.

58. Canada, Auditor General, *Report of the Auditor General of Canada to the House of Commons, Fiscal Year ended 31 March 1984*, (Ottawa: Supply and Services Canada, 1984). See chapter 12 on the Department of National Defence.

59. Canada, *Report of the Auditor General of Canada* (1984), sec. 12.16.

60. Bland, *The Administration of Defence Policy in Canada 1947 to 1985*, pp. 179, 182.

61. These "capability components" included: general-purpose maritime forces (including maritime air); general-purpose land forces in Canada (including tactical helicopters); general-purpose air forces in Canada (including tactical air forces, air defence forces, and support); forces stationed in Europe (including land forces and helicopters, tactical air forces, and theatre support); general support forces (air transport, search and rescue); command, control, communications, and intelligence; personnel support; and matériel support. See Colonel W.N. Russell, "The Management of Canada's Defence Resources," p. 18.

62. Colin S. Gray, "Defence Policy and the Military Profession: What Are Canada's Soldiers To Do?", in *Canadian Military Professionalism: the Search for Identity*, eds. R.B. Byers and Colin S. Gray, Wellesley Paper 2 (Toronto: Canadian Institute of International Affairs, February 1973), p. 79.

63. R.B. Byers, "Canadian Security and Defence: The Legacy and the Challenges," *Adelphi Papers* 214 (Winter 1986), p. 59.

64. See, for example, Kenneth N. Waltz, *Foreign Policy and Democratic Politics* (Boston: Little Brown & Co., 1967) and Max Beloff, *Foreign Policy and the Democratic Process* (Baltimore: Johns Hopkins University Press, 1955).

65. Edward S. Corwin as quoted in Arthur Schlesinger, Jr., "Congress and the Making of American Foreign Policy," *Foreign Affairs* 51, no. 1 (October 1972): 82.

66. See Thomas M. Franck and Edward M. Weisband, *Foreign Policy by Congress* (New York: Oxford University Press, 1979); Samuel P. Huntington, *The Common Defense: Strategic Programs in National Policy* (New York: Columbia University Press, 1961); Richard Haas, "Congressional Power: Implications for American Security Policy," *Adelphi Papers* 153 (Summer 1979).

67. David Taras, "From Bystander to Participant," in *Parliament and Canadian Foreign Policy*, ed. David Taras (Toronto: Canadian Institute of International Affairs, 1985). See also Nossal, *The Politics of Canadian Foreign Policy*, ch. 5; W.M. Dobell, "Foreign Policy in Parliament," *International Perspectives*, (January/February 1985).

68. Byers, "Canadian Security and Defence," p. 60.

69. See Chapters 5 and 7.

70. On the role of parliamentary committees, see W.M. Dobell, "Parliament's Foreign Policy Committees" and Don Page, "The Standing Committee on External Affairs 1945–1983—Who Participates When?", *Parliament and Canadian Foreign Policy*, ed. David Taras.

71. Canada, House of Commons, SCEAND, *Tenth Report of the Standing Committee on External Affairs and National Defence Respecting Maritime Forces* (Ottawa: Queen's Printer, 1970).

72. Dobell, "Parliament's Foreign Policy Committees," p. 24.

73. Dobell, "Parliament's Foreign Policy Committees," p. 25.

74. Canada, House of Commons, SCEAND, NORAD *1986: Canada–U.S. Defence Cooperation and the 1986 Renewal of the NORAD Agreement* 14 February 1986.

75. R.P. Pattee and Paul G. Thomas, "The Senate and Defence Policy: Subcommittee Report on Canada's Maritime Defence," *Parliament and Canadian Foreign Policy*, ed. David Taras, p. 104.

76. Examples of its reports are: Canada, Senate, Standing Committee on Foreign Affairs, *Canadian–United States Relations* (Ottawa: Queen's Printer, 1975); Senate, Standing Committee on Foreign Affairs, *Report on Canada's Relations with the Countries of the Middle East and North Africa* (Ottawa: Supply and Services Canada, 1985).

77. The reports produced by the Sub-committee (later the Special Committee) on National Defence of the Standing Committee on Foreign Affairs were: *Manpower in Canada's Armed Forces* (January 1982); *Canada's Maritime Defence* (May 1983); *Canada's Territorial Air Defence* (January 1985); *Military Air Transport* (February 1986). See also Byers, "Canadian Security and Defence," p. 3 and Pattee and Thomas, "The Senate and Defence Policy."

78. Canada, Secretary of State for External Affairs, *Competitiveness and Security: Directions for Canada's International Relations* (Ottawa: Supply and Services Canada, May 1985).

79. Canada, Special Joint Committee on Canada's International Relations, *Interim Report Pertaining to Bilateral Trade with the United States and Canada's Participation in Research on the Strategic Defense Initiative* (Ottawa, 23 August 1985).

80. Canada, SCEAND, NORAD *1986*, p. 78.

81. Canada, Special Joint Committee on Canada's International Relations, *Independence and Internationalism* (Ottawa: Supply and Services Canada, 1986).

82. Canada, Department of External Affairs, *Canada's International Relations: Response of the Government of Canada to the Report of the Special Joint Committee of the Senate and the House of Commons* (Ottawa: Supply and Services Canada, 1986).

83. Canada, SCEAND, *NORAD 1986*, p. 81.

5

THE DOMESTIC POLICY-MAKING ENVIRONMENT

Introduction

Moving outward from the crucial inner circle of policy makers, we now come to the broader public dimension of Canadian defence policy. We might expect that Canadians would take a great interest in defence matters: after all, the fundamental duty of the modern state is to ensure the survival, security, and independence of its populace. The military establishment obviously plays a vital role in this task, and it can also be used to help achieve other national goals. We might therefore presume that the Canadian public would want to have a voice in determining which societal values should be protected and how this should be done.

Most commentators agree, however, that generally this has not been the case in Canada, at least until fairly recently. By and large, Canadians have not been greatly interested in defence policy issues. Analysts point to the fact that since World War II—with the possible exception of the 1963 federal election, precipitated by Prime Minister Diefenbaker's inept handling of the acquisition of nuclear warheads for Canadian weapons—no government has risen or fallen on defence issues.

Notwithstanding this striking fact, scholars have been hard pressed to provide convincing explanations for it. Some have seen its causes in the essentially "unmilitary" character of the Canadian people, while others have simply repeated, with little concrete evidence, the time-worn cliché about the apathy of Canadians on the issue of defence.

Other reasons can be adduced. For example, because governments have little cause to fear retribution at the polls over defence questions, politicians generally have not taken the initiative in raising defence issues for public debate. The fact that Canada has had only three major defence policy White papers since World War II suggests that the government has not considered public education to be a priority concern in the defence area. Moreover, as we demonstrated in Chapter 4, Parliament itself has not been very successful in providing a forum for informed and sustained public debate on defence policy, although this situation may indeed change in time. Politicians on the whole have little background in, or concern for, military matters. Parliament, as well as the public, on the other hand, has been denied adequate access to the data and information on the basis of which the executive makes its defence decisions. This has proved to be a serious obstacle to those individuals and groups seeking to influence government defence policy making; the all-encompassing constraint imposed by national security considerations is by now a familiar one to many Canadians.

Finally, the military itself has become increasingly isolated from the society that it serves and in which it operates. Canada maintains a relatively small (in relation to total population), all-volunteer, regular force whose primary postwar role has been oriented toward operations in NATO Europe. Furthermore, even the CF's North American defence activities are largely invisible to the Canadian public. Finally, the actual military "presence" in Canadian national life has declined with the dwindling numbers of the geographically scattered regular force, and, more importantly, with the drastic shrinkage of the size and roles of the reserves.

Thus, for the vast majority of Canadians who have never served in the forces and who are not regularly exposed to, or invited to participate in, the formulation of defence policy, the military, and consequently its roles and problems, have become less directly relevant to their daily concerns. On the surface, then, the domestic environment would appear to be less important than the federal and external environments of Canadian defence policy making.

But this is not an entirely accurate picture. Certain sections of the Canadian public are most interested in defence policy and have indeed sought to influence the policy-making process. The domestic environment is not comprised of a single, homogeneous "public." There are many different sectors of the public pursuing a variety of different interests. The interests and opinions of the sector concerned with defence policy have not been entirely neglected.

No government can formulate defence policy with complete disregard for its public consequences. Thus, it is in this more specifically defined domestic environment that the important debates on defence policy take place, and it is here that the government and DND must promote their policy decisions to win the hearts and minds—and pocketbooks!—of the Canadians who must ultimately support those policies and subsidize defence.

This chapter seeks to identify the sectors of the public that act on the various issues and the stages in the policy-making process at which they are involved and to determine their relative influence—both individually and collectively—on the formulation and implementation of Canadian defence policy.

Public Opinion

Very little systematic research has been carried out regarding the relationship between public opinion and defence policy in Canada. Empirical evidence is therefore sketchy and is based largely on analyses of public opinion polls. Nevertheless, these studies, whose findings should be regarded as suggestive rather than conclusive, generally do reflect the traditional view that Canadians by and large have supported the basic principles, objectives, and broad directions of Canadian defence policy in the postwar era.

This apparent consensus has been reflected in the general pattern of public acceptance of Canada's commitment to, and participation in, NATO, NORAD, and UN peacekeeping operations. Canadians perceive themselves to be Western-aligned, and, while the majority favours the concept of arms control, it rejects the notion of unilateral Western disarmament. As a corollary, the general public accepts the need for an adequately armed military establishment to carry out Canada's international defence responsibilities.[1]

But questions arise as to whether this consensus is real; that is, whether it reflects active agreement by the Canadian public or merely passive acquiescence or even indifference and apathy about policies decided by the government. In short, is public opinion a significant determining factor in the making of Canadian defence policy?

The evidence suggests that there are indeed nuances and shades of opinion among the various components that comprise the Canadian public. Thus, it is appropriate to differentiate between the so-called attentive public—a small elite possessing the professional training or inclination to concern itself on a more or less continuing basis with defence policy[2]—and the mass public, composed of ordinary citizens with no sustained interest in these matters. But while the consensus is not monolithic, it is nevertheless real insofar as there has been a significant degree of agreement among these sectors of the public regarding the fundamental orientation and tenets of postwar Canadian defence policies.

At the same time, however, the nature of this consensus has ebbed and flowed according to the changing state of East-West relations and the type of defence issues that have arisen for public consideration as a result. What do opinion polls reveal about Canadian views regarding the prospect of nuclear war, the relationship between arms and national security, and the possibilities of arms control and disarmament?

The attitudes of Canadians have shifted subtly on these and related issues over time. Compared to the period from the late 1940s to the early 1960s, Canadians in the past two decades have been less disposed to view the Soviet Union as the sole or even main threat to their security. They are more prone to adopt a sceptical view of American military policies, both as they impinge on Canadian defence policies directly and as they affect Canadian concerns indirectly in the course of superpower strategic relations. Moreover, more Canadians now express a growing concern about the risks and dangers of nuclear war. At the same time, the public continues to support Canadian participation in collective self-defence arrangements and recognizes the need for increased defence expenditures to re-equip the armed forces.

Therefore, depending on the issue and the international context in which it is perceived, the breadth and intensity of the public consensus on Canadian defence policy has fluctuated considerably. Public opinion has ranged from quiet support or passive (and at times reluctant) acquiescence to outright opposition by a visible and voluble minority. Without question, the general consensus on defence has proved most susceptible to fragmentation and even dissolution when issues pertaining to nuclear weapons have come before the government. Indeed, beginning in the early 1960s, nuclear issues have tended to evoke a high degree of ambivalence and ambiguity both in government policies and in the Canadian public psyche. A strong and direct correlation exists between Ottawa's handling of nuclear issues on the one hand and Canadian public attitudes on the other.

The substance of these nuclear issues has varied over time: in the early 1960s it concerned the acquisition of nuclear warheads for several weapons systems procured for the armed forces; in the early 1980s it involved the testing of ALCMs in Canadian airspace by the USAF; in the mid-1980s it concerned Canada's participation in the U.S. SDI program to develop defences against nuclear-armed ballistic missiles; and most recently it has focussed on DND's planned acquisition of nuclear-powered submarines (SSNs).

There are elements common to each of these issues and the public controversies they have given rise to in Canada. First, they were all precipitated by major changes, usually of a technological nature, in the external environment. Canadian policy makers were confronted by these changes and placed in the position of having to respond to them. In these circumstances, the government's policy responses were sometimes hesitant and ambivalent, and public opinion consequently took longer to crystallize into a new consensus.[3] Second, they all involved, in one form or another, Canada's involvement with U.S. nuclear technology or military doctrine. Thus, to an increasingly nationalistic and independently minded Canadian public, they all raised the spectre of Canada's symbolic subordination to U.S. interests and pressures. In this respect, these nuclear issues tapped elements both of a latent anti-Americanism and of a self-image of moral rectitude in the Canadian body politic. This in itself was often sufficient to spark public debate in Canada.

But did Canada's defence policy makers act on the basis of, or in spite of, the prevailing public sentiment in these cases? The 1960–63 warheads controversy represented the clearest expression of Canada's ambivalent approach to nuclear issues. In seeking to improve the capabilities of the Canadian military, the Diefenbaker government had purchased a series of weapons systems that required nuclear warheads for effective operation. At the same time, Diefenbaker, prompted by his crusading secretary of state for external affairs, Howard Green, who was in turn assisted by his experienced deputy minister, Norman Robertson, was promoting the cause of nuclear disarmament at the United Nations.

In this confused environment of apparently contradictory policy objectives, Diefenbaker sought to stall the decision on acquiring the warheads—an action dictated in part by his reading of public opinion. Unfortunately for him, he took counsel from the wrong opinion—his personal mail, the antinuclear, anti-American views of which were being orchestrated by a concerted letter-writing campaign. Had he consulted public opinion polls, Diefenbaker would have found a substantial, if slightly eroding, majority in favour of the acquisition of the nuclear warheads.[4]

Diefenbaker's indecisive handling of the nuclear issue probably contributed more to the Conservatives' demise in the 1963 federal election than did the substance of the issue itself. By that time, opposition to the purchase was clearly growing among the public, but ironically, Pearson's Liberal government decided to defuse the controversy by accepting the nuclear warheads from the Americans. Evidently Pearson's clear resolve to accept the warheads and *then* to examine the prospect of negotiating out of a nuclear role for Canada was preferred by the Canadian public over Diefenbaker's prolonged waffling.

In any event, the 1960s debate marked a clear turning point in public and governmental attitudes toward the acquisition of nuclear weaponry. In 1971, when the Trudeau government announced that Canada would be dropping its nuclear-strike role in NATO and closing its Bomarc bases, there was no public objection. Since then Canada has not contemplated new nuclear roles for its armed forces, and there was no public opposition at all to the government's announcement, when it signed the CF-18 fighter contract, that it would not be acquiring nuclear-capable missiles for this aircraft.

By the 1980s the nature of the public debate over nuclear weapons had taken a different form. Both the cruise-missile testing and the SDI issues raised questions in the public's mind about the extent to which Canada's close military ties with the United States entailed an implicit (or explicit) acceptance of what were perceived by some as potentially destabilizing, "war-fighting" U.S. strategic doctrines. While Canadians were no doubt concerned by the "hawkish" attitude of the Reagan administration, the real focus of their attention was the risk of nuclear war and Canada's complicity in fuelling the nuclear arms race. Compared to the mid-1960s, a growing percentage of Canadians now believed that the chances of nuclear war had increased significantly and that their government should be doing more to reduce this risk.[5]

The emergence of this "new cold war" pessimism in Canadian public opinion made it difficult for the government to arrive at a firm consensus on Canada's nuclear-related policies. The Trudeau government was clearly caught off guard by the initially strong opposition to the ALCM testing agreement with the United States—one which Ottawa had at first tried to keep secret. Later it floundered somewhat in finding a politically acceptable rationale for its decision— namely, that it was "a necessary and fair contribution to NATO security by Canada."[6] Nevertheless, the Trudeau government had agreed to the testing arrangement despite polling evidence showing that a majority of Canadians (52 percent) were opposed to it just prior to the time the decision was taken. Clearly, the government was not governed by public opinion in taking this particular decision. On the other hand, the 1983 cruise debate did sensitize the Canadian public to the broader strategic and arms-control considerations relating to nuclear issues involving Canada. Moreover, from the government's perspective, the legacy of this debate was that Ottawa could no longer take for granted docile public acceptance of nuclear decisions: nuclear weapons and arms control were now permanently ensconced in the government's defence decision-making agenda.

Recognizing this, the Mulroney government adopted a more openly solicitous approach on the issue of possible Canadian participation in the U.S. SDI research and development program. Not only did the government decide to hold a series of cross-country parliamentary hearings prior to making its decision in 1985, but it also commissioned comprehensive opinion polls through DEA on a range of foreign policy issues. The August 1985 Decima poll found that, while there was a narrow majority in favour of SDI, there was "no great enthusiasm" for the program "in large part because of fears related to a renewed arms race."[7] Other polls taken in 1985 found a similar guarded consensus in favour of limited Canadian participation in the SDI research program. Perhaps not surprisingly, a higher percentage of Canadians were prepared to support SDI if it meant more jobs for Canadians.[8] These results, and not the overwhelmingly negative views on SDI expressed before the joint parliamentary committee, evidently convinced the Mulroney government to adopt its somewhat ambivalent decision on 7 September 1985, ruling out direct, government-to-government participation in SDI research, but leaving open the possibility of non-governmental participation. In this case, expectations of economic gain appeared to outweigh moral considerations in the public's attitudes.

The Mulroney government also privately canvassed public opinion prior to announcing its intention to acquire a fleet of nuclear-powered submarines in the 1987 White Paper on Defence. The government, through its DND-commissioned polls, learned that there was a broad foundation of public support for the acquisition of SSNs, especially if the program was sold on the merits of the need to do more to protect Canadian sovereignty in the Arctic.[9] Once again, the government's initial justification for its program corresponded closely with the public consensus its polls had indicated in support of this decision.

Although Canadian governments have increasingly recognized the need to monitor the nation's attitudinal pulse, and even occasionally to heed the beat thus registered, they have shown themselves to be notably resistant to public opinion in one important area. Over the past two decades, a majority of Canadians have indicated that they would support increased defence spending to improve the conventional capabilities of the CF; indeed, in a March 1987 Decima poll for DND, 70 percent of the respondents replied that the government should spend more money on defence.[10] Despite this prevailing view, governments have been reluctant to increase defence expenditures except in marginal increments, and often despite electoral pledges to major increases.

The preceding analysis suggests several conclusions. First, defence issues have only occasionally sparked divisive public debates in Canada, and when they have, they have tended to revolve around matters pertaining to nuclear weapons and strategy. Second, Canadian governments can normally rely on a reasonably solid consensus in support of their defence policies, even on contentious issues: the majority of Canadians rarely coalesce in united and sustained opposition to these policies and generally support clear, firm decisions of any sort from the government. Third, there is a certain ambivalence in Canadian opinion when the government's support for specific U.S. and NATO policies and doctrines appears to be inconsistent with its espousal of the cause of arms control and disarmament. Fourth, this ambivalence is often intensified by public perceptions that the government of the day is following U.S. policies and doctrines too slavishly; Canadians appear to be very sensitive to defence policies that suggest a junior, "satellite" status for Canada. Finally, on the whole, Canadian governments have not been greatly swayed by public opinion in formulating and implementing defence policy.

If public opinion has played a role in defence policy making, it has been in establishing the broad parameters within which Canadian political leaders and bureaucrats must operate. Public opinion often functions as a negative indicator in that it draws the boundaries beyond which the political executive must *not* transgress; rarely does it illuminate the path that the Canadian people believe the government *ought* to follow. In this sense, Canadian public opinion is essentially a reaction to policies and decisions already taken or contemplated by the government. While it is true that these decisions usually represent Canadian responses to external developments over which Ottawa exercises little control, the government, because of its decisive advantage in expertise and information, normally acts as the interpreter of these developments to the Canadian public. In this respect, it is Ottawa, not public opinion, that defines the terms of the debate on defence policy within the domestic environment.

Interest Groups

Within the Canadian domestic environment, there are groups that organize for the purpose of enabling their members to act collectively to influence government policy in the direction of their common interest. These groups, which for the sake of convenience we shall label "interest groups," vary greatly in their degree of organizational rigour, the scope and depth of their interests and objectives, and the type of political behaviour to which they resort in impressing their interests on the government.[11]

Regrettably, the academic community has almost completely ignored the role of such groups in the Canadian defence policy-making process.[12] This is surprising insofar as, in other countries, groups associated with the so-called military–industrial complex or with the peace movement have attracted a great deal of scholarly attention. Nevertheless, the very dearth of such studies in Canada might suggest that interest groups play only a minor and peripheral role in the making of Canadian defence policy.

However, this may be changing as the government finds that it must maintain a broad consensus of support for greater expenditures on defence and for policy responses dictated by an ever-shifting international strategic environment. To do so, the political leadership has found it expedient to grant greater access to the policy process to a broader range of public-interest groups; and this access, once granted, will become increasingly difficult to deny altogether in the future.

If the number and membership of groups were the only criteria, then one might conclude that the potential for interest-group involvement in defence policy making is high. Nossal notes the existence of "a well-organized military lobby" in Canada, numbering somewhere between 500 000 and 3 000 000 members.[13] Another study indicates that the number of peace groups in Canada has increased from a few dozen in the early 1970s to over 1000, with some 300 000 members in the late 1980s.[14] As defined by the nature of their interests and objectives, defence-oriented interest groups fall into two broad categories: those that are generally in favour of a strong national military establishment, and those that oppose a military buildup and support arms control.

The former include a variety of groups pursuing different interests. Some espouse employee-welfare interests such as veterans' rights and benefits (the Royal Canadian Legion), while others seek to reinforce the government's overall commitment to defence (the Federation of Military and United Service Institutes of Canada). Others focus on service-specific interests relating to the organizational concerns and operational requirements of particular environmental elements (sea, air, land) of the CF. (Examples are: The Navy League of Canada and the Naval Officers Associations of Canada; the Royal Canadian Air Force Association; and ten corps associations representing the land element. These corps associations, along with several other affiliated groups representing the Air and Naval Reserves, and some other associations, now meet annually in an umbrella organization, the Conference of Defence Associations [CDA]).[15] Finally, there are corporate groups with defence-related interests, especially those concerning DND's general capital expenditures and specific equipment-procurement programs (Aerospace Industries Association of Canada, the Canadian Maritime Industries Association, the Canadian Manufacturers' Association, and the Business Council on National Issues). Other pro-defence groups, including "think tanks" and advocacy organizations (Canadian Institute for Strategic Studies, the Canadian Conservative Centre, the Canadian Council for Peace in Freedom, the Strategic Analysis Group, and the Coalition of Peace Through Strength) have been established in recent years.

At the other end of the spectrum, numerous peace groups have emerged to counter what they generally perceive to be a pro-military bias among the groups cited above. While it is difficult to categorize their interests precisely, in the main they advocate pro-disarmament, antinuclear, anti-alliance, or distinctly pacifist views. There are well over 200 major Canadian peace organizations, many of which rely for their vitality on local branch affiliates.[16] The most active of the earliest of these groups were the Canadian Peace Congress and Voice of Women, but many new groups have arisen in the past decade to give expression to their concerns about nuclear war and Canada's nuclear policies. Among the most prominent of these organizations are: the Canadian Peace Alliance; Project Ploughshares; Operation Dismantle; Physicians for Social Responsibility; Lawyers for Social Responsibility; the Canadian Peace Research and Education Association; Veterans Against Nuclear Arms; The Group of 78; the Peace Research Institute—Dundas; and the Institute of Peace and Conflict Studies.[17]

Although many of the early peace groups were oriented toward single issues and focussed on such concerns as protesting Canada's cruise-missile testing agreement with the United States in the early 1980s, most are now institutionalized in varying degrees, rely extensively on co-operative networking activities with other groups, and strive to attract a broad cross-section of Canadians to their causes. Beginning with the SCEAND hearings on Canada's policies regarding the United Nations Special Session on Disarmament in 1982, more of these peace groups have become actively involved in testifying before, and making prepared submissions to, parliamentary committees. This increased level of participation was especially evident during the SCEAND hearings on the NORAD renewal and the special joint committee hearings on Canada's role in SDI, both in 1985.

For example, while 22 peace groups, together with 44 government officials, 8 business groups, and 25 academics and research-institute representatives appeared before SCEAND's NORAD hearings in 1985, only two of the peace groups testifying (Voice of Women and Project Ploughshares) had appeared before SCEAND's hearings on the 1980 NORAD renewal issue. Also in marked contrast to the 1980 hearings, the special joint committee of 1985 heard from 115 groups of all different sizes and political orientations. In all, 99 individuals appeared before this committee, and 17 academics and research institutes submitted briefs, while only 3 business groups participated. It is worth noting that 109 of the 115 groups opposed Canadian involvement in the SDI program.[18]

But the mere size and activity levels of interest groups are not necessarily indicative of their influence in the defence policy-making process. The Mulroney government's decisions on the NORAD and SDI issues, as well as those represented in its defence White Paper, reveal that the traditional themes, orientations, and substance of Canadian defence policy have remained largely unaffected by interest-group efforts. Although the government, no doubt sensitized by the Liberals' uncomfortable experience with the ALCM testing debate, obviously perceived a need to gauge the range and depth of group concerns on these issues through more extensive, open, and accessible parliamentary hearings and ministerial consultations, this did not result in fundamental changes in Canadian defence policy.

Indeed, there are few documented cases in which pressure-group activity has altered specific governmental policy decisions. On the surface, the Trudeau government's 1976 decision to reverse its 1971 White Paper announcement that Canada would not acquire a new main battle tank for the CF appeared to be a lobbying victory for the Royal Canadian Armoured Corps Association. However, it now appears that pressure from allies in favour of Canada retaining a heavy armoured role in Europe combined with Trudeau's pursuit of a contractual link with the EEC played a much more important role than did the interest groups in the government's about-face on the tank issue.[19]

In a broader sense, interest groups have been more successful in keeping issues alive in the public's mind than they have been in influencing specific policy decisions. For the pro-defence groups this has usually taken the form of drawing public attention to the deteriorating state of the CF and of conducting "holding" operations against dramatic cutbacks in defence spending.[20] For the peace groups this has been reflected in their continuing efforts to publicize the cause of arms control and disarmament and to prevent these issues from being dropped from the government's policy-making agenda.

Why have interest groups not played a more influential role in Canadian defence policy making? Part of the explanation lies in the structure and organization of these groups. As noted earlier, a predominant characteristic of defence-related interest groups, whether of the pro-defence or peace-movement variety, is the heterogeneity of their concerns. There is no single "defence" or "peace" movement in Canada. Rather there are numerous, yet disparate, issue-specific and quasi-institutionalized groups and organizations that are loosely oriented to a variety of overlapping concerns. For example, the peace movement consists of many small, local disarmament branches, coalitions, and networks whose activities are only occasionally co-ordinated in nation-wide campaigns. Because their financial resources are limited, most rely on volunteer workers and only a few can afford full-time organizers and researchers. Given their organizational weaknesses and diverse interests, the peace groups have encountered difficulties in defining common policies and tactics. In these circumstances, for many peace activists, disarmament has tended to become "an all-encompassing goal" obscuring the real divisions among different groups.[21]

Most of these groups are removed from the policy-making process, and for many peace groups this distancing represents a philosophical preference. Most groups tend to "preach to the converted," engaging in marches, rallies, and petitions of a high-profile, albeit usually short-lived, nature. At both ends of the spectrum interest groups have tended to target the general public and a few members of the political leadership in public-education lobbying efforts, rather than to focus on the less accessible defence bureaucracy. To date, few groups have attempted to mobilize their members to take more directly political action during federal election campaigns, although this may change as the peace groups prepare their "Peace Pledge" campaign for future elections.[22]

Finally, for the most part, defence policy makers have maintained a warily sceptical view of the efforts of these groups. From the perspective of those formulating defence policy, few groups have attempted to offer concrete, substantive, and politically feasible proposals that might guide decision making. While many in the peace movement protest the iniquities of the nuclear-arms race and militarism and preach the virtues of disarmament, nuclear-weapons-free zones, and neutralism, those in the pro-defence groups belabour the growing Soviet threat and urge dramatic increases in defence spending as a panacea. Because their recommendations are perceived as either irrelevant or unrealistic, the impact of these groups on the defence policy-making process is further diluted and minimized.

Provincial and Municipal Governments

Below the federal level, there are many other governmental actors with a direct or indirect interest in Canadian defence policy. This interest may take either a legal–political or socio-economic form. Canada's provincial governments, through their respective attorney generals, are empowered to request the services of the CF "in the aid of the civil power" to suppress "a riot or disturbance of the peace" under Section 233 of the National Defence Act.[23] Provinces have resorted to such requisitioning of troops on only two occasions since World War II—during the Montreal police strike in 1969 and during the October 1970 FLQ crisis in Quebec. Moreover, while DND is obligated to respond to such provincial requests, the determination of the number and type of troops dispatched lies within the discretion of the CDS.

The socio-economic impact of Canadian defence expenditures has been a more persistent concern of the provincial governments. Although this concern has historically manifested itself in provincial resistance to the closure of military bases, especially in the poorer Maritime provinces, more recently it has taken an increasingly overt acquisitive bent. Beginning in the mid-1970s, as the federal government gradually began to increase defence funding in the wake of the DSR, and as DND began allocating a steadily expanding share of its budget to re-equipment needs, the provinces have taken a more active interest in DND's capital-acquisition programs. This in turn has resulted in a more politicized defence policy-making process, as the provinces compete with one another for their "fair share" of DND's equipment procurement and maintenance contracts. In short, the provincial governments, on behalf of their defence-industry constituents, have now become active participants, or lobbyists, in the contract-definition-and-implementation phases of Ottawa's defence procurement process.

This trend became pronounced during the contract negotiations for the long-range patrol aircraft (LRPA) program in the early 1970s. This was the first DND program involving contractually stipulated "industrial benefits." As part of Ottawa's strategy to use defence procurement as an economic policy instrument, the program sought to achieve "the widest possible regional distribution of industrial benefits." However, when it became clear that the bulk of the industrial benefits would go to Quebec-based Canadair Limited (on a subcontract from Lockheed, the prime contractor), Manitoba's Premier, Ed Schreyer, charged that Ottawa's procurement policy was "rotten, biased and heavily prejudiced" in favour of aerospace firms in central Canada. Apparently, Schreyer wanted a "fair share" of the Lockheed subcontracts—where "fair" meant a percentage of the contracts proportional to Manitoba's share of the national population.[24]

Since the LRPA decision in 1976, provincial competition for DND weapons-procurement contracts has become more heated. Industrial lobbies (such as the Manitoba Aerospace Group and the Ontario Aerospace Consortium) have been established to pool their resources and improve their chances in soliciting defence contracts. These lobby groups have occasionally received support from their respective provincial governments in what has become a highly politicized bidding war for defence industrial benefits.[25]

DND's new fighter aircraft program (NFA) provides a good example of just how volatile this interprovincial competition has become.[26] By December 1979, despite an intervening federal election that placed a new Conservative government in office, the NFA Project Office had decided to recommend the selection of the McDonnell Douglas F-18A Hornet to the Clark cabinet. Just before cabinet could act on this recommendation, however, the government was defeated in the House of Commons, and the NFA decision was deferred pending the results of the ensuing federal election. After the Liberal victory, the NFA program became the focus of intensive provincial lobbying and debate. The two prime contractors, McDonnell Douglas and General Dynamics, lobbied the new Liberal caucus through their Canadian affiliates and prospective co-production partners in abrasive, and sometimes disingenuous, appeals to public opinion and media support.

The central concern of these efforts was the provincial distribution of industrial benefits contained in the contractors' bids. General Dynamics, in particular, waged a scurrilous media campaign, alleging that its proposal contained better economic benefits for Quebec than did those of Ontario-based McDonnell Douglas, and playing to the political sensitivities of Premier René Lévesque's Parti Québécois, which was then engaged in an already contentious debate with the federal government over the coming sovereignty-association referendum. General Dynamics' media blitz succeeded in splitting the Liberal caucus in Quebec and forced a meeting with the new MND, Gilles Lamontagne, other ministers, DND officials, and company representatives, in which the respective merits of the two contending contract proposals were debated. Ultimately, the interprovincial wrangling was defused, with the CF-18A selection being confirmed, but not until Industry Minister Herb Gray had taken the unprecedented step of declassifying and publishing his department's analysis of the superior industrial benefits of McDonnell's offer in order to allay Quebec's suspicions of unfair treatment in DND's procurement process.

The NFA example has come to typify the extent to which non-military regional and provincial concerns have permeated defence procurement decision making in Canada. Virtually no major weapons-acquisition program is now exempt from some sort of highly publicized intrusion by provincial politicians, often aided and abetted by their regional counterparts at the federal level as well as by defence firms located within their jurisdictions. Charges of untoward political interference and regional discrimination abound during the selection process, while evidence of past political favouritism is conveniently forgotten. For example, while Quebec cried "foul" over the original CF-18A decision, it was curiously silent in 1986 when Manitoba Premier Howard Pawley railed against the blatantly political factors at work in the government's decision to award the CF-18 maintenance contract to Canadair of Montreal against the advice of the project evaluation team, which judged the bid of Winnipeg's Bristol Aerospace to be significantly better on cost and technical grounds.[27] Nevertheless, this victory for Quebec did not prevent Premier Robert Bourassa and his cabinet colleagues from lobbying furiously in late 1987 for a share in the production of the second batch of naval frigates, or from expressing displeasure at the loss of jobs entailed when the contract was awarded to Saint John Shipbuilding of New Brunswick in December 1987. (See Chapter 7.)

These examples suggest that DND equipment contracts have become "political footballs" in the ongoing federal–provincial and interprovincial power struggle. Astute foreign prime contractors have skilfully used the prospect of regional subcontract work to play one province off against another in an attempt to garner better tax breaks and subsidies for their Canadianized operations. This was most aptly illustrated by Litton Systems' courting of the Maritime provinces as potential sites for a new radar-production facility following DND's low-level air defence system contract award. For DND, the intrusion of such non-military political and economic considerations into the procurement process has tended to complicate decision making by creating the possibility of politically induced delays and by adding substantial financial premiums to the contracts eventually awarded.

At the local level, governments have at times played a role in defence policy making, albeit a relatively minor one. Defence spending can have a disproportionately large impact on the life of certain communities, especially those located in high-unemployment areas of the country which have become dependent on the socio-economic spinoffs of military bases. This historical dependency has made it difficult for DND to close or relocate its bases on cost-effectiveness grounds. For example, one government study noted that at least seven of 33 DND bases, as well as a substantial number of stations, could be closed "if military requirements were the only criterion."[28]

This problem was evident in the fierce resistance mounted against the Liberal government's 1982 decision to disband a CF-101 Voodoo fighter squadron at CFB Chatham, New Brunswick by the end of 1984. So adamant was the local outcry against the prospect of losing almost 1400 jobs in an area where unemployment exceeded 40 percent that both the federal Liberals and later the Progressive Conservatives announced measures, including the establishment of a low-level air-defence training school and a mobile anti-aircraft battery, and the relocation of a CF-5 tactical fighter squadron there, to prevent any disruption in the $30 million in annual disposable income generated by the base.

In a relatively new phenomenon, local governments have also become the targets of campaigns mounted by local branches of peace groups. By the end of 1987, these groups had succeeded in persuading some 170 municipalities across Canada, as well as the governments of Ontario, Manitoba, and the Northwest Territories, to declare themselves nuclear-weapons-free zones. Notwithstanding the success of these groups locally, they have not succeeded in convincing the federal government in Ottawa to follow their example.

The Media and Public Information

As one analyst has noted, "Canadians are media junkies."[29] Given the prevalence of the media in the daily lives of the general populace, it is not surprising that it would play a major role in determining the defence issues that concern the Canadian public and in influencing the public's perceptions of and attitudes toward these issues. By extension, we could expect the media to be influential in bringing defence issues to the attention of other actors in the domestic policy-making environment, in publicizing the views and preferences of these actors, and in relaying these views to the government. In short, the media appears to occupy a pivotal position in the defence policy-making process in Canada, and serves to inform and educate the general public and other interest groups and to help establish the broad parameters within which the political leadership and the bureaucracy must act.

The media, especially the print media, has been influential in defining, and reciprocally, in reflecting, the broad contours of what is acceptable to the Canadian public in security matters. Munton notes that in the 1980s the media appears to have been instrumental in reversing a core assumption held by Canadians about the relationship between nuclear arms and security: the public is now disposed to regard nuclear weapons as a chief source of insecurity, one which must be eradicated through arms control.[30] Furthermore, the media played a key role in publicizing, and thereby politicizing, the cruise-missile testing issue in the early 1980s. However, while in this case the media helped set the government's policy agenda, it did not cause it to adopt a different policy.

The media has been less successful in informing and educating the public about defence policy issues. For the most part, the media has not been greatly interested in these issues. There are few writers or reporters who have made Canadian defence policy a major professional concern.[31] Thus, while the media does occasionally publicize and dramatize defence issues, especially those that serve to embarrass the government of the day—by revealing the contradictions in official policy, lapses in fulfilling electoral and other pledges, and serious shortcomings in the equipment or operations of the forces—they do so only on an intermittent basis and their coverage usually lacks depth and balance.

Because the media fails to take a leadership role in providing continuous and reliable information on defence issues or in discussing the policy options and implications of such issues, Canadians on the whole have remained undereducated about important defence policy matters.[32]

This comparative public ignorance has made it difficult for Canadian governments to communicate their policies to the population at large or to fashion a solid consensus around them. In part the government has been the victim of its own negligence in this respect. For years Ottawa had adopted a passive-reactive approach to public information on defence policy. It had been reluctant to volunteer anything but the barest of information on the goals, commitments, and activities of the forces, and had entrusted the bulk of the task of informing and educating the public to an ill-equipped and generally uninterested media.

Recognizing the problems that it had created for itself through this approach, the government has recently assumed a more active public-education role to get its defence message through to the Canadian populace.[33] Evidence of this new activism can be seen in several measures implemented by the government (and by DND itself) to rectify what was perceived to be a deficient public-information system. The specific catalyst for this new approach was the extent of public reaction to Ottawa's cruise-missile testing policy, which the government had been unable to contain. Under DND's Director General Information, a new Communications Program on Deterrence, Arms Control, and Disarmament (DAD) was established. Beginning with its "Facts about the Cruise Missile" (October 1983), DAD produced a series of brochures explaining different aspects of Canadian defence policy. Shortly thereafter, DND instituted a DAD Speakers Bureau, which involved senior officers and DND officials explaining governmental defence policies to the Canadian public. Since late 1986 this function has been reconfigured as the National Defence Speakers Bureau, with a ministerial mandate to encourage more active participation by senior military personnel, both serving and retired, in a much enlarged and better co-ordinated campaign to address issues relating to Canadian defence policy more frankly, and to a much broader cross-section of specially targeted audiences (especially at the secondary-school level).

In addition, in 1984 the government established, by an act of Parliament, the Canadian Institute for International Peace and Security. Funded jointly by DEA and DND, the institute acts as a government think-tank to increase public awareness and understanding of peace and security issues through the wide variety of information, research, and publication programs operated under its aegis. DND also partly funds the Canadian Institute of Strategic Studies, another think-tank, albeit one with a more conservative, pro-defence bias. Finally, in December 1986 DND set up a new Directorate of Public Policy under the assistant deputy minister (policy) to take over responsibility for DND's well-established Military and Strategic Studies Program and to help articulate defence policy to the Canadian public.

Through these and related measures, the government has acknowledged that it must accept responsibility for communicating its defence policies to Canadians on a more regular and broader basis than before. To accomplish this, Ottawa has in effect institutionalized its public information and education activities within the defence policy-making process. The intention is not only to provide the public with more and better information regarding government defence policies, but also to convey the message that the search for peace and security is not solely the prerogative of the peace movement.

Notes

1. Much of the analysis in this section is drawn from R.B. Byers and Don Munton, "Canadian Defence, Nuclear Arms and Public Opinion: Consensus and Controversy" (Paper presented to the Annual Meeting of the Canadian Political Science Association, Vancouver, B.C., June 1983). Another useful source is Don Munton, "Public Opinion and the Media in Canada from Cold War to Détente to New Cold War," *International Journal*, 39 no. 1 (Winter 1983/84): 170–213.
2. For a more detailed definition, see A. Paul Pross, *Group Politics and Public Policy* (Toronto: Oxford University Press, 1986), p. 99.
3. Byers and Munton, "Canadian Defence, Nuclear Arms and Public Opinion," p. 25.
4. Byers and Munton, "Canadian Defence, Nuclear Arms and Public Opinion," pp. 13–15. See also J.L. Granatstein, *Canada 1957–1967: The Years of Uncertainty and Innovation* (Toronto: McClelland and Stewart, 1986), pp. 112, 122.
5. Byers and Munton, "Canadian Defence, Nuclear Arms and Public Opinion," p. 21. Also Munton, "Public opinion and the media," pp. 193–96.
6. John Barrett and Douglas Ross, "The Air-Launched Cruise Missile and Canadian Arms Control Policy," *Canadian Public Policy* 11, no. 4

(December 1985): 718. See also David Cox, "The Cruise Testing Agreement," *International Perspectives* (July/August 1983), pp. 3–5.

7. Christopher Waddell, "Polls Alerted Ottawa to Lack of Support for Star Wars Role," *Globe and Mail*, 9 March 1987, p. A9. See also P.H. Chapin, "The Canadian Public and Foreign Policy," *International Perspectives* (January/February 1986), pp. 14–16.

8. A Globe CROP poll reported that 65 percent of Canadians would support the SDI program if participation meant more jobs for Canadians. *Globe and Mail*, 10 August 1985, p. A1.

9. Under an access-to-information request, in 1987 DND released the results of two Decima polls taken in December 1986 and March 1987. In the March poll, 59 percent of the respondents supported the building of nuclear-powered submarines to defend Canadian sovereignty in the Atlantic, Pacific, and particularly the Arctic oceans. A later Decima poll, conducted in May 1987, revealed that support for the SSN program had declined to 53 percent of adult Canadians. A memo to DND from the polling firm, dated 3 June 1987, cautioned that it would be "quite damaging" if Canadians perceived that decisions about the defence of the Canadian North were being made jointly with the United States. The memo warned that the SSN issue "continues to be very delicate. . . . Opinions are fluid and are neither deeply nor consistently divided. Prevailing in the debate, therefore, depends upon careful positioning and being able to set the terms of the discussion." Halifax *Chronicle-Herald*, 11 December 1987, p. 28.

10. See also Byers and Munton, "Canadian Defence, Nuclear Arms and Public Opinion," p. 18.

11. For the most comprehensive recent scholarly treatment of this subject in the Canadian context, see A. Paul Pross, *Group Politics and Public Policy*. See also Don Munton, *Groups and Governments in Canadian Foreign Policy* (Toronto: Canadian Institute of International Affairs, 1985); Kim Richard Nossal, *The Politics of Canadian Foreign Policy* (Scarborough, Ont.: Prentice-Hall Canada, 1985), ch. 2; Elizabeth Riddell-Dixon, *The Domestic Mosaic: Domestic Groups and Canadian Foreign Policy* (Toronto: Canadian Institute of International Affairs, 1985); and "Domestic Sources of Canada's Foreign Policy," special theme issue of *International Journal* 39 no. 1 (Winter 1983/84).

12. Only a few recent studies exist. The most general is by Kim Richard Nossal, "On the Periphery: Interest Groups and Canadian Defence Policy in the 1970s," unpublished paper presented to the Conference on Domestic Groups and Foreign Policy sponsored by the Canadian Institute of International Affairs, Ottawa, 9–11 June 1982. This paper was later summarized, with some commentary, in Don Munton, *Groups and Governments in Canadian Foreign Policy*. There is also a specific group history by Major W. Alexander Morrison, *The Voice of Defence: The History of the Conference of Defence Associations—The First Fifty Years 1932–1982* (Ottawa: Department of National Defence, 1982). See also Ernie Regehr and Simon Rosenblum, "The Canadian Peace Movement," in *Canada and the Nuclear Arms Race*, eds. Ernie Regehr and Simon Rosenblum (Toronto: James Lorimer, 1983), pp. 225–30. Finally, and perhaps indicative of a direction to be followed by the next generation of academics, see Toby C.D. Lennox, "Pressure

Groups and Canadian Security Policy: The Case of the SDI and NORAD Decisions," unpublished M.A. thesis, Department of Political Science, Dalhousie University, Halifax, September 1986.

13. Nossal, "On the Periphery," p. 1. It is not clear whether the higher estimate includes members of the numerous Canadian peace groups. Nossal tends to exclude "antimilitary" interest groups from his analysis, and concentrates more on those organizations promoting the cause of national defence in Canada.

14. North Atlantic Assembly, Civilian Affairs Committee, *Interim Report of the Subcommittee on Public Information on Defence and Security: The Netherlands, Turkey and Canada* (Brussels: International Secretariat, North Atlantic Assembly, September 1987), p. 50.

15. For details of the organizational evolution and composition of the CDA, see Morrison, *The Voice of Defence.* While its constituent groups individually seek to promote specific service interests, the CDA as a whole now functions more as a vehicle for the advancement of broader, employee-welfare oriented, defence issues. According to its constitution: "The objects of the Conference are to consider the problems of National Defence, to assist the Government of Canada in placing these problems before the people of Canada, to coordinate the activities of the service associations in matters of common interest in all branches of the Canadian Armed Forces, to make such recommendations to the Government of Canada through the Minister of National Defence as may appear expedient, and generally to promote the *efficiency and well-being* of the Canadian Armed Forces." Morrison, p. 239 (emphasis in the original).

16. A comprehensive "Directory of Canadian Peace Organizations with International Concerns" is maintained by Peace on Earth, c/o the Mennonite Central Committee in Winnipeg, Man.

17. For a brief review of the interests and activities of these groups, see Regehr and Rosenblum, "The Canadian Peace Movement."

18. See Toby Lennox, "Pressure Groups and Canadian Security Policy," pp. 89–91.

19. See Nossal, "On the Periphery," pp. 22–23; Michael Tucker, *Canadian Foreign Policy: Contemporary Issues and Themes* (Toronto: McGraw-Hill Ryerson, 1980), pp. 130–33; and Martin Shadwick, "The Relationship between Defence Policy and Defence Procurement in Canadian Practice," unpublished paper, York University, June 1978.

20. Munton, *Groups and Governments in Canadian Foreign Policy,* p. 43.

21. Lennox, "Pressure Groups and Canadian Security Policy," p. 140. See also Tony Rogers, "Dilemmas for the Canadian Peace Movement," *Peace & Security* 3, no. 1 (Spring 1988): 10–11.

22. See Alexandra Radkewycz, "Peace Groups Take Aim at Voters," *Globe and Mail,* 2 November 1987, p. A10.

23. For a discussion of this domestic role of the military, see Brian Cuthbertson, *Canadian Military Independence in the Age of the Superpowers* (Toronto: Fitzhenry & Whiteside, 1977), ch. 8, especially pp. 243–44.

24. Dan Middlemiss, "Military Procurement as an Instrument of Canadian Economic Policy: The Case of the Long Range Patrol Aircraft," unpublished paper, Centre for Strategic Studies, University of Alberta, Edmonton, April 1979, p. 36.

25. For example, Manitoba's New Fighter Aircraft (NFA) Task Force set a public target of 10 percent, or about $250–$300 million, in industrial benefits for Manitoba under this program. See *Manitoba Business Review* 2 no. 5 (Spring 1978), p. 4 and the *Financial Post*, 29 April 1978, p. 19. Ontario's Ministry of Industry and Tourism commissioned a sector analysis of the province's aerospace industry in October 1975 to determine the needs and potential of this industry in bidding on future government contracts. The Research Program in Strategic Studies, York University, also completed a study in March 1986, entitled "Developing Defence-Industrial Opportunities for Ontario: Prospects and Perspectives," to assist Ontario industry in this area.

26. For details of the CF-18 procurement process, see Lieutenant-Colonel Frank L. Boyd, Jr., "The Politics of Canadian Defence Procurement: The New Fighter Aircraft Decision" (Paper presented to the conference on the Canadian Defence Industrial Base, Domestic and International Issues and Interests, Centre for International Relations, Queen's University, 18–19 June 1987); Sister Maureen Cronin, "A Case of Hornets: The Controversial CF-18A," *American Review of Canadian Studies* 12, no. 3 (Fall 1982): 17–28; Michael M. Atkinson and Kim Richard Nossal, "Bureaucratic Politics and the New Fighter Aircraft Decisions," *Canadian Public Administration* 24, no. 4 (Winter 1981): 531–58; and W.M. Dobell, "Parliament's Role in Choosing the New Fighter Aircraft," *International Perspectives* (September/October 1981), pp. 10–13.

27. Pawley's charges were substantiated many months later by documents obtained under federal freedom-of-information legislation. See Jeff Sallot, "Ottawa Didn't Heed Own Experts' Advice on CF-18 Contract," *Globe and Mail*, 6 January 1988, p. A-1. Other evidence suggests that the Mulroney government deliberately delayed announcing Canadair's selection until after the 1986 Saskatchewan provincial election to protect the chances of Conservative Premier Grant Devine. See Jeff Sallot, "Tories Stalled Jet Contract to Aid Devine, Book Claims," *Globe and Mail*, 26 October 1987, p. A-1.

28. Canada, *A Study Team Report to the Task Force on Program Review, Management of Government—Real Property, May 1985* (Ottawa: Supply and Services Canada, 1986), p. 394.

29. Munton, "Public Opinion and the Media in Canada," p. 209.

30. Munton, "Public Opinion and the Media in Canada," p. 209.

31. Rod Byers, "Canadian Security and Defence: The Legacy and the Challenges," *Adelphi Papers* 214 (Winter 1986), p. 67.

32. This is illustrated by the finding that, while a high percentage of Canadians approved of Canadian involvement in NATO, a fairly large proportion either did not know, or were unsure of, what NATO was. See North Atlantic Assembly, *Interim Report of the Subcommittee on Public Information* (September 1987), p. 47.

33. This section is drawn in part from the analysis in the North Atlantic Assembly's *Interim Report*, pp. 49–50.

6

THE EXTERNAL
POLICY-MAKING
ENVIRONMENT

Introduction

Even if one acknowledges the complexity of the Canadian defence policy-making environment and the importance of the domestic factors, there is the temptation to ask, in effect, what difference does it all make? No matter what Canada's defence policy is, no matter what weapons it buys and how much it spends, it will be no more secure against its major potential threat—a strategic nuclear attack by the Soviet Union on North America. Moreover, since Canada has decided to seek its security in alliance with a superpower as well as with other countries of greater military and geographic importance, there is little of substance left to decide in Canadian defence policy. The international environment and membership in NATO and NORAD have determined Canada's entire defence policy.

Though frequently heard in Canada, this line of reasoning fails to capture and explain the true impact of external factors on Canadian defence policy. It is undoubtedly true that for Canada alliance commitments and the nature of international relations have been major influences on the content of defence policy. But this should not be surprising since defence policy, as an element in external policy, must almost by definition be formulated with reference to the character of international relations and the policies of foreign governments, both friend and foe. In this, Canada does not differ from any other state, even the superpowers. To be sure, Canada's ability to influence the behaviour of other countries and to use its military for this purpose is not great relative to that of some other countries. Yet this has not meant that decisions need not be made or that choices are not available in the conduct of defence policy. Indeed, as the evolution of defence policy has shown, the constraints Ottawa has confronted in the external environment have compelled it to make significant decisions and choices in defence policy. This has applied not only to Canada's place in Western collective defence, but also to its role in peace-keeping and sovereignty protection.

The International Strategic Environment and Canada

Canada's *de facto* and *de jure* independence in foreign affairs, won from London during the interwar period, was partially obscured by its World War II alliances. But even before the war had ended, Canada signalled its intention to build upon these gains. Backed by a growing confidence and a productive economy, Canada stepped out onto the international stage as a truly independent world actor whose external policies, including those relating to defence, would be determined independently, by Ottawa. The international strategic environment in which Canada sought to determine its own security policies was, however, markedly different than that which had preceded the war. It is one of the ironies of Canadian history that just when Canada obtained the ability to conduct an independent defence policy, the capacity of all nations to secure themselves against military attack became greatly diminished. In the nuclear age, the very nature and meaning of security and military power were to be altered.

A year after the first (and only) atomic bombs were used by the United States to end the war against Japan, the noted academic strategist, Bernard Brodie, wrote in his book, *The Absolute Weapon*:

> Thus, the first and most vital step in any American security program for the age of atomic bombs is to take measures to guarantee to ourselves in case of attack the possibility of retaliation in kind. The writer in making that statement is not for the moment concerned about who will win the next war in which atomic bombs are used. Thus far the chief purpose of our military establishment has been to win wars. From now on its chief purpose must be to avert them. It can have almost no other useful purpose.[1]

In 1946 there were only a handful of atomic bombs, all in the possession of the United States. Within three years, contrary to expectations, the Soviet Union had tested its first atomic bomb, and four years after that both countries had hydrogen, or thermonuclear, weapons whose destructive power was to be measured in the millions of tons of TNT. By the mid-1960s, the United States and the USSR not only possessed thousands of nuclear weapons but also the means for intercontinental delivery from silos in the ground, from submarines at sea, and from strategic bombers. In addition, the two superpowers had a panoply of shorter-range, lower-yield, tactical and theatre nuclear weapons. During the 1970s and 1980s, despite progress in arms control, nuclear arsenals became more sophisticated. With the advent of MIRVs (multiple independently targeted re-entry vehicles), a single ICBM or SLBM could hit ten or more targets with as many nuclear warheads. Air-, sea-, and ground-launched cruise missiles (ALCM, SLCM, and GLCM) began to appear. Today, the prospect of a new arms race in space looms as the United States pursues its SDI program and the Soviets threaten to step up their own research into space weapons unless SDI is terminated. Also to be considered is the emergence of other nuclear powers—Great Britain, France, China, and India—as well as those states that are believed to have (or be close to having) atomic bombs, such as Israel and South Africa. Thus, if what Bernard Brodie said about the revolutionary impact of the atomic bomb on international politics was valid in 1946, it seems even more so 43 years into the nuclear age.

The impact of nuclear weapons on international strategic relations, and hence on Canadian security, can be understood by briefly examining how these weapons have (or have not) changed the roles of war and force in global politics. In the pre-nuclear age, war or the threat of war was a frequent means by which states attempted to secure their interests. In times of peace, states armed for war, trying to maintain a balance of power with other states in order to deter attack or to win if war came. States entered into alliances for mutual defence or mutual aggrandizement at the expense of other states. War seemed to be the logical outcome of this system of sovereign states, each attempting to secure its interests, if necessary by force of arms.[2] This anarchic, Hobbesian environment of all against all seemed very much to be the condition of great power relations, resulting in two world wars within a span of 25 years.

The impact of nuclear weapons on the international system can be appreciated by first recognizing that these weapons are significantly different from all other weapons used by states in earlier times. They differ in a number of ways.

First, there is the potential of mass destruction by a small number of weapons. In 1967, U.S. Secretary of Defense Robert S. McNamara told Congress that "a mere 400 one megaton weapons, if delivered on the Soviet Union, would be sufficient to destroy over one-third of her population and one-half of her industry."[3] The impact of an attack would extend beyond the blast area, with radiation and fall-out affecting millions of people hundreds of miles distant. The second difference lies in the means of delivery. Most nuclear weapons are carried on ICBMS and SLBMS whose flight times are measured in minutes and against which there exists no effective defence. A third difference is that a nuclear war would require no mobilization of forces. It could be fought with existing arsenals, large parts of which are always kept on a high state of alert.

A fourth major difference is the target. Nuclear weapons are generally targeted on other nuclear weapons and military facilities. But they are also deliberately targeted on civilian population centres. Indeed, the ability to inflict mass civilian deaths on an adversary, even after he has struck first, is considered essential for deterring such an attack. The capacity to deter by threatening mass civilian deaths is a result of a fifth unique characteristic of the nuclear age, what the Harvard Nuclear Study Group has called "the crystal ball effect." Because of what the world saw at Hiroshima and Nagasaki and what it witnessed in the atmospheric tests of the 1950s, we know the consequences of nuclear war. No one can predict with certainty what it would be like, but we are almost certain that a strategic nuclear war would destroy life on this planet as we have known it. In the nuclear age, statesmen live day-to-day with a horrific picture of what a war would look like.[4]

Because there have never been weapons like nuclear weapons before, new meaning has been given to the concept of deterrence in international relations. In past ages, states have sought to dissuade other states from taking certain actions by threatening to inflict damage believed to be unacceptable. The known characteristics of nuclear weapons have made them the instruments of deterrence *par excellence*. Nuclear weapons deter because they hold out the near-certain prospect of "assured destruction." With both superpowers deploying roughly equal strategic nuclear capabilities, assured destruction would work both ways, making "mutual assured destruction" (MAD) the likely outcome of any war between the superpowers and their allies. In a MAD world, each side has attempted to maintain deterrence

by creating retaliatory forces capable of inflicting unacceptable damage even after being subjected to a first strike:

> (W)e must be able to absorb the total weight of nuclear attack
> on our country—on our strike-back forces; on our command
> and control apparatus; on our industrial capacity; and on our
> population—and still be fully capable of destroying the aggres-
> sor to the point that his society is simply no longer viable in
> any meaningful 20th century sense. That is what deterrence to
> nuclear aggression means. It means the certainty of suicide to
> the aggressor—not merely to his military forces but to his so-
> ciety as a whole.[5]

Nuclear weapons have made it difficult to view war as
simply the continuation of politics by other means because
war has become an unacceptable option for the powers who
possess the new means. But these weapons have not eliminated politics and rivalry among states, especially among
the great powers. The international system is still anarchic,
with the United Nations serving as a forum for diplomacy
but not as a supranational authority able to impose its will
on states. Since 1945 scores of new states have emerged and,
like others before them, struggle and compete with each
other, sometimes violently. Europe, where the major wars
of the past were fought, has been at peace. Yet, the struggle
for mastery in Europe has continued; indeed, the international strategic environment remains largely Eurocentric.
The combination of nuclear weapons and an international
system of competing states is what has made the post-1945
period seem so dangerous.

Yet the international system is not exactly the same as
it was in the pre-nuclear age. Along with the advent of nuclear weapons came the rise of the United States and the
Soviet Union to a status so different from that held by any
other states before them that a new term had to be coined—
superpower. In the 19th and early 20th centuries the world
was still multipolar, with several roughly equal great powers
who balanced each other and combined when one single
power threatened hegemony over all. Since 1945, the international system has been bipolar. There are no other states
that can balance the overall power of the United States and
the USSR. The Soviet-American global rivalry has dominated international politics for over 40 years. It is a rivalry
that would have existed without the advent of nuclear weapons but that has taken on an unprecedented character because of the nuclear arsenal each side maintains. Humanity

literally hangs breathless on the fate of superpower relations.

While the combination of nuclear weapons, a still anarchic international system, and the Soviet–American rivalry has raised the spectre of a global holocaust, it has also introduced a measure of stability and predictability into international relations. In previous ages, the great powers frequently fought wars as they jostled for security and influence. War was a plausible instrument of policy because defeat usually did not carry with it the prospect of total annihilation. In the nuclear age, war between the superpowers could bring such a catastrophic end. Thus, the probability of a U.S.–Soviet war is low. The other major European powers are not likely to fight each other as they did in the past. There are rivalries between China and the West, and between China and the USSR, but these too are constrained by the fear of nuclear war as well as by China's still secondary position relative to the superpowers.

It is because in a largely bipolar system nuclear weapons have been viewed as providing for deterrence and stability that they are considered both useful and necessary. They are credited with achieving certain goals for both East and West—mainly security from direct attack and reduction of the likelihood of war. All of this may sound paradoxical. How can rational national leaders maintain arsenals that would be suicidal to use but that are deemed essential to national security if *not* used? Indeed, the impact of nuclear weapons on international politics may be best appreciated by seeing it as a series of paradoxes.

Nuclear weapons deter only if there is a possibility that they will be used, but they must not be made so usable that anyone would be tempted to use them.[6] Mutual deterrence ultimately rests on estimates of what would happen if these weapons were ever employed, and on speculations about the adversary's willingness to "pull the nuclear trigger" under certain circumstances. At the same time, it would be extremely dangerous if political and military leaders viewed nuclear weapons as useful in a traditional military sense, because this would tempt them to pull the trigger too readily. The superpowers believe they can deter direct attacks on their homelands by threatening to use their nuclear weapons in a retaliatory blow. The usability problem arises in situations where the nuclear deterrent has been extended to cover areas and countries outside the

United States and the USSR themselves, mainly in Western and Eastern Europe. Here, both sides have deployed a range of tactical and theatre nuclear weapons, integrated into conventional forces, whose use might appear more plausible. And indeed, NATO has not disavowed the first use of nuclear weapons should it find itself losing a conventional war. It is NATO's hope that by stating this policy it will deter any Soviet attack, because the Soviets will fear escalation to the strategic nuclear level. Yet, the usability paradox, and its dangers, remain.

The presence of American nuclear weapons in Europe is meant to couple European security with that of the United States. This brings up another paradox. While it would appear that no rational national interest could be served by nuclear war, both East and West have made political commitments to the effect that goals other than the direct defence of the homeland are worth the risk of nuclear war. It is the belief that the willingness to run this risk will be taken seriously by the other side which is supposed to lend credibility to those commitments. Thus, the United States has committed itself to the territorial integrity of NATO allies in Western Europe. This commitment is backed by the American capability to destroy the Soviet Union should it attack any of these allies. In essence, what the United States is saying to the Soviets is, "Western Europe is not worth a nuclear war to you because you will be annihilated in such a war." But, paradoxically, this threat is only credible to the extent that the Soviets believe the defence of Western Europe is worth a nuclear war for the United States. It works the other way as well. The NATO allies were unlikely to come to the aid of anti-Soviet insurgents in Hungary in 1956 or Czechoslovakia in 1968 because of the fear of war and nuclear escalation—that is, due to the perception that the Soviets were prepared to defend Eastern Europe at all costs.

Backing up the possibility of nuclear use and the credibility of nuclear guarantees are weapons and strategies to engage in nuclear war. Thus, another paradox: while both sides might agree that a nuclear war must never be fought and can never be won, both believe that their deterrent postures require preparations to fight. And since it is not the habit of military or political leaders to plan to lose wars, such preparations seek to achieve victory should deterrence fail. In fact, some argue that such planning is necessary for deterrence to work because "any deterrent strategy that does not consider how the war will be fought and terminated is a hollow shell."[7] Given what is known about the effects of nuclear weapons, "victory" may have no meaning in a nuclear war; in fact, its possibility contradicts the basic premise that mutual deterrence rests on the certainty of mutual assured destruction.

Nevertheless, even in a purely MAD approach to nuclear strategy, there must be weapons development, force posturing, and planning. Since deterrence rests on the ability to retaliate even after suffering a first strike by opposing nuclear forces, both sides must try to ensure the survivability of sufficient weapons and command and control facilities to direct the retaliatory blow. The deployment of ballistic missile submarines (SSBNs) greatly increases not only the number of nuclear weapons but also the assuredness of retaliation, since SSBNs are largely invulnerable to a first strike. Thus, preparing for a nuclear war is not inconsistent with deterring one. The problem arises when such plans appear to make a war more likely because weapons and strategy refinements might, under certain circumstances, persuade military and political leaders that assured destruction will not be the inevitable result of a nuclear war, or that a limited, nuclear war might be possible. For example, both the Soviets and Americans have sought to acquire a "counterforce" capability that would, in theory, allow them to destroy the other side's nuclear weapons and other military facilities rather than its cities, thereby avoiding, or at least postponing, an attack on population centres. The USSR has favoured counterforce because its nuclear doctrine has long advocated the quick destruction of the enemy's forces should nuclear war seem unavoidable, while the United States has long sought to increase its options and flexibility in the event of hostilities. In either case, such plans, and the weapons to back them up, could undermine mutual deterrence. On the other hand, would the world be safer if the only response available to superpowers is one exclusively directed at cities?

To the uncertainties and paradoxes of nuclear weapons must be added the role of conventional forces, particularly in the context of the East–West rivalry. The post-1945 period has witnessed a nuclear arms race and a conventional-arms race on land, at sea, and in the air. But what role can these weapons have when a nuclear war would destroy entire countries in a matter of days if not hours? What need can there be, for example, for submarines to cut sea lines of communication or for ASW forces to protect shipping, when the harbours for which the shipping is destined can be destroyed with a single missile?

Conventional forces exist, in part, because of the existence of nuclear weapons and the uncertainties that surround them. Neither East nor West has wanted to rely exclusively on nuclear deterrence for its security because the threat of nuclear retaliation is not considered to be credible under all circumstances. NATO's strategy of flexible response seeks to extend deterrence below the nuclear threshold in order to convince the Soviets that they cannot expect to win a quick conventional victory should they attack. And for nearly forty years, the large Soviet land armies in Eastern Europe have deterred direct Western interference in affairs there. Conventional forces also exist for the same reason that counterforce weapons and theatre nuclear weapons exist, because political and military leaders on both sides want options in the event of war, short of a strategic nuclear response. The war plans of both sides envision the use of conventional forces before and during the use of nuclear weapons. For example, the Soviets might want to pave the way for the advance of their tank armies by using nuclear weapons first. Or, if NATO were to find its conventional forces being overwhelmed by a Soviet conventional attack, it might resort to nuclear bombardment behind Soviet lines, yet it would still have to maintain conventional combat.

While conventional forces are partially a response to the uncertainties of nuclear weapons, the presence of nuclear weapons endows conventional forces with uncertainties as well. Can an East-West conventional war be fought at all? Would not either or both sides use their nuclear weapons rather than wait upon the outcome of a conventional conflict? Is it even true that conventional forces provide options in the event of war, or do they simply make war more likely because they are viewed as being more usable? American thinking on flexible response has tended to regard conventional forces as steps on a ladder of escalation, steps that can be climbed deliberately according to the nature of a Soviet attack. The Europeans have tended to see both their own and U.S. conventional forces in Europe in a different way. Their own forces help to guarantee the extended deterrent of the United States' strategic nuclear forces, while the presence of U.S. troops in Europe is meant to convince the Soviets that an attack on Western Europe will mean nuclear war. Where the United States sees a ladder of escalation as necessary to make deterrence credible, the Europeans prefer a rapidly moving escalator that cannot be stopped. It is not surprising, therefore, that one analyst has described flexible response as "less a strategy than an agreement not to disagree over strategy."[8]

The inconsistency of flexible response and the uncertainties of conventional deterrence in Europe are unlikely to persuade either East or West to do away with their conventional forces. Indeed, reductions in nuclear weapons, especially those in Europe, such as will take place under the Intermediate-Range Nuclear Force (INF) Treaty signed by the United States and the Soviet Union in December 1987, are likely to increase the importance of conventional forces for NATO because of what is still considered to be a large Soviet advantage in that area. Both superpowers, and some NATO allies, also maintain large conventional forces to support their policies outside the European theatre. The United States relies on a vast array of conventional forces to secure its interests in nearly every corner of the globe, while the Soviets have also developed forces capable of operating in distant areas. France and Britain continue to use armed forces in the Third World and, in 1987, along with the United States, deployed naval forces to the Persian Gulf.

Canada conducts its defence policies in an unprecedented strategic environment because of the impact of nuclear weapons and the continuing but uncertain role of conventional forces, all operating in the context of the Soviet–American global rivalry. But since 1945 this environment has also been relatively stable; a stability for which nuclear weapons, conventional weapons, and bipolarity are seen as being responsible. Outside Europe and the North Atlantic region, there have been many wars since 1945, usually involving countries that gained their independence or that came into existence with the break-up of the European empires. Civil wars and numerous insurgencies have also plagued the Third World.

But the Soviet Union and the United States have not engaged in any direct armed conflict, and the instances of crises, such as that of the 1950s, which climaxed in the Cuban missile crisis of 1962, have actually declined. Threats, including both overt nuclear and conventional threats, have been made. Outside Europe, the Soviets and Americans have backed rival regimes that have been engaged in war and that, as in the case of the 1973 Middle East war, did bring the superpowers close to armed confrontation. But they have always exercised great caution and drawn away from the brink. The possibility that such situations could get out of hand and end in a nuclear war by miscalculation or misperception has imposed mutual restraint. As Brodie noted, "It is a curious paradox of our time that one of the foremost factors making deterrence really work and work well is the lurking fear that in some massive confrontation crisis it might fail. Under these circumstances one does not tempt fate."[9]

The mutual deterrence that persuades East and West not to tempt fate, and thereby results in a measure of international stability, is seen as being dependent on the maintenance of a stable balance of nuclear and conventional forces such that neither side would perceive an advantage in trying to secure its interests through war. How this balance is to be maintained and what its exact nature is to be are subjects of considerable debate. For the West, does it mean "balance" in the sense of financial accounts, where a surplus of nuclear forces is maintained to balance Soviet conventional forces and perceived Soviet aggressive designs? Is it the Soviets who need nuclear and conventional superiority because they are surrounded by hostile countries on nearly all their borders? Or does it make a difference anymore as long as both sides have an assured retaliatory capability? As former U.S. Secretary of State Henry Kissinger once observed: "What in the name of God is strategic superiority? What is the significance of it, politically, militarily, operationally, at these levels of numbers? What do you do with it?"[10]

Doubts about the utility of ever-increasing numbers of nuclear weapons have prompted efforts at arms control. In the first and second Strategic Arms Limitation Talks (SALT), the Soviets and Americans did place numerical limits on certain systems. But these agreements were possible only because they left both sides with large numbers of retaliatory forces. Nor did they halt further weapons developments, such as MIRVs and cruise missiles. The INF Treaty of 1987 was the first to actually eliminate a certain class of nuclear weapons. Yet strategic nuclear forces as well as other theatre-tactical weapons remain committed to Europe by both the United States and the USSR. Far from setting the stage for the total eradication of nuclear forces, arms-control agreements thus far have tended to build these weapons even more firmly into the international system.

Arms limitation has not been "an alternative to giving nuclear weapons a major role in international politics, but merely one way of defining that role."[11]

In recent years, particularly with the rise to power of Soviet leader Mikhail Gorbachev, there has been discussion of large cuts in strategic systems and even mutual nuclear disarmament. Given the importance of these weapons to both sides, and the uncertainties about stability in a still bipolar world in which the knowledge of how to build nuclear weapons remains, the prospect of total disarmament in the near future is remote. The numbers of weapons may be reduced and agreement might be reached to prevent a race in strategic defences, but nuclear weapons, as well as conventional forces, are likely to continue as important components in the worldwide balance of power.

In the global calculus of this balance, Canada does not figure highly. But its security is dependent on it, and its defence policy is oriented toward helping to maintain it. Since 1945 this has drawn Canada into an alliance with the United States and the NATO countries of Western Europe; that is, Canada has sought to secure itself from attack by contributing to the collective nuclear and conventional deterrent posture of the West. In so doing, Canada has hoped not only that aggression would be deterred and war prevented, but also that the international stability thereby achieved would allow it to pursue its economic and political interests at home and abroad. Canada shares these goals with its allies, with whom it also shares a commitment to democratic values and institutions. Over the years, Ottawa, in the pursuit of peace and stability, has also promoted negotiations between East and West, détente, efforts to achieve verifiable arms control, the peaceful resolution of international disputes, and the rule of law internationally. There has been, as well, a concern for the protection and assertion of sovereignty over the lands and waters to which Canada holds claim and in the airspace above. All these objectives have been pursued simultaneously through contributions to Western defence and deterrence.

In making these contributions, Canada finds itself in a unique situation not without its own paradoxes. The greatest threat to Canadian security comes from a strategic nuclear attack by the Soviet Union. Paradoxically, this threat is not directed against Canada in the first instance, but against the United States. Thus, Canada finds itself vulnerable because of simple geography: no other western ally is in this position. Yet, because of its position, Canada also finds that, far more than other allies, it enjoys the security afforded by the American strategic nuclear retaliatory force to which it does not contribute offensive weapons. So long as the strategic nuclear balance makes war an extremely unlikely possibility, Canada's security is assured.

But a direct attack by the Soviets against the United States would likely occur only as a result of an East-West confrontation outside North America. To this extent, Canadian security is dependent on the maintenance of a global balance of conventional and nuclear power and on the continuing ability of the superpowers to manage their rivalry, and not tempt fate, whenever their interests clash. The most important region for the superpowers is Europe, where their forces and those of their allies directly face each other. Thus, again paradoxically, Canadian security is affected by a conventional threat that does not threaten it directly but that, because of the risk of escalation, could result in a nuclear war from which Canada could not hope to escape. As former Canadian ambassador to NATO John Halstead has observed, "North America is where Canadian security will be at risk if the U.S. nuclear deterrent fails, yet Europe is still the place where the global East-West balance is at stake."[12] An unarmed neutral Canada would still confront this paradox; it would simply be leaving its defence, in Europe and especially in North America, entirely to others— a situation inconsistent with national sovereignty and independence. Thus, it is not surprising that in helping to maintain the East-West balance of power, Canada is the only Western ally, apart from the United States, that contributes to the defence of North America as well as to that of Western Europe.

The Defence of North America

Canada's involvement in North American defence is conditioned by the nature of the threat to the continent. The primary threat comes from ICBMs and SLBMs, with lesser threats posed by manned bombers and SSNs, carrying ALCMs and SLCMs respectively. There is virtually no conventional land threat to North America, although it might be possible for small Soviet units to land in remote areas.

Reflecting the nature of the threat, U.S.-Canadian defence co-operation is centred on NORAD. To the extent that NORAD is directed against the bomber, ALCM, ICBM, as well as the

SLBM and SLCM threats, it deals with the aerospace and maritime defence of the continent. However, maritime defence is primarily the responsibility of the Canadian and U.S. navies, which co-operate without a joint-command arrangement but in conjunction with NATO's Atlantic Command. There are also agreements to co-ordinate the territorial land defence of North America, but given the absence of a concrete threat, these have received far less attention and draw upon few resources from either country.

As we described earlier, one of the paradoxes of North American defence is that there is really no defence against the greatest threat—a strategic nuclear attack by ICBMs and SLBMs—because once fired, these missiles cannot be stopped. North America is wide open, as is the Soviet Union. In this mutual vulnerability rests strategic stability. Since neither side can attack the other without suffering a devastating counter-strike, MAD seems to be the only certain consequence of a nuclear war, and expectations of MAD ensure that such a war is an unlikely possibility. Thus, while the threat to North America is infinitely great, the chances of this threat being carried out are small.

In this sense, the real defence of North America rests upon the ability of the United States to destroy the Soviet Union even after it has suffered a Soviet first strike. It is the U.S. deterrent that ultimately defends both Canada and the United States by reducing the likelihood of attack. In so deterring an attack, the American deterrent also negates any overt Soviet threats of attack that might be made to exact some political concession unfavourable to the United States and Canada.

By being able to reduce the Soviet threat to North America, the United States is also able to extend its deterrent umbrella to distant allies across the seas. That is, the United States offers protection to these allies against Soviet attacks and threats of attack by linking their security to that of the United States. This extension of the deterrent is only credible, however, if the deterrent itself remains credible, meaning that the United States can indeed retaliate after suffering a first strike.

Elements of the retaliatory force posture can be distinguished. The United States relies on ICBMs, SLBMs, manned bombers carrying ALCMs, and SLCMs to deliver nuclear weapons against the Soviet Union. Of these, only the ICBMs and a portion of the bomber/ALCM forces would be launched from American territory. The rest can be launched from other bases or from the world's oceans. This is especially the case with the SLBMs, which constitute the primary secure second-strike capability upon which the credibility of the U.S. deterrent rests. Thus, even if the entire U.S. ICBM force were destroyed in a Soviet first strike, U.S. SSBNs and other forces outside North America could still inflict a devastating retaliatory blow against the Soviet Union.

The credibility of the deterrent is also linked to the effectiveness of command, control, communications, and intelligence systems (C³I) and the ability of enough of these systems to survive a first strike and assist in the launching of the retaliatory blow. Closely related to the protection of C³I is surveillance, warning, and attack assessment. Without the continuous ability to monitor Soviet activity and to provide warning and assessment of possible attack, the United States could be attacked in such a way that it could not effectively retaliate.

It might seem that in a strategic nuclear war it would not matter much if the United States could retaliate with total effectiveness, because even if a small portion of its forces were launched, the impact on the Soviet Union would be devastating. Moreover, what surveillance really provides is the option to launch on warning, to get U.S. ICBMs out of their silos before they are destroyed in them. Deterrence does rest on the assuredness of retaliation, even in the case of a first strike "out of the blue."

But the stability of the nuclear balance also rests on the ability to verify, on a day-to-day, indeed minute-to-minute, basis, that no attack is taking place: hence the need for surveillance and warning facilities that confirm the peaceful activities of the Soviets. It would be extremely dangerous to have nuclear weapons on heightened states of alert without an ability to detect a possible attack. Thus, it is crucial for western security and for global stability that the United States be able to monitor the approaches to North America.

Where does Canada fit into this picture? Canada does not possess strategic nuclear weapons and no U.S. retaliatory forces are based in Canada. But Canada lies between the United States and the Soviet Union and thus its air and sea space are possible avenues of attack. As President Franklin Roosevelt declared in 1938, the United States would not "stand idly by" if Canada was threatened. And as Prime Minister Mackenzie King responded a few days later, Canada's obligations as a good and friendly neighbour required that it make itself as immune from attack as possible, so that enemy forces could not reach the United States through its territory. The United States has a security interest in Canada, and Canada has an interest in not becoming a strategic liability for the United States. This is the basis of bilateral co-operation in the defence of North America.

The situation now, however, is more complicated than it was in 1938. In the first place, as noted above, the United States is the prime target. The defence of the continent really means the defence of the American retaliatory capabilities against a first-strike, knock-out blow by the USSR. Thus, Canada's role in North American defence comes down to the question of "what ought Canada to do to make the United States apparatus of deterrence and defence as effective as possible?"[13] Second, with regard to the main means by which a first strike would be carried out—ICBMs and SLBMs—Canadian territory is almost irrelevant. There is as yet no defence, but there are also no missile-warning facilities in Canada. Thus, as far as a missile threat is concerned, Canada is not crucial to North American defence.

The threat to the continent comes not only from ballistic missiles, however, and that brings us to the third point: there is more to maintaining the credibility of deterrence than having missiles capable of retaliation. The Soviet Union could strike at North America using its manned bombers armed with gravity bombs or ALCMs. It would also be likely to deploy long-range, land-attack SLCMs on various classes of its attack submarines. Relative to the ICBM and SLBM threat, the bomber and cruise-missile threats appear marginal. If the Soviets decided to attack North America, it is likely that they would use their most powerful weapons to destroy as much of the U.S. retaliatory force as possible. Yet the possibility exists that the Soviets would attempt a limited strike against American C^{3}I facilities using bombers and cruise missiles. This could be a "decapitation" strike whereby the USSR hoped to "deny or severely disrupt the U.S. ability to launch retaliatory strikes by decapitating the political and military leadership from the nuclear forces." Such a strike might also be a "precursor" attack designed to blind U.S. defences to a Soviet follow-on ballistic-missile attack, again with the intention of disrupting the retaliatory blows.[14]

For Canada, the important point about these attack scenarios is that the bombers and cruise missiles could transit Canadian land, sea, and air space. Since such "air-breathing" threats continue to exist, it is important to maintain a continual surveillance against them. Moreover, in the case of bombers, an active defence—interception and destruction by fighter aircraft—is possible. For SLCMs, antisubmarine warfare techniques, which involve locating and, if necessary, destroying attack submarines, are also important. Furthermore, it may still become possible to detect and perhaps destroy cruise missiles once they are fired.

While Canadian territory and Canadian forces are relevant to the defence of the continent because of the nature of the strategic environment, the environment itself does not dictate precisely how Canada's contributions to North American defence should be structured. This is determined by the arrangements that have been made for bilateral strategic co-operation through NORAD and through less formal arrangements, such as those covering maritime threats. But it should be stressed that the decision (or rather the series of decisions made over the years) to approach North American defence from a joint perspective was taken deliberately by Ottawa. That is, while the international strategic environment has imposed constraints on Canadian defence policy with regard to North America, other constraints have been self-imposed, because Canada essentially chose the route of alliance for its own direct defence.

This approach was selected, and continues to be followed, for various reasons. Since there is really no threat to North America apart from the Soviet direct threat to the United States, and since Canada bases its security on the credibility of the U.S. deterrent posture, "going it alone" would have made no sense.

It might appear that close military ties with a superpower would undermine sovereignty, especially since, for strategic purposes, the North American continent is considered a single unit. NORAD places Canadian forces in Canada under the operational control of an American air force general. Under certain alert conditions, U.S. aircraft might enter Canadian airspace. Any steps Canada takes with regard to both the air and maritime defence of its own territory will have to be co-ordinated with those of the United States. Thus to a certain extent, bilateral co-operation does impose limits on Canadian defence policy. Yet, Canada has acted as a sovereign nation in its agreement to such constraints. Moreover, most international agreements and treaties entail some compromise on sovereignty. This is as true in the strategic arena as it is in the international economic sphere.

While concerns about sovereignty are ever-present in the bilateral defence relationship, they have been matched by concerns about other aspects of sovereignty that have made a joint approach to the defence of North America attractive to Canada. NORAD affords Ottawa "a voice in enterprises which would be carried out by the U.S. regardless of Canadian wishes."[15] Although lacking the formal multilateral political oversight of the NATO commands, NORAD affords Canada a say in matters directly related to its own security. Under the agreement, the commander-in-chief (CINCNORAD) is directly responsible to both the U.S. and Canadian governments. He by no means has a completely free hand to conduct operations in Canada. His deputy (DCINCNORAD) is a Canadian general, and other Canadian officers also hold important posts in the command. NORAD participation also gives Canada access to information not available to it even as a NATO ally.

None of this, however, translates into special Canadian influence over U.S. defence policy decisions, even during crisis situations. NORAD gives Canada a seat at the console, not a seat on the U.S. President's National Security Council. Still, NORAD and other bilateral institutions, such as the PJBD, the MCC, and the various arrangements for the land and sea defence of North America, give Ottawa formal institutional structures in which to conduct bilateral defence relations. In this sense, although continentalist in approach, such structures help to discipline the forces of continentalism by staking out and protecting the Canadian interest in a "lopsided continent."[16]

Bilateral co-operation in North American defence has necessitated the provision of forces: to this extent, again, such co-operation has partly determined the content of Canadian defence policy. But it has certainly not limited Canada in the number and type of forces it has deployed for more national purposes. Canada has been free to buy more interceptors, build more radar stations, or commission more patrol ships to further assert its sovereignty. The fact is, however, that Ottawa has relied on bilateral defence co-operation to reduce expenditures on Canadian-based defence forces. This has allowed it to meet its perceived sovereignty needs at lower cost. Traditionally, Canada has paid ten percent of NORAD's expenses, reflecting the relative difference in the size of the populations and economies of the two countries. The 1980 report of SCEAND concluded that "the most efficient and cost-effective way for Canada to contribute to the defence of North American airspace while assuring the protection of Canadian sovereignty and reaffirming the Canadian commitment to the joint defence of the continent, is to renew the NORAD agreement."[17] Canada will pay approximately 12 percent of the NORAD modernization to which it agreed in 1985. For the NWS, Canada is committed to pay 40 percent.

Not only has bilateral defence co-operation been viewed as cost-effective and supportive of Canadian sovereignty, it has imposed fewer constraints on Canadian defence policy and demanded fewer resources than has Canada's involvement in European defence. There are two key, related, reasons for this: overall U.S. strategy, and technology.

The defence of North America has never been a high priority for the United States, indeed, even for the USAF. Since the beginning of the nuclear age, the United States, and by automatic extension, Canada, were to be defended by the threat of retaliation. NORAD's *raison d'être* came to be its role in defending the deterrent, not providing protection for American and Canadian cities and populations. Not until President Reagan launched his SDI in March 1983 did strategic defence receive high-level attention within the U.S. military. In part, the previous neglect of strategic defence reflected the preferences of the U.S. services: the American air force, navy, and army were not interested in devoting substantial resources to North American defence.

More important were technological developments, both Soviet and American. Early-1950s predictions about the growth of the Soviet bomber force proved grossly overestimated, and there were doubts about how effective air defences could actually be. By the time NORAD was established, and at its peak in terms of resources, the ballistic missile had emerged as the main threat. The U.S. reaction in the early 1960s was not to engage in a massive ABM program, hence NORAD never assumed this function. Instead, the United States built only missile-surveillance-and-warning systems.

Technology also influenced the maritime defence of the continent. Until the mid-1960s the Soviets did not have the capability to threaten North America from the sea. With the advent of their ballistic-missile submarine, however, they acquired this capability, and it became necessary to monitor Soviet SSBN movements. Yet as the range of Soviet SLBMs increased, the need for these SSBNs to come close to North America declined. Continual surveillance of the ocean approaches to the continent remained necessary. The United States deployed undersea sensors as part of its sound surveillance system, in which Canada participated. But the strategic maritime defence of North America was never a high priority for the U.S. Navy and did not require specifically designated resources from Canada.

These strategic and technological trends influenced Canadian defence policy in that they allowed Canada to reduce progressively the resources it had committed to North American defence. By the late 1970s Canada had only 36 aircraft dedicated to NORAD, down from 200 in the early 1960s. All nuclear-armed, surface-to-air Bomarc missiles were dismantled, as was the entire Mid-Canada radar line and most of the Cadin-Pinetree line. Unlike the Americans, however, the Canadians were not shifting resources to missile warning and surveillance. As a 1985 Senate report noted, "Canada was scarcely involved in the new missile warning and space surveillance functions" of NORAD.[18] There were only two Spacetrack (Baker-Nunn) camera sites in Canada, both scheduled for de-activation by the late 1980s, and no Ballistic Missile Early Warning System (BMEWS) radars were constructed by the United States in Canada. At sea, Canada did not allocate new resources to counter the SSBN threat. The 1971 White Paper on Defence stated that

> Although an anti-submarine warfare capability will be maintained as part of the general purpose maritime forces, the present degree of emphasis on anti-submarine warfare directed against submarine launched ballistic missiles will be reduced in favour of other roles.[19]

By the mid-1980s strategic and technological trends appeared to be giving renewed importance to North American defence. American strategy was emphasizing the need for flexibility and endurance in a nuclear war and Reagan's SDI created renewed interest in ballistic-missile defence. Space, already heavily used by both superpowers for surveillance and communications, was opening up as a new strategic frontier. In 1985 the United States established a unified Space Command (USSPACECOM). Air defence was also receiving more attention. The condition of NORAD's existing systems had made the 1985 modernization necessary, but concerns about Soviet ALCMs and SLCMs have not only increased the importance of Canadian air and maritime space, but have prompted the United States to launch an ADI to develop new technologies for defence against bombers and cruise missiles.

These trends could generate increased demands on Canadian resources and impose new constraints on future defence options.[20] As noted in Chapter 3, the 1987 White Paper appears to have anticipated this and suggests a shift in the focus of Canadian defence policy from Europe to North America.

Canada and the Defence of Europe

This recent shift in emphasis from European to North American and maritime roles is particularly significant because, for most of the period since 1945, the defence of Europe has been a much more important influence on defence policy than the direct defence of Canada or bilateral co-operation with the United States in continental defence. During the height of the Cold War rearmament, Canada deployed air and land forces to Europe even as U.S. forces assumed air defence roles in Canada. The weapons purchases that emerged out of the DSR, such as the Leopard tanks, the Aurora ASW aircraft, the patrol frigates, and even the CF-18, were meant primarily to fulfil NATO roles.

Canada's interest in the defence of Europe predates the nuclear age and the formation of NATO. In both world wars Canada fought to oppose the domination of Europe and the North Atlantic ocean by a single, hostile power. In the postwar era, Canadian defence policy continued to be based on this Eurocentric approach. Ottawa shares the American and Western European view that the deterrence of a Soviet attack on Western Europe, and the negation of Soviet influence through the maintenance of a credible deterrent posture, is necessary for peace and stability. For Europe, as for North America, deterrence rests on the strategic nuclear arsenal of the United States. These weapons, together with the American theatre and tactical nuclear forces deployed in Europe, and the French and British nuclear forces, are meant to deter not only a Soviet nuclear attack but any possible assault with conventional forces. In Europe, however, unlike in North America, the Western deterrent posture has also relied on conventional forces, especially since the adoption of the flexible-response strategy in 1967. The continuing importance in the nuclear age of conventional forces in the crucial European theatre has had the most profound impact on Canadian defence policy. Without NATO and its strategic assumptions, there would be far less of a requirement for Canada to maintain armoured land forces, ASW naval forces, and air forces with air-to-surface, ground-attack capabilities.

Since such forces are not needed for North American defence, their prime justification is to fulfil the roles that Canada has assumed in NATO.

An example of how NATO can influence Canadian decision
making is the Trudeau government's 1983 decision to proceed with the construction of six ASW frigates. The primary
role of these ships was to be ASW in support of NATO's Atlantic
Command, in order to keep the sea lines of communication
(SLOCs) open between North America and Europe in the event
of war. But the importance of the SLOCs rests upon certain
strategic assumptions of the flexible-response strategy: (1)
that there will be enough warning time to begin a trans-
Atlantic sealift of reinforcements and supplies; (2) that there
will be a long enough period of conventional hostilities for
sealift to have an impact; (3) that NATO's ground and air forces will be able to hold at the conventional level during this
period; (4) that ports will be usable once the convoys reach
Europe; and (5) that nuclear weapons will not be used at
sea. To be sure, there are no certainties here, although it
seems safe to assume that without ASW forces, NATO would
be unable to secure the SLOCs at all.[21] The important point
is that assumptions such as these determine much of the
Canadian defence posture—a posture that is largely geared
to fighting a conventional war in Europe and in the North
Atlantic.

The impact of NATO strategies on Canadian defence policies has been so great because of the way Canada has approached the alliance. Ottawa has been a "good" ally in that
it has not only maintained its nominal membership, but
has participated fully in all aspects of NATO. Unlike Iceland,
Canada has maintained armed forces and made them available to the alliance. Unlike France, it has remained within
the integrated military-command structure and participates
in the complex array of allied agencies. Canada has also
contributed its territory for the training of NATO air and land
forces. For example, the German army conducts tank training at Shilo, Manitoba, while its air force, along with those
of Britain and the Netherlands, conducts low-level flying exercises at Goose Bay, Labrador.

Canada decided in the early 1950s to assume sea, air,
and land roles within NATO, the latter two involving the stationing of Canadian forces in Germany. This has continued
to be NATO's most crucial area; thus, Canada's original decision to remain has necessarily affected later choices, including the retention of the armoured role in the 1970s. Canada's commitments to Norway and to the AMF(L), made in

the 1960s, also to a certain extent determined decisions in the 1970s.

Yet, even with these constraints, Canada has had some leeway in determining the exact nature of its NATO contributions. At sea, Canada offered only ASW forces to the alliance and, even here, gradually confined itself to surface ships and land-based patrol aircraft, having scrapped its lone aircraft carrier and acquired only three submarines. The land forces in Germany were cut by half in 1969 and moved into a reserve counter-attack role. Both the land and air forces in Europe shed their nuclear weapons in the early 1970s. Canada decided to take on the Norwegian role in 1968 and then to withdraw from it in 1987, having done little to make it a credible commitment. Under the 1987 White Paper, both the air and ground units previously committed to Norway are to reinforce Canadian forces in Germany. Canada has retained AMF(L) in the north, but in 1968 dropped a similar commitment to NATO's southern flank.[22]

With the exception of those forces exclusively dedicated to NORAD, nearly all of Canada's land, sea, and air forces are available to NATO. In this regard, the nearly $1 billion per year that Canada spends on the air and ground units permanently stationed in Europe in fact understates the cost to the country of alliance participation.[23] It also does not adequately reflect the importance of NATO to Canada and its influence on defence policy. Among the allies, Canada ranks sixth in total defence expenditures and fifth on a per capita basis.[24] At the same time, Canada is widely regarded, both abroad and at home, as not pulling its weight or contributing its fair share given its relative wealth and prosperity.[25]

Whether or not Canada should be doing more is a matter of debate. But spending levels have been a crucial part of defence decision making, and in general, over the past thirty years Canadian governments, both Liberal and Conservative, have decided that the country cannot afford to spend much above two percent of GDP on defence. Thus, while NATO participation has generated demands for certain kinds of weapons and spending that would not otherwise exist, Ottawa has had some latitude in determining how much is enough.

Over the years, Canada has gone along with continual improvements to the allied conventional posture, not because it believes its contributions will make a significant difference to the balance of military power in Europe, but because such expenditures are viewed as necessary to maintain the political cohesion of NATO. Under constant pressure from the United States, the European allies have maintained large conventional forces not only for the sake of conventional deterrence and flexible response, but also to secure the American nuclear guarantee. Canada need not spend on conventional forces to fall under the protection of the U.S. nuclear umbrella. Yet Ottawa has a stake in keeping the allies united, and thus it has demonstrated its support for conventional deterrence by continuing its conventional contributions to the defence of Europe.

These contributions are also viewed as giving added weight to Canada's voice in allied councils. This is particularly true of the forces in Germany. In a long-standing Canadian tradition going back to the Imperial War Cabinet of World War I, Canada's political leaders use contributions to European defence as an instrument of statecraft. As the 1987 White Paper argued, "the presence of Canadian armed forces in Western Europe contributes to the defence of Canada and, what is more, ensures that we will have a say in how key security issues are decided."[26] In having a say in allied councils, Ottawa does not put forth major policy initiatives. Rather, Canada attempts to foster consensus and mutual understanding and "maximize common ground" among the allies.[27] Canada's ability to act in this capacity is viewed as being partially dependent on its willingness to make material contributions to the common defence.

Here, again, it can be seen that NATO constraints on Canadian defence policy decision making are, in a real and fundamental sense, self-imposed, or at least the direct result of prior political decisions that successive Canadian governments have reaffirmed. For example, even Prime Minister Trudeau decided to keep Canadian forces in Europe in the belief that they enhanced Ottawa's diplomatic standing and influence there.

The preference of Canada's political leadership for NATO contributions, especially in Germany, has supported and complemented the preferences of the military bureaucracy. Active participation in NATO's collective conventional deterrent gave each branch of the CF a credible military role in the nuclear age. In addition to its role in North American defence, the air force contributed to the alliance's tactical airpower. The navy may have preferred a more "balanced" fleet than the ASW force dedicated to NATO, but it was unlikely that Canada's sailors would have had much of a navy at all were it not for the alliance. Most of all, the army benefited because it could justify the maintenance of heavy armoured units. For all the services, NATO afforded the opportunity to collaborate closely with the larger and more sophisticated forces of the United States and the Europeans, and thus provided the Canadian forces with a measure of satisfaction and professionalism. The maintenance of all these allied roles, even during the period of unification and cutbacks in defence spending, resulted in the commitment–capability gap of the 1970s. At the same time, it also helped sustain the forces' morale during these years. The combination of political and military preferences, as well as those of diplomats in DEA, has made NATO the most important external influence on Canadian defence policy decision making.

Although the 1987 White Paper eliminated Canada's commitment to Norway and suggested a shift in emphasis away from European defence, the future impact of NATO on Canadian defence policy could still be significant. The retention of both the armoured and air roles in Germany, and the redirection of forces previously committed to Norway to these roles, reaffirmed Canada's support for the flexible-response strategy. It will also tie Canada into elaborations on the strategy, such as the Follow-On Forces Attack (FOFA) approach, which places particular importance on attacking forces behind Warsaw Pact front-lines in the event of war. If Canada does remain in Germany, new tanks and other highly sophisticated—and costly—equipment will be required to keep the forces compatible with the allies. The INF Treaty has refocussed attention on what NATO regards as the continuing conventional imbalance, and the allies, including Canada, have pledged to implement a Conventional Defence Improvements (CDI) action plan. In addition, Canada is to retain its commitment to supply forces for theAMF(L). Finally, the ambitious maritime rebuilding program of the White Paper is intended to create a modern navy able to fulfil NATO tasks in the North Atlantic as well as to meet new demands in the Pacific and the Arctic. Thus, as is the case with North American defence, evolving NATO strategies and technologies will influence Canadian defence policy. But this will be so because Ottawa has decided to remain actively involved in the defence of Europe.[28]

Canadian Defence Policy and Arms Control

To the extent that East–West arms-control efforts can slow the arms race, ease tensions, promote stability, and perhaps reduce the chances of nuclear war, Canada's interest in arms control is much like that of any other nation. And, as with the majority of other nations, Canada's ability to influence the course of international arms control is limited. Nevertheless, the progress or lack of progress in arms control, especially between the superpowers, has long been of vital interest to Canada. Changes in the composition of the Soviet and American nuclear arsenals and in the NATO and Warsaw Pact conventional balances can influence the environment in which Ottawa pursues its security and formulates its defence policies. Arms control is of immediate concern to Canada because its defence policy is so closely bound up with the strategies and postures of the United States and the West European allies. This has turned Canada's participation in NATO and NORAD into arms-control issues for some groups in Canada. Such participation, it is argued, not only makes Canada a party to dangerous immoral strategies, but also prevents Ottawa from taking a more active role in multilateral disarmament efforts for fear of allied reactions.

Arms control is a part of national and collective security, and DND has been involved with it consistently since the 1950s. In general, though, DND is not the lead department: DEA has the primary responsibility for arms control, with DND and the military acting in an important, but mainly advisory and secondary, capacity. DND advises DEA on such issues as Canada's position on Soviet–American strategic-nuclear and theatre-nuclear arms-reduction negotiations, the East–West Mutual and Balanced Force Reduction talks on conventional forces in Europe, efforts to curtail the spread of nuclear weapons as required by the multinational Non-Proliferation Treaty, and other United Nations disarmament initiatives.[29]

One reason that strategic arms-control policy has not been considered a matter of defence policy is that Canada does not possess nuclear weapons and therefore has no claim to be a party to negotiations on their control or limitation. Only the Soviet Union and the United States participated in the 1970s Strategic Arms Limitation Talks (SALT) and the current Strategic Arms Reduction Talks (START). Nor were other NATO allies party to the INF negotiations and treaty, even though the nuclear weapons involved were based in Europe. Thus it would be unrealistic to expect that Canada could play an influential role in nuclear arms control. Moreover, every recent Canadian government has held that, far from being a detriment to whatever influence Canada might exercise, participation in NATO affords Canada a greater opportunity to be heard on nuclear arms control than it would have if it were neutral. For example, in the course of its negotiations, the United States regularly briefs and consults with its NATO allies.

It is not clear how receptive Washington is to Canada's views and how much weight is given to them compared to those of the larger allies in Europe. A case can be made that Canada might take a more independent stand if it did not have to support an allied consensus on some issues, such as proceeding with the deployment of GLCM and Pershing II missiles in 1983. Others have argued that Ottawa would often rather hide behind the excuse of allied solidarity than disagree openly with the United States.[30]

On East-West arms-control issues, Canada has tended not to specify exactly what kind of arms reductions it prefers. Ottawa does favour the types of reductions that have been discussed by the superpowers since 1985, but appears ready to support any agreement that the two can conclude. At the same time, Canada, like other Western allies, has approached the question of nuclear arms reduction with caution and in the context of its security needs. The 1985 DEA Green Paper on foreign policy stressed the "need for patience and diligence in negotiating agreements which are to stand the test of time and verification to ensure that the agreements are honoured and generate confidence rather than suspicion." The statement also emphasized that "although our ultimate goal is the complete elimination of nuclear weapons, we may have to live [with] and rely on them for many years to come."[31]

Historically, successful arms-control agreements have had little impact on defence policy decision making in Canada. And this too is a reason why DND has not taken a greater interest in arms control. The SALT I and II agreements placed numerical limits on some strategic nuclear weapons. But they did not alter the basic composition of the Soviet-American balance of power and left ICBMs, SLBMs, and bombers as threats to North America. Thus, Canada's role in NORAD remained unchanged. Although the 1972 ABM Treaty did limit both sides to the protection of one site with missile defences, Canada had already had a clause written into the NORAD renewal agreement of 1968 precluding its participation in any ABM system. In any event, the United States did not proceed with the system allowed it under the treaty, and the possibility of a ballistic missile defence (BMD) role for NORAD became moot, at least until the SDI program in 1983.

On the conventional level, there have been no agreements to reduce forces in the European theatre where Canada has committed nearly half its fighter aircraft and the bulk of its ground forces. Various confidence-building measures taken and agreements reached under the umbrella of the Conference on Security and Co-operation in Europe (in which Canada participates) have helped to stabilize the situation there, but the MBFR talks have resulted in no changes in over a decade. As noted earlier, however, the success of negotiations on intermediate-range nuclear weapons in Europe may well give impetus to new efforts to improve NATO's conventional posture.

No arms-control agreement to date has affected Canada's maritime forces. Even radical reductions in the number of Soviet SSBNs would not have much of an impact on the navy's needs and roles. This is so because although its forces are primarily tasked with antisubmarine warfare, this role is not specifically directed against Soviet SSBNs. As DND explained to a Senate committee in 1984, "Canada's contribution to collective defence and the defence of North America ... require[s] the capability to detect and if necessary neutralize hostile submarines operating in ocean areas for which Canada is responsible as well as those operating in the maritime approaches to North America."[32] Because Soviet SSBNs are expected to remain close to the USSR and because SSNs are more of a threat to trans-Atlantic SLOCs and to North American waters, the altered size of the Soviet SSBN fleet after any possible arms-control agreement would not likely reduce the Canadian navy's North American surveillance and NATO responsibilities.

The 50 percent reductions in offensive strategic nuclear systems being discussed by the superpowers as a result of the December 1987 Washington summit will not appreciably alter the roles of the CF as long as the nature of the weapons remains the same. Some technological and strategic trends, however, if they remain unaltered by arms control, could have a measurable impact on Canadian defence policy.

The 1987 White Paper on Defence referred to the advent of both ALCMs and SLCMs as posing new threats to North America. The modernization of NORAD has been justified partly by the need to provide better protection against such cruise missiles. Although it is likely that the improvements now underway would have been initiated even without this new threat, further efforts may be tied to estimates of Soviet ALCM and SLCM development. Such further efforts would include the airborne and space-based surveillance and defence systems currently being researched under the ADI. This research, in turn, is linked to SDI and trends in U.S. strategy that emphasize strategic defence. If the United States proceeds with a BMD system, the character of North American aerospace defence will change. Equally, an unrestricted SLCM arms race may well require even more maritime forces than those called for by the White Paper. Surveillance and protection of the Arctic might also become more complex if current Soviet and American strategic trends pertaining to this area continue.

Thus, as some in Canada have argued, Ottawa should press the United States to limit its cruise-missile development and seek reductions of these weapons, lest Canada be drawn into more costly defence efforts that will do little to enhance its own, or the world's, security. Similarly, with regard to SDI and the Arctic, there have been calls for Ottawa to take the lead in promoting demilitarization.[33] In these cases, there is a direct link between arms control and Canada's defence posture as it relates to forces operating in, over, and around Canada itself. Even if Ottawa were to press these concerns, however, it would have to reckon with the real possibility that it might not be successful, or that arms-control agreements would not completely do away with ALCMs, SLCMs, or superpower Arctic operations. Given that even the existing threats to North America are deemed to require an enhanced Canadian effort, limited success may not very much change the requirements of the CF. Finally, even the total elimination of cruise missiles and an East-West agreement to stay out of each other's Arctic areas would still require Canadian efforts for North American defence, and improvements similar to those advocated by the White Paper would still be necessary. Indeed, if Canada wanted independently to verify compliance with arms-control measures pertaining to its own territory, its requirements for additional air and sea surveillance might well increase. Thus, progress in arms control would not relieve Canada of the need for many of the same types of armed forces that it has already long deployed.

Defence Policy and Sovereignty

If Canada's alliance commitments have been criticized for hampering an active role for the country in arms control, NATO and NORAD have also been criticized for drawing defence resources away from the protection of Canadian sovereignty. And, if political and military leaders have downplayed the role of arms control in defence decisions, they have also cast doubt on the importance of sovereignty protection— defined in non-military terms—in the making of defence policy. There have been three reasons for this. First, there have been few direct challenges to Canadian sovereignty claims by other nations. For Canada, the external environment has been relatively benign with respect to its territorial integrity, national airspace, and even its maritime approaches. Second, in dealing with actual challenges, Ottawa has not regarded the use of military force as the primary or best response. Third, those forces that Canada has deployed to meet collective-defence commitments have also served a sovereignty-protection role, and have been available to back up the civil authority when necessary. Thus, there has been no pressing need to acquire forces specifically for sovereignty-protection purposes.

Sovereignty may be defined as the idea that there exists a "final and absolute political authority in the political community . . . and no final and absolute authority exists elsewhere."[34] In international politics, nations claim this absolute and exclusive authority over their territories, airspace, and parts of the ocean areas extending out from their coasts. To the extent that other nations do not challenge these claims, in word or deed, it may be said that a country's sovereignty is recognized. Thus, for example, Israel's claim to sovereignty over East Jerusalem is not widely recognized, even by countries friendly to it. Furthermore, Arab states do not recognize Israel's claim to the rest of the country, and have attempted by force of arms to recover the territory. Pakistan and India have conflicting claims over Kashmir, while Argentina still does not recognize Britain's sovereignty over the Falklands.

Happily, Canada faces almost no such challenges. Few countries in the world object to the exercise of absolute political authority by Ottawa over most of the land and sea areas that the country claims. There are certain celebrated cases, however, in which disputes have arisen. Canada continues to encounter disputes over fishing rights with other nations, such as France. Also, the United States does not agree with Canada's assertion that the Northwest Passage is an internal Canadian waterway, and instead holds that it is an international strait. But Washington does recognize the application of Canadian environmental, criminal, and other laws over the passage and in January 1988 agreed to seek Ottawa's permission for transits by American Coast Guard icebreakers.[35]

When such sovereignty disputes have arisen, Canada and the challenging nation have sought a negotiated settlement or—if this failed—international arbitration, as in the case of the maritime boundary dispute with the United States over Georges Bank. In the present international environment, those nations most likely to dispute Canada's claims are its military allies, the Europeans or the United States. None of these countries has ever used force to support its claims. For Canada and these other nations, the issues at stake are simply not worth the political costs of armed conflict. It would hardly further the interest of collective defence if the United States were to go to war with Canada over rival fishing claims. While the CF have been used to assert Canadian laws and claims by "showing the flag" and by occasionally apprehending boats fishing illegally, Ottawa's claims are not such that would require securing international recognition at the point of a gun. Canadian sovereignty concerns, to the extent that they do arise from the international environment, have essentially constituted international legal problems, best resolved by political negotiations and judicial processes.

Given the very favourable international environment that Canada faces, it is surprising that sovereignty should be an issue at all in defence policy. In fact, it has become something of an issue not so much because of the international environment, but because of the domestic policy-making environment. Sovereignty disputes, especially those with the United States, tend to be viewed in the context of Canadian independence, autonomy, and national pride. As was the case in the Northwest Passage dispute, many Canadians believe that anything less than full U.S. recognition of Canada's claims constitutes a challenge to the very ability of the party in power to govern. The same view is being applied in the case of contending Canadian and French claims to rich offshore fishing grounds near Newfoundland. Strong emotions are aroused as sovereignty claims come to be identified with nationhood and with the need to "stand up to the Yankees" (or to other foreigners).

Political leaders in Ottawa may sense these domestic pressures from time to time, and may feel obliged to respond, as in the case of the decision to construct a new Arctic icebreaker. But it is difficult to translate this emotional concern over sovereignty into defence policy decisions and procurements that are distinct from those associated with Canada's collective-defence roles. It is also difficult to decide what role DND and the CF should play in sovereignty protection, as opposed to that played by other governmental agencies, such as those concerned with fisheries, transportation, and the environment.

These difficulties became apparent when the Trudeau government shifted emphasis from collective defence to sovereignty in the early 1970s. It was unclear from the beginning what amount of effort the forces were to devote to sovereignty roles as opposed to traditional, alliance-oriented defence tasks. Nor was the "appropriate relationship between the responsibilities of the Minister of National Defence and of the Canadian Armed Forces for the protection of sovereignty, and the responsibilities vested by statute in other ministers and in the departments and agencies reporting to them," precisely specified.[36] As outlined in Chapter 3, this emphasis on sovereignty was further complicated by the fact that no allied commitment had been dropped. Thus, by 1975, NATO and NORAD continued to drive defence decisions, especially those involving major expenditures.

In the absence of a serious threat to Canadian sovereignty, apart from the military threat to North America, it is difficult to formulate a defence policy or procurement program on national sovereignty-protection grounds alone.

But DND does not dismiss sovereignty concerns or the use of the armed forces to back up the civil power in asserting Canadian claims and laws. Rather, what defence officials have argued is that, given the need to "ensure an optimum allocation of limited resources," Canada cannot afford forces dedicated exclusively to fulfil sovereignty-protection roles. And, since the "more demanding" collective-defence tasks "usually subsume the capabilities for less demanding activities and commitments," priority has been given to NATO and NORAD roles in making force-posture decisions.[37] Canada's surface ships and long-range maritime patrol aircraft, for example, are primarily tasked with ASW missions in support of NATO and North American defence roles. But, on a day-to-day basis, as they carry out their surveillance of Soviet submarines, they also serve to affirm Canada's sovereignty and are able to come to the aid of the civil power if necessary. An unarmed fisheries patrol boat might be able to do the latter, but it would not be able to perform effectively in an ASW role. Equally, an unarmed executive-type jet might be able to identify intruders into Canadian airspace, but would be less useful to NORAD in an active air-defence role against Soviet bombers. Collective-defence commitments do constrain defence policy in the sense that NATO and NORAD, and not sovereignty protection, drive spending decisions. But, this does not mean that Canada thereby entirely lacks forces for non-military sovereignty protection needs.[38]

There is another sense in which collective-defence forces assist in protecting Canadian sovereignty. This is what has been called the "defence against help" role of the armed forces, and it applies especially to North American defence.[39] In this role, the forces respond to domestic sovereignty concerns by fulfilling collective-defence tasks. It is based on the premise that, without a Canadian military contribution to the defence of North America at sea and particularly in the air, the whole burden for the continent's defence would be assumed by the armed forces of the United States. Given that the major threat is ballistic missiles, against which there is no defence and, currently, no warning system in Canada, this would not lead to hordes of American forces being stationed in Canada. Yet it would mean that Canada would be unaware of measures that the United States might be planning for the defence of the continent. Strategic defence may not yet be a priority for the United States, but Washington could never stand idly by.

It has long been DND's view that a failure to contribute to collective defence could undermine both Canada's sovereignty and its sense of nationhood. As a commander of the Air Command told a Senate committee:

> I instinctively, as I think most Canadians do, have a feeling that unless we have the capability of controlling our airspace—that is, of knowing of the presence of an intruder and being able to intercept and identify that intruder to enforce our sovereignty in airspace—there is something lacking in the composition of the Canadian nation. It is a difficult question [and one that calls, not for] a military expression of the need but essentially a political one.[40]

A similar theme was struck by Minister of National Defence Perrin Beatty when, at the tabling of the 1987 White Paper, he rejected the suggestion that Canada "contract out" its defence to others. The government was prepared to discuss all aspects of North American defence, but as a "partner with our allies and not a dependent."[41] Given the nature of the international strategic environment, Canada could never be an equal partner. The emphasis that the White Paper puts on North American and maritime roles, however, suggests that Ottawa is concerned about an erosion of sovereignty resulting from the elevation of the strategic defence of North America in U.S. strategy and the consequent need for Canada to take steps so that it does not become irrelevant to its own defence. To this extent, the posture called for in the White Paper may be as much a "political expression" of Canada's security and sovereignty needs as it is a military one.

Canada and Peacekeeping

It is another of the ironies and paradoxes of Canadian foreign and defence policy since 1945 that Canada has been more actively engaged in monitoring transborder violations in the Third World than in North America or even in Europe. Cliché or not, the Canada–U.S. border is indeed the longest undefended frontier in the world. While the possibility always exists that some Soviet troops may land along Canada's coastline, territorial defence is not a high priority. In Europe, Canada is committed to the territorial integrity of the NATO nations, but there has been no hostile attack from the East in over forty years. On the other hand, there have been numerous clashes across national frontiers during this period in the Third World. For while the East–West balance of nuclear and conventional power has made war an unlikely eventuality in the Europe–Atlantic region, the stable international environment that Canada and its allies enjoy does not include large parts of the rest of the world.

Since the Korean War, Canada has not been a belligerent in Third World conflicts. However, the Canadian military has been involved in these struggles as part of multinational peacekeeping forces. Peacekeeping "is the use of military personnel to monitor and supervise a cease-fire between belligerents."[42] It involves both observing that neither side is violating a cease-fire line or national boundary and taking limited steps to prevent violations. Peacekeeping forces, es-

pecially those operating under United Nations auspices, operate only with the consent of the belligerents on whose
territory they may be based. These forces do not keep the
peace by force of arms. They are only lightly armed and
may use their weapons only in self-defence. Peace is meant
to be ensured not by the peacekeeping forces but by the
diplomatic negotiations that are supposed to accompany the
deployment of the multinational contingents. "The expectation is that once a cease-fire has been assured, the political
climate will become more conducive to diplomatic negotiation and possible settlement" through the UN or some
other third party.[43]

The record of peacekeeping operations in facilitating the
resolution of long-standing disputes is not good. Peacekeeping forces have been stationed along the Arab–Israeli borders
for over forty years. In 1967, Egypt ordered the UN force
off its territory and war with Israel followed quickly. A United
Nations force has been on Cyprus since 1964 because of the
continuing dispute between the Greek and Turkish communities. In Indochina, peacekeeping failed after the 1954 set-
tlements and again after the 1973 accords. Nevertheless,
these forces do afford some opportunity for diplomacy and,
in the case of Cyprus, have at least succeeded in defusing
tensions. A non-UN Multinational Force and Observers (MFO)
has been monitoring the Sinai desert pursuant to the Egyptian–Israeli peace treaty of 1979.

Because of its many frustrations and restrictions, peacekeeping may be no job for a soldier, but only a soldier can
do it. The awarding of the 1988 Nobel Peace Prize to UN peacekeeping forces was recognition of the contribution of the
forces to global peace and stability. Canada's soldiers can
rightly claim a lion's share of the credit, having become
peacekeepers *par excellence*, utilizing their skills in communications and logistics, in particular, to support the multinational forces. Since 1947, Canada has participated in
every major peacekeeping operation mounted by the United
Nations, as well as in several others outside the UN framework. At the height of Canadian involvement in international
peacekeeping in the mid-1960s, there were over 2100 Canadian personnel involved. Some indication of the importance that the Canadian government still attaches to peacekeeping can be seen in the numbers involved: in 1987 over
800 members of the CF were active in four peacekeeping
operations, with 515 in Cyprus alone.[44]

The need and opportunity for Canada to contribute to
peacekeeping operations arises out of the nature of the

international environment. But that environment does not automatically require that Canada respond. Of all the defence roles assumed by the Canadian Forces, peacekeeping is the most discretionary in that Canada has complete freedom to refuse requests for its services and to avoid involvement. Unlike Canadian involvement in NATO and North American defence, participation in peacekeeping is something that is not determined by the external environment.

In fact, Canada accepted and often pursued peacekeeping roles with a zeal not often present in other defence and external activities. Indeed, it was Canada's secretary of state for external affairs in 1956, Lester B. Pearson, who originated the concept of large multinational peacekeeping forces during the Suez crisis. Because Canada quickly became identified with peacekeeping, its contributions have been requested frequently by the UN and other countries. Sometimes, as in the case of the 1973 Vietnam accords, Canada found it difficult to refuse. To this extent, past decisions again constrained future policy options.

The key decisions relating to peacekeeping—which requests to accept and under what terms—are not issues for DND but rather for DEA and ultimately for the prime minister and cabinet. For the most part, Canada has responded quickly and positively to requests. Peacekeeping has been attractive for a number of reasons. First, it has been consistent with the basic internationalist approach that has been the foundation of Canadian foreign policy since 1945. In this approach, Canada has identified its interests with the broader goal of global stability; hence, anything Canada might do to enhance stability, such as by contributing to the peaceful resolution of disputes, can be said to be in the national interest. Where a Third World conflict draws in the superpowers, as it has in the Arab–Israeli conflict, there is the possibility of a major East–West crisis and the ever-present danger of escalation to armed confrontation. Thus, peacekeeping can be related directly to the security of Canada as well.

Second, peacekeeping has afforded Canada the opportunity to play a role in world affairs somewhat outside the framework of its military alliances and its collective-defence tasks. It has been the case that almost all the major peacekeeping operations in which Canada has participated have had the political, and often financial, support of the United States. Nevertheless, peacekeeping has been popular as something of an independent, uniquely Canadian aspect of defence policy. As a *Globe and Mail* editorial argued at the time of the Congo operation in 1960, "Canada's involvement with humanity and history should express itself in something more effective than radar lines, anti-aircraft rockets . . . ."[45] Viewed in this context, there has been a large measure of domestic support for peacekeeping, thereby making the dispatch of forces a relatively easy decision for the government.

While peacekeeping has enabled Canada to play a distinctive international role, a third reason why it has been attractive to Ottawa is that it has not been inconsistent with collective-defence obligations. Quite the contrary: Canada's allies, especially the United States, have welcomed and encouraged Ottawa to assist both UN and non-UN operations. The forces on Cyprus are particularly important because of the potential for conflict between two NATO allies. Canada's forces deployed with the MFO in the Sinai contribute to the American and NATO goal of maintaining peace between Egypt and Israel.

Finally, peacekeeping, while involving thousands of members of the CF over the years, has not represented a serious drain on the resources allocated to defence. Canada has been able to recover some of its expenses from the UN or sponsoring countries. During the period that covered the most active years—1949 to 1980—the net cost to Canada for peacekeeping was about $266 million or roughly 0.4 percent of the total DND budget during that time.[46] The approximately 2000 members of the CF who may be called upon for peacekeeping duties are drawn from Canadian-based units, but not ones specifically maintained for peacekeeping duties.

The 1964 White Paper, with its emphasis on the creation of highly mobile units that would be available for quick dispatch in peacekeeping operations, was the only attempt to suggest that this role should be a major determinant in force-posture decisions. But it did not work out this way because Canada still retained all its allied commitments, and these continued to determine the forces' overall posture. Yet, the 1971 White Paper's attempt to downplay peacekeeping did not last long either. Within two years, Canadian troops found themselves back in the jungles of Vietnam and the deserts of the Middle East. And all this was accommodated amidst steadily declining personnel levels and budget freezes.

In sum, peacekeeping, although one of the longest-standing roles for the CF since 1945, has been of only marginal importance in the formulation of defence policy and the shaping of the military's posture. It has become something that the forces are expected to be able to do along with their other tasks. It is the other roles, those related to the defence of North America and Europe, that generate not only the greatest demands on the forces but also the most difficult decisions for policy makers as they seek to cope with a relatively stable, yet always uncertain, external environment.

Notes

1. Bernard Brodie, ed., *The Absolute Weapon: Atomic Power and World Order* (New York: Harcourt, Brace, and Company, 1946), p. 76.

2. This approach to international relations is taken from Kenneth N. Waltz, *Man, the State and War: A Theoretical Analysis* (New York: Columbia University Press, 1954).

3. P. Edward Haley, David M. Keithly, Jack Merritt, eds., *Nuclear Strategy, Arms Control and the Future* (Boulder, Colo.: Westview Press, 1985), p. 79.

4. Harvard Nuclear Study Group, *Living with Nuclear Weapons* (New York: Bantam, 1983), p. 44.

5. Haley et al., *Nuclear Strategy*, p. 78. On the role of deterrence in the U.S. strategy and foreign policy, see Alexander L. George and Richard Smoke, *Deterrence in American Foreign Policy: Theory and Practice* (New York: Columbia University Press, 1974); and Henry A. Kissinger, *Nuclear Weapons and Foreign Policy* (New York: Council on Foreign Relations, 1957).

6. Harvard Nuclear Study Group, *Living with Nuclear Weapons*, p. 34.

7. F.J. West, "Maritime Strategy and NATO Deterrence," *Naval War College Review* 38, no. 5, (September/October 1985): 7. See also Colin S. Gray, "Nuclear Strategy: A Regrettable Necessity," *SAIS Review* 3, no. 1 (1983), pp. 13-28.

8. Leon V. Sigal, *Nuclear Forces in Europe: Enduring Dilemmas, Present Prospects* (Washington, D.C.: The Brookings Institution, 1984), p. 14. On flexible response, see also David N. Schwartz, *NATO's Nuclear Dilemmas* (Washington, D.C.: The Brookings Institution, 1983), pp. 136-92; Richard K. Betts, *Surprise Attack: Lessons for Defence Planning*, (Washington, D.C.: The Brookings Institution, 1982), pp. 153-227.

9. Bernard Brodie, *War and Politics* (New York: Macmillan, 1973), pp. 430-31.

10. Henry Kissinger, *Years of Upheaval* (Boston: Little Brown, 1982), p. 1175. See also Robert Jervis, "Why Nuclear Superiority Doesn't Matter," in *The Use of Force: International Politics and Foreign Policy*, 2nd ed., eds. Robert J. Art and Kenneth N. Waltz (Lanham, Md.: University Press of America, 1983), pp. 498-515.

11. Laurence Martin, "The Role of Military Force in the Nuclear Age," in *Strategic Thought in the Nuclear Age*, ed. Laurence Martin (Baltimore: Johns Hopkins University Press, 1979), pp. 5-6.

12. Joseph T. Jockel and Joel J. Sokolsky, *Canada and Collective Security: Odd Man Out*, The Washington Papers, no. 121 (New York: Praeger, 1986), p. viii.

13. James Eayrs, "Military Policy and Middle Power: The Canadian Experience," in *Canada's Role as a Middle Power*, ed. J. King Gordon (Toronto: The Canadian Institute of International Affairs, 1965), p. 73.

14. David G. Haglund, *Soviet Air-Launched Cruise Missiles and the Geopolitics of North American Air Defence: The Canadian North in Changing Perspective*, Occasional Paper, no. 16 (Kingston: Centre for International Relations, Queen's University, 1987), p. 20. See also Paul Bracken, *The Command and Control of Nuclear Forces* (New Haven: Yale University Press, 1985); Ashton B. Carter, Johns Steinbruner, Charles A. Zraket, eds., *Managing Nuclear Operations* (Washington, D.C.: The Brookings Institution, 1987).

15. Cynthia Cannizzo as quoted in Canada, House of Commons, SCEAND, Report, *Canada–U.S. Defence Cooperation and the 1986 Renewal of the NORAD Agreement*, 1986, p. 17. See also Roger F. Swanson, "NORAD: Origins and Operations of Canada's Ambivalent Symbol," *International Perspectives* (November/December, 1972), pp. 3–8; Joseph T. Jockel, *No Boundaries Upstairs: Canada, the United States and the Origins of North American Air Defence, 1945–1958* (Vancouver: University of British Columbia Press, 1987); David Cox, *Canada and NORAD 1958–1978: A Cautionary Retrospective*, Aurora Papers 1 (Ottawa: Canadian Centre for Arms Control and Disarmament, 1985).

16. John Holmes as quoted in SCEAND, *Minutes of Proceedings and Evidence*, Issue no. 37, 10 October 1985, p. 37:25.

17. SCEAND, *Report on NORAD* (1980), recommendation 2.

18. Canada, Senate, Special Committee on National Defence, *Report on Canada's Territorial Air Defence* (1985), p. 10. See also Joel J. Sokolsky, "Changing Strategies, Technologies and Organization: The Continuing Debate on NORAD and the Strategic Defence Initiative," *Canadian Journal of Political Science* 19, no. 4 (December 1986): 751–74.

19. Canada, Department of National Defence, *Defence in the 70s* (Ottawa: Information Canada, 1971), p. 28.

20. On future trends in North American defence, see David Cox, *Trends in Continental Defence: A Canadian Perspective*, Occasional Papers 2 (Ottawa: Canadian Institute for International Peace and Security, 1986); G.R. Lindsey et al., *Aerospace Defence and Canada's Future Role*, Wellesley Papers 9 (Toronto: Canadian Institute of International Affairs, 1985); John C. Toomay, "Warning and Assessment Sensors," in *Managing Nuclear Operations*, eds. Ashton Carter et al., pp. 282–321.

21. Joel J. Sokolsky, "Canada's Maritime Forces: Strategic Assumptions, Commitments, Priorities," *Canadian Defence Quarterly* 15, no. 3 (Winter, 1985/86), pp. 28–29.

22. Joseph T. Jockel, *Canada and NATO's Northern Flank* (Toronto: Centre for International and Strategic Studies, York University, 1986), pp. 2–22.

23. Canada, Department of National Defence, *Defence 86* (Ottawa: Minister of Supply and Services, 1987), p. 4.

24. Canada, Department of National Defence, *Challenge and Commitment: A Defence Policy for Canada* (Ottawa: Supply and Services, Canada, 1987), pp. 46–47.

25. This, at least, was the view of one of Canada's allies: see United States, Department of Defense, *Report on Allied Contributions to the Common Defense* (Washington, D.C.: Department of Defense, 1986), pp. 18–20, 23. But Canadian parliamentarians have also criticized Canada's contribution to the alliance. In the early 1980s, committees of the Senate issued several reports highlighting what they regarded as serious weaknesses in the Canadian Forces. See Standing Committee on Foreign Affairs, Subcommittee on National Defence, *Manpower in Canada's Armed Forces* (Ottawa: Supply and Services Canada, 1982), and *Canada's Maritime Defence* (Ottawa: Supply and Services Canada, 1983); Special Committee on National Defence, *Canada's Territorial Air Defence* (Ottawa: Supply and Services Canada, 1985) and *Military Air Transport* (Ottawa: Supply and Services Canada, 1986). See also Canada, Special Joint Committee of the Senate and the House of Commons on Canada's International Relations, *Independence and Internationalism* (Ottawa: Supply and Services Canada , 1986).

26. Canada, Department of National Defence, *Challenge and Commitment*, p. 6.

27. John G.H. Halstead, "Canada's Security in the 1980s: Options and Pitfalls," *Behind the Headlines* 41, no. 1 (September 1983): 12.

28. On trends in NATO, see Andrew J. Pierre, ed., *The Conventional Defense of Europe: New Technologies and New Strategies* (New York: Council on Foreign Relations, 1986); Stanley R. Sloan *NATO's Future: Toward a New Transatlantic Bargain* (Washington, D.C.: National Defense University Press, 1985); Gerald Wright, "Canada and the Reform of NATO," eds. John W. Holmes et al. in *No Other Way: Canada and International Security Institutions,* (Toronto: University of Toronto, Centre for International Studies, 1986).

29. For background on Canada and arms control, see George Ignatieff, "Canadian Aims and Perspectives in the Negotiation of International Agreements on Arms Control and Disarmament," in *Canadian Perspectives on International Law and Organization*, eds. R. St. John MacDonald et al. (Toronto: University of Toronto Press, 1974) and Fen Osler Hampson, "Arms Control and East West Relations", in *Canada Among Nations 1986: Talking Trade*, eds. Brian W. Tomlin and Maureen Appel Molot (Toronto: James Lorimer, 1986).

30. For this approach, see Simon Rosenblum, *Misguided Missiles: Canada, the Cruise and Star Wars* (Toronto: James Lorimer, 1985).

31. Canada, Department of External Affairs, *Competitiveness and Security: Directions for Canada's International Relations* (Ottawa: Supply and Services Canada, 1985), p. 39.

32. Canada, Senate, Special Committee on National Defence, *Proceedings*, Issue no. 8, 17 April 1984, p. 8A:9.

33. For a discussion of arms-control options relating to cruise missiles and the Arctic, see Ronald G. Purver, *Arms Control Options in the Arctic*, Issue Brief no. 7 (Ottawa: Canadian Centre for Arms Control and Disarmament, 1987).

34. F.H. Hinsley, *Sovereignty* (London: Watts, 1966), p. 26.

35. On Canada and the law of the sea, see Douglas M. Johnston *Canada and the New International Law of the Sea* (Toronto: University of Toronto Press, 1985). Johnston's book is volume 58 in the series of studies commissioned as part of the research program of the Royal Commission on the Economic Union and Development Prospects for

Canada. On the special problems of the Arctic and the Northwest Passage, see another study written for the commission, entitled *The North*, research co-ordinator, Michael S. Whittington (Toronto: University of Toronto Press, 1985), especially Donat Pharand's essay "Sovereignty and the Canadian North," pp. 141–64.

36. J.C. Arnell and J.F. Anderson, "Program Management in the Department of National Defence," *Canadian Defence Quarterly* 1 no.2 (Autumn 1971): 31–32.

37. Canada, Senate, Special Committee on National Defence, *Proceedings*, Issue no 8, 17 April 1984, p. 8A:6.

38. For a discussion of how allied tasks outweighed non-military sovereignty considerations in a defence procurement decision, see Michael Tucker, "Sovereignty and Defence Policy: The Case of the 'Aurora'," *Canadian Foreign Policy: Contemporary Issues and Themes* (Toronto: McGraw-Hill Ryerson, 1980), pp. 141–74.

39. For a discussion of the "defence against help" concept in Canadian defence policy, see Nils Orvik, "The Basic Issue in Canadian National Security: Defence Against Help, Defence to Help Others," *Canadian Defence Quarterly* 11 no. 1 (Summer 1981): 8–15.

40. As quoted in Canada, Senate, Special Committee on National Defence, *Canada's Territorial Air Defence* (Ottawa: Supply and Services Canada, 1985), p. 32.

41. The Honourable Perrin Beatty, Minister of National Defence, "Address Upon the Tabling of the Defence White Paper in the House of Commons," June 5, 1987.

42. Henry Wiseman, *Peacekeeping and the Management of International Conflict*, Background Paper 15 (Ottawa: Canadian Institute for International Peace and Security, 1987), p. 1.

43. Wiseman, *Peacekeeping*, p. 1. See also D. Wainhouse, *International Peacekeeping at the Crossroads* (Baltimore: Johns Hopkins University Press, 1973) and Michael Comay, UN *Peacekeeping in the Arab–Israeli Conflict, 1948–1975* (Jerusalem: The Leonard Davis Institute for International Relations, 1976).

44. Canada, Department of National Defence, *Challenge and Commitment: A Defence Policy for Canada* (Ottawa: Supply and Services Canada, 1987), p. 25. For background on Canadian peacekeeping, see A. Taylor, D. Cox, and Jack L. Granatstein, *Peacekeeping: International Challenge and Canadian Response* (Toronto: Canadian Institute of International Affairs, 1968); Colwyn D. Williams, "International Peacekeeping: Canada's Role," in *Canadian Perspectives on International Law and Organization*, eds. R. St. John MacDonald et al., pp. 645–89; and John Sigler, ed., *International Peacekeeping in the Eighties: Global Outlook and Canadian Priorities*, Carleton International Proceedings (Ottawa: Norman Paterson School of International Affairs, Carleton University, Fall 1982). On Canada's peacekeeping in Vietnam, see James Eayrs, *In Defence of Canada*, vol. 5, *Indochina: Roots of Complicity* (Toronto: University of Toronto Press, 1983) and Douglas A. Ross, *In the Interest of Peace: Canada and Vietnam, 1954–1973* (Toronto: University of Toronto Press, 1984).

45. Editorial, *Globe and Mail*, 14 July 1960, p. A7.

46. Albert Legault, "Canada's Contribution to Peacekeeping Operations," in *International Peacekeeping in the Eighties*, ed. Sigler, p. 19.

7

CASE STUDIES

IN CANADIAN DEFENCE

POLICY MAKING

The relative impact of the governmental, domestic, and external environments on Canadian defence policy decision making will vary according to the issue involved. This chapter examines three case studies in order to illustrate the various influences on defence decisions. In the first part, two commitment and posture decisions are reviewed: the 1986 renewal of the NORAD agreement and the 1987 decision to end the CAST brigade group and air commitments to Norway. The second part looks at decisions on funding and procurement with particular reference to the Canadian Patrol Frigate (CPF) program.

Commitment and Posture Decisions

The 1986 NORAD Renewal At their March 1986 summit meeting, Prime Minister Mulroney and President Reagan renewed the NORAD agreement for another five years. There had been little doubt that the two countries would elect to continue the joint command structure and co-operative arrangements for the aerospace defence of the continent. By the mid-1970s, NORAD's main function had become warning and assessment of missile attack, with a residual and declining role in detecting and intercepting bombers. This reflected the nature of the Soviet threat, in which ICBMs and SLBMs predominated. NORAD had also assumed a space monitoring function. Although Canadian personnel were present at U.S. missile-warning facilities and worked in the space-surveillance sections at NORAD Headquarters, Canada was only minimally involved in these activities. Its main interest was in airspace surveillance, where NORAD's arrangements to counter Soviet bombers also contributed to the protection of Canadian air sovereignty. As the 1971 White Paper noted, though, Ottawa was not going to put substantial resources into the air-defence role.[1]

Nevertheless, because Canada had a continuing interest in NORAD's air surveillance role, the closing down by the United States of radar stations in Canada presented Ottawa with the prospect of inadequate coverage of Canadian airspace. Thus it was Canada which, in 1975, suggested to the United States that NORAD's radars be modernized. While a bilateral team was formed to examine the problem, the Pentagon was not very interested because the United States had adequate coverage for civilian and military purposes with its Joint Surveillance System.

Toward the end of the 1970s, however, the state of NORAD's air-defence capabilities was drawing more attention in Washington. A new Joint United States–Canada Air Defence Study (JUSCADS) was undertaken. The study, completed in 1979, revealed that there were significant gaps in NORAD's bomber-warning systems. That same year Congress directed the Department of Defense (DoD) to develop a plan for improving continental air defences. The USAF proposal, known as the Air Defense Master Plan (ADMP), was directed against a continuing Soviet bomber threat and what the United States expected to be a growing threat from Soviet ALCMs and SLCMs. As a congressional study observed, over the years Pentagon planners paid little attention to, and Congress provided little money for, "defenses that could ward off ALCM, SLCM and bomber attacks against the United States."[2]

These "air-breathing" weapons did not fundamentally alter the balance of power or seriously call into question the credibility of the U.S. nuclear deterrent. Rather the ADMP was concerned with the possibility of an undetected, surprise "precursor" strike by Soviet bombers and cruise missiles against a small number of targets, especially C^3I facilities. Such an attack was now considered an option open to the Soviets, given the obsolescence of North American air defences. If successful, it could partially blind the United States and prevent warning of follow-on ICBM–SLBM attack as well as delay any retaliation. This threat had been considered unlikely in view of the other options open to the Soviets, such as a first strike with ballistic missiles. Nevertheless, "the precursor strike . . . was used for planning purposes because it was large enough, given the assumption of surprise, to be a significant threat. Equally, such a strike was considered small enough so that a reasonable defensive system might be considered 'affordable'."[3]

It was considered affordable by the Reagan administration, which incorporated the ADMP into its strategic modernization program of 1981. The Canadian government likewise considered the ADMP reasonable, for it would not only modernize NORAD's air defences, but also, in the process, enhance Canadian territorial air sovereignty by upgrading Canada-based systems. In 1982 Ottawa accepted the ADMP as a blueprint for the overhaul of North American air defences. Negotiations on the ADMP culminated in the signing, by Prime Minister Mulroney and President Reagan, of an agreement on NORAD modernization at their March 1985 meeting—that is, a year before the NORAD renewal.

The bulk of the improvements to be undertaken as a result of the agreement will be located in, and paid for by, the United States. This includes the installation of over-the-horizon backscatter radars (OTH-Bs) in the continental United States and the upgrading of interceptor squadrons. In the north, the old DEW Line is to be replaced by the new NWS, a series of long- and short-range radars, most of which will be located in Canada. The Canadian NWS radars, unlike those of the earlier DEW Line when it was first deployed, will be entirely owned and operated by Canada. There will be Canadian personnel at some of the U.S. OTH-B sites. Because of limits on the coverage of the OTH-Bs, it will also be necessary to construct additional coastal radars in Canada. Backing up the NWS will be improved northern airfields to provide FOLs for Canadian interceptors, and DOBs for U.S. AWAC aircraft that Canada will help man. Canada will pay roughly 12 percent of the approximately $7 billion cost of the modernization, mainly by assuming 40 percent of the cost of the NWS. The United States will pay some of the costs of the FOLs. It is expected that all the different components of the system will be in place by 1994.[4]

Given this background, it was not surprising that the prime minister and his cabinet readily agreed to renew NORAD without making changes to the agreement. The strategic environment was such that the air defence of North America was still necessary, and Canadian territory continued to be important for this task. As in the past, contributing to NORAD's resources served Canadian sovereignty interests by providing the means to monitor Canadian airspace and by affording Canada a role in the defence of the continent.

The NORAD modernization would mean additional costs; but, even if Canada's share amounted to $1 billion (adding in the FOLS), it was a manageable sum when spread out over several years.

Adding to these immediate factors supporting renewal was the weight of past decisions. The NORAD agreement had been renewed four times before—in 1968, 1973, 1975, and 1981, with an interim one-year extension in 1980. While the NORAD boundaries had been redrawn, placing all Canadian airspace under Region Operations Control Centres (ROCC) located in Canada, the country was in no position to "go it alone" on air defence if NORAD was terminated. Another factor was that the CF-18 aircraft, whose procurement had been decided in 1980 for both the NATO and NORAD roles, was now coming into service in large numbers. For Ottawa, the decision to renew in 1986 was just the continuation of bilateral "business as usual" with only some marginal technological and deployment improvements added.

Although the decision to renew was never in doubt, the government found itself having to justify that decision in the face of some of the strongest domestic criticism that had ever been mounted against NORAD. This criticism was not directed at NORAD itself, nor at Canada's air-defence role within the joint command. Instead, it focussed more on the place that NORAD would occupy in the U.S. defence posture given the emerging strategic, technological, and organizational trends in American defence policy under President Reagan. In essence, critics were saying that the external environment had altered sufficiently to give Canada pause before agreeing to renew, without change, the NORAD agreement.

President Reagan's SDI program quickly became the lightning-rod for this criticism. But even before the launching of SDI in March 1983, there was criticism to the effect that NORAD would drag Canada into new and dangerous U.S. nuclear strategies. This "nuclear revisionism," begun during the Carter administration, but accelerating under Reagan, was seen as a turning away from deterrence and MAD toward a nuclear war-fighting posture. In 1982, Douglas Ross argued that, in renewing the NORAD agreement in 1981, the Canadian government had failed to take proper notice of these changes in United States strategy. The new emphasis on active air defence, as set forth in the ADMP, was part of this revisionism because it suggested the possibility of fighting a nuclear war at an acceptable cost. Thus, according to Ross, a stronger role for Canada in air defence would constitute tacit collaboration in an inherently provocative, and therefore irresponsible, approach to strategic doctrine and deployment.[5]

The goal of the SDI is to provide the United States with the technologies that would allow for BMD, perhaps from systems located in space. Since the late 1960s government officials and academics have debated the issue of whether BMD is stabilizing or destabilizing. Opponents argued that the existence of BMD systems would undermine the mutual deterrent effect of nuclear weapons with their guarantee of MAD. Military and political leaders, having both offensive and defensive strategic systems at their disposal, might be tempted to pull the nuclear trigger. Supporters of BMD contended that not only would defences against missiles be stabilizing—because they would complicate an attack, thereby helping deter it—but that with more BMD systems, real reductions in offensive weapons would be possible.[6] The debate was resolved through an arms-control measure. In 1972 and 1974 the United States and the USSR had agreed, in the ABM Treaty, to limit themselves to one BMD system each with up to 100 missiles. The USSR deployed its system around Moscow, but the United States did not go ahead with its Safeguard system, planned for deployment near an ICBM base.[7]

When the Reagan SDI announcement of March 1983 reopened the BMD debate, it had particular meaning for Canada. At the time of the first NORAD renewal in 1968, Ottawa had Washington agree to a clause that specified that NORAD would "not involve in any way a Canadian commitment to participate in an active ballistic missile defence."[8] In general, Canada shared the view that BMD was destabilizing and would not enhance deterrence. But in the 1981 renewal, when NORAD's title changed from North American Air Defence Command to North American Aerospace Defence Command, this clause was dropped. The official DND explanation was that, because of the ABM Treaty and the fact that the United States had not deployed the one ABM system allowed it, there was no need for the clause.[9] With the advent of SDI, this deletion assumed greater significance during the debate over the 1986 renewal. Some disarmament groups suggested that DND knew the direction of U.S. thinking and did not want to foreclose any option. Reinsertion of the clause became a major objective for a number of interest groups, including some supportive of NORAD itself.[10]

Whether NORAD would become involved in BMD as a result of the research begun under SDI was unclear. If the United States moved ahead with ground- or space-based systems requiring facilities on Canadian territory, it would pose problems for Canada. On the other hand, if technologies allowed for BMD deployments that did not involve Canadian territory, as was the case with most of the existing missile-warning capabilities, then it could be kept separate from NORAD.

Of more immediate concern was the link between SDI and air defence, an activity in which Canada was still involved and with which it associated a national sovereignty interest. Would the deployment of ballistic-missile defences by the United States prompt the Soviets into building up their bomber, ALCM, and SLCM forces—thus requiring a major improvement in North American air-defence capabilities beyond those agreed to under the ADMP, to complement BMD? In one of its first reports to Congress, the SDI Organization (SDIO) had noted that there was no link between planned improvements to North American air defences and SDI, but that "continuing progress in the area of the Strategic Defense Initiative will permit the addressing of . . . the interrelationship between SDI and strategic air defense."[11] Congress' own initial assessment of SDI noted that some technologies applicable to BMD could be applied to bomber and cruise defences: "a BMD system does not have to be able to attack aircraft. However, should one be developed, the advantages of also providing it with anti-aircraft capability may be compelling."[12]

That the United States was already looking into the link between BMD and air defence came out during the parliamentary hearings on the 1986 NORAD renewal. DND explained that in the fall of 1982, prior to the initiation of the SDI, the U.S. Department of Defense began the Strategic Defense Architecture 2000 (SDA 2000) studies on the future of integrated defences against bombers, cruise missiles, and ballistic missiles. Canada was involved in Phase I of SDA 2000, which looked primarily at air defence. Phase I was completed in the spring of 1985 and became a long-range planning annex to the ADMP. Canada was not involved in Phase II of SDA 2000, which looked at missile defences. But out of Phase I came the ADI, which is researching new technologies, especially space-based ones, for meeting the air-breathing threat.[13]

Adding to the potential changes in strategy and technology that might affect Canada's role in NORAD were organizational changes to the U.S. command structure relating to aerospace activities. In September 1985, the Pentagon established the USSPACECOM, a unified command drawing on many of the space assets of three services. Among those assets are the U.S. Air Force missile-warning and space-surveillance systems that support NORAD. The commander-in-chief of USSPACECOM was also to serve as commander-in-chief of NORAD. Reorganization of the U.S. side of NORAD seemed at once to put Canada too close to possible BMD involvement via USSPACECOM, yet it also appeared to reduce NORAD to an organization subordinate to the new American unified command (although CINCNORAD remained accountable directly to the Canadian government regardless of his new U.S. command responsibilities).[14] In sum, as the 1986 SCEAND report observed, the "comfortable certainties and familiar assumptions" of North American aerospace defence were being challenged.[15]

All these trends became issues during the 1986 NORAD renewal process when they were publicized in the course of two parliamentary reviews agreed to by the Mulroney government. In the summer of 1985 the Special Joint Committee of the Senate and the House of Commons on Canada's International Relations was asked to review and recommend whether Ottawa should accept the U.S. invitation to co-operate in SDI research. The joint committee's hearings provided a forum for all kinds of opposition to SDI and Canadian involvement. But in the end, the committee was divided on the issue and said it lacked sufficient information to make a recommendation to the government.[16] In September 1985, the Mulroney government decided not to accept the American invitation for official co-operation on SDI. It did, however, call SDI "prudent" and said that private Canadian interests would be free to compete for SDI contracts.

But many of the same issues raised before the special joint committee resurfaced before SCEAND in its review of NORAD. Again parliamentarians heard from arms-control, specialist, and peace groups concerned about possible links with SDI, the impact of SDI on air defence, the command changes in the U.S., and trends in American strategy. Few groups, however, opposed NORAD's existing functions and Canada's role in them. SCEAND also heard extensive testimony from DND officials, both civilian and military, as well as from the U.S. Air Force general who served as CINCNORAD. The result was that these hearings provided a valuable forum to bolster the case for renewal, notwithstanding potential strategic, technological, and organizational changes.

With a Progressive Conservative majority, it was not surprising that SCEAND recommended renewal of NORAD. It rejected recommendations that Canada ask for the reinsertion of the ABM clause, although it did recommend that the Canadian government invite the U.S. government to issue a joint declaration affirming its support for the ABM Treaty. Both the Liberal and NDP committee members issued statements of dissent.

The Mulroney government did not need the support of SCEAND to proceed with renewal and it did not act upon the recommendation about seeking a joint declaration of support for the ABM Treaty. It was not that the government was unaware of the trends in the U.S. that were causing concern in Canada. Testifying before SCEAND, DND's ADM(Pol), John Anderson, acknowledged that even if no BMD systems were deployed in Canada, they would have a profound impact upon Canada–U.S. security relations. They would signal a shift away from the traditional deterrence based on offensive systems toward a posture resting primarily on defensive capabilities. This "could alter the nature of the arrangements necessary in the context of the defence of this continent between Canada and the United States. Canada would, therefore, have to re-examine its place in the overall strategy."[17]

But Anderson and other DND officials argued that it was too soon to tell what the impact of SDI would be, and therefore that NORAD should be renewed in the context of the existing external strategic environment. Moreover, DND argued that the trends cited by critics need not automatically entangle Canada in military undertakings in which it had no interest and with which it did not agree. Indeed, just the opposite could occur. That is, the United States might, because of shifts in strategy and technology, conclude that it no longer needed Canada's participation in continental defence. The SCEAND report echoed this concern when it observed that BMD and related technologies might allow the U.S. to "dispense not only with Canada's geography but with Canada's good will and counsel as well . . . ."[18] This was of particular concern to the Canadian air force, which felt that trends and organizational changes on the U.S. side might eventually make it difficult for Canada to participate in "ventures that should be of interest" to it.[19] These would include space-based radar surveillance, which is now being researched under the ADI.

Thus, despite all the emotion generated by the advent of SDI, the Canadian government found the decision to renew fairly easy. The external strategic environment offered no compelling reason not to renew based on the existing situation and likely changes over the five-year term of the renewal. Strategic, technological, and organizational trends in the United States did suggest problems, but there was still a great deal of uncertainty about the future direction of these trends. If anything, this uncertainty probably persuaded DND that renewal was all the more necessary, because only by remaining within a joint framework for continental defence could Canada keep itself informed on trends that might affect how Washington would approach continental defence against both missiles and air-breathing threats. Continued participation in NORAD would also put Canada in a better position to keep abreast of air-defence technologies that would be of interest to it. For example, the 1987 White Paper announced that Canada would co-operate in ADI, something that would have been difficult had NORAD not been renewed.

In making its decision to renew, cabinet did not consider itself constrained by the domestic environment. Public-opinion polls indicated broad support for continued defence co-operation with the United States,[20] and the public hearings had not brought forth substantial opposition to NORAD itself. For most critics, the real problem was SDI. But the government believed it had already dispensed with the SDI question in its September 1985 decision. The link between SDI and NORAD was a problem for the future, if it was one at all. To have asked the United States for a statement of support for the ABM Treaty merely to appease some interest groups in Canada would hardly have been well received in Washington. Nor would it have meant any appreciable gain in Progressive Conservative popularity, because the general public would neither have understood the meaning of such a joint statement nor credited the Conservatives for obtaining it.

In sum, the NORAD commitment was retained by Canada in 1986 because the government came to the simple conclusion that the agreement still served Canada's interests. The external environment had not altered in such a way as to make either dismantling or significantly changing NORAD, necessary. The domestic environment, although more active than usual, did not generate great pressure for change either. Whether the decision to renew in 1991 will be as easy will depend on the course of external trends evident in 1986, the reaction of domestic groups to those trends and, not least, the political party that will be in power at that time and that will have to make the decision.

The Norwegian Commitment   In the case of the 1986 renewal of the NORAD commitment, the Canadian government made a decision to keep a commitment whose ramifications had touched off considerable public debate. A little over a year later, in the 1987 White Paper, Ottawa announced it was abandoning a commitment that had never generated much interest. For two decades after assuming a role on NATO's northern flank in 1968, the federal government virtually had a free hand in deciding how to fulfil it. This applied not only to the domestic policy environment in Canada, but also to the external environment, which did not have decisive influence on the making, and eventual unmaking, of this Canadian commitment.

At the time of the 1987 White Paper, Canada had several commitments to NATO's northern flank. AIRCOM's 433 Tactical Fighter Squadron, based in Bagotville, Quebec, and 434 Tactical Fighter Squadron, based at Chatham, New Brunswick (both squadrons being re-equipped with CF-18s), were tasked with a rapid-reactor role to northern Norway. One battalion of the Royal Canadian Regiment, based in London, Ontario, was tasked to join other NATO rapid-deployment forces as part of AMF(L). This battalion was to move from Canada to Norway or to Denmark. The 4000-man CAST brigade group based at Valcartier, Quebec, committed to the defence of northern Norway, was slated to be deployed prior to the outbreak of hostilities. Although some of the brigade group's equipment had been pre-positioned, the bulk of it, including helicopters from other Canadian-based units, would have to come by sea. Additional medical and support units were also committed.

This Canadian commitment of ground and air forces to the northern flank and especially to Norway was consistent with NATO's strategy of flexible response. That strategy, adopted in 1967, had placed particular emphasis on the need to bolster deterrence by improving allied conventional capabilities. This included the ability of the alliance to mobilize rapidly and deploy in the face of overt Soviet threats and mobilization. The allies hoped a quick response would persuade the Soviets not to attack, but if war came, the NATO mobilization might deny the Soviets a quick conventional victory and reduce the risk of nuclear escalation.

The need for NATO to move quickly was recognized as being particularly acute on the northern flank, especially in Norway. Here, a NATO ally shares a border with the USSR itself. While Norway maintains a strong military force relative to its size, its defence would require the introduction of allied reinforcements early on—indeed, prior to the outbreak of hostilities. For reasons of prudence and sensitivity, Norway does not allow the stationing of foreign forces on its soil in peacetime.

Not only does Norway confront the USSR directly, but the Soviet Union maintains one of the largest concentrations of air and naval forces in the region, as well as considerable ground forces. Should Norway be overrun, air and naval units would be in a position to dominate the Norwegian Sea and perhaps to threaten allied SLOCs across the Atlantic, thereby jeopardizing the reinforcement of the central front. In a conventional war between NATO and the Warsaw Pact, the loss of Norway might therefore seriously undermine the ability of the alliance to maintain conventional resistance. Even under normal peacetime conditions, the perceived ability of Soviets to cut Norway off in war could undermine the political ties between Norway and the rest of NATO. For deterrence and for assurance, the ability of the allies to reinforce Norway was considered important when Canada assumed its Norwegian commitments in the mid-1960s and became even more so in subsequent years.[21]

It appears, though, that these external considerations were quite secondary in Canada's decision to undertake a role in Norway and to keep it. This was so because the commitments to the northern flank were assumed at a time when Ottawa was actually looking for ways to reduce the burden of its NATO commitments and viewed the reinforcement roles to Norway and Denmark as the least costly alternative to the ground and air forces that comprised CFE in Germany.

The 1964 White Paper had emphasized the need to reduce the heavy armour component of Canada-based forces to allow for the greater mobility required for peacekeeping roles as well as for NATO. Although CFE's air and ground units were retained at their then current strength, Canada did earmark a battalion for the AMF(L) in the north and another for the AMF(L) in the south. But as the Canada-based forces available for NATO began to move to a more mobile and flexible posture, questions arose about their ability to reinforce the ground units in Germany that had retained their heavy-armour role. In 1968, the problem was eliminated through the Trudeau government's termination of Canada's commitment to send heavy reinforcements to Germany by sea.

The CFE reinforcement commitment was replaced by CAST in the fall of 1968. To include the battalion earmarked for the AMF(L), the CAST group was designated for deployment to either Norway or Denmark. The commitment to the AMF(L) south was dropped. Subsequently, Canada did commit two Canada-based air squadrons to the northern flank. These new commitments were, however, assumed at the same time as cutbacks were being made elsewhere in the CF's overall posture. Following the termination of the reinforcement commitment to CFE and its replacement by the CAST commitment, the Trudeau government announced that the air and ground units in Germany would be cut in half. Both were to shed their nuclear weapons, and the ground units were to lose their heavy tanks and be moved off the front line. All of this took place amid a freeze in defence spending and cuts in personnel levels. And the 1971 White Paper shifted defence emphasis from allied roles toward national sovereignty-protection functions for the armed forces.[22]

These changes suggest that the external environment was not the main factor behind the decision to assume an expanded Canadian role on NATO's northern flank. Instead, the Trudeau government was interested in reducing defence spending primarily by reducing the amount of resources allocated to collective-defence roles. Recognizing the symbolic importance of maintaining forces in Germany, the government had not abandoned CFE entirely. The reinforcement commitments assumed in Norway appear to have been similarly politically motivated. They showed the allies that Canadian forces were still going to be dispatched to Europe in the event of war. (This is something that the Europeans worry about a great deal with respect to U.S. forces, but they extend the concern to Canada as well.)

Having made a largely politically motivated commitment, one that was only secondarily related to the strategic importance of the northern flank, the military realities of the role quickly called its wisdom into question. The major concern was the lack of adequate sealift for the CAST brigade group. By 1975 the minister of national defence himself was casting doubt on the CAST brigade's ability to get to Norway and Denmark in a reasonable time after an allied mobilization call. In Denmark, there was a further problem, because there Canada would need heavier armour than planned for the CAST brigade. In 1976 the Denmark deployment option was dropped. Canada also reached agreement with Norway to pre-position some equipment there and to have Norwegian ships transport the rest.

Despite these improvements, DND remained sceptical about the CAST commitment. This was especially true among the military itself, some of whom viewed it as a wholly unsupportable undertaking in the event of war.[23] The problem for Canada was that NATO had come to count on the CAST brigade group as the only external reinforcement specifically earmarked for Norway. The other allied forces planned for the region, such as those of the United States and Britain, might be needed elsewhere. Moreover, with high-quality Canadian personnel supplementing the relatively small numbers of Norwegian forces, a pre-hostilities deployment could have an important deterrent impact and, if necessary, provide for the early defence of Norway. As one U.S. government official put it, the CAST group

> is of the size, training and equipment needed to have a major impact upon the battle and is also experienced in the arctic conditions of northern Norway. It is equipped to survive and fight effectively in that kind of weather and terrain, having a large component of oversnow vehicles. It has significant fire support, anti-armor potential and, unlike most other potential NATO reinforcements, also has some organic air defence.[24]

But by the early 1980s the problem of getting this fine fighting force to Norway on time, and of sustaining it once it was there, persisted. Once a decision was made to reinforce, it would take three to four weeks for the non–pre-positioned equipment to arrive and marry up with the air-lifted troops. An early pre-hostilities movement might improve the situation, but "it is difficult to imagine the Canadian and Norwegian governments agreeing to deploy the CAST three or four weeks in advance of hostilities."[25] The only other solution would be a pre-positioning of all the CAST group's equipment. This, however, would mean that Canada would have to acquire an entire duplicate set of equipment for use in Canada during peacetime. Still another problem with CAST was that one of its battalions was still earmarked for the AMF(L) and might be initially sent to Denmark. The only effective part of Canada's Norwegian commitment was the air component, soon to be enhanced with the acquisition of the CF-18s. The Norwegian role, which had become a politically important symbol of Canada's continued support for NATO, and which, if effective, would also be of strategic significance, had become another element in the commitment–capability gap that plagued the CF.

When it came into office in September 1984 pledging to close this gap, the Mulroney government appeared to support the continuation of the Norwegian commitment. It ended the double-tasking of the battalion that was committed to both the CAST group and the AMF(L), and planned to mount a full-scale exercise—the first ever for this group—of the CAST brigade group. The government also said it would close the gap in CFE, and began by adding 1200 personnel there. It also moved ahead with a new low-level air-defence system, and continued the naval modernization program of the later Trudeau years. All of this, however, was to be accomplished with defence spending increases no greater (and indeed a little smaller) than had been projected by the Liberals before they lost power.[26]

If defence spending was not going to increase significantly, then the commitment–capability gap could be narrowed only by reducing commitments. In the fall of 1985, the Conservative government approached several NATO allies with the suggestion that Canada withdraw its air and ground forces from Germany and concentrate on the northern flank, especially in Norway. The reaction of the Germans, the Americans, and the Norwegians themselves was unanimously negative. Washington and Bonn were both worried that Canada would withdraw actual forces from the politically important central front in exchange for unspecified pledges to reinforce Norway—pledges to which Canada had not lived up previously. The allies were also concerned that the Canadian move would set a precedent for other smaller allies wishing to unburden themselves. For their part, the Norwegians did not want to be in the position of "stealing" Canadian forces from Germany. Nor were they willing to change their stand on foreign basing and allow Canada to station troops permanently in Norway.[27]

Thus rebuffed by the allies, the Mulroney government dropped the idea of consolidating the European commitments in Norway. But the Brave Lion exercise in September

1986, while successful, revealed many continuing difficulties with the CAST commitment.[28] The new MND, Perrin Beatty, who had set out to produce a new White Paper that summer, appeared doubtful about the northern flank commitment, and in this he was supported by a large part of the military bureaucracy.

Without the concurrence of its allies, Canada announced in the 1987 White Paper that it would be terminating its commitments to send the CAST brigade and the two air squadrons to Norway. The battalion commitment to the AMF(L) would be retained and the equipment pre-positioned in Norway would remain for use by this battalion. As explained in the White Paper, Canada could no longer assume two widely spread European commitments, neither of which could be adequately supported in time of war, without spending considerably more on both. Given the existing infrastructure in Germany, it made sense to consolidate there "as the best way to achieve a more credible, effective and sustainable contribution to the common defence in Europe."[29] Thus, the units formerly earmarked for the CAST group, together with the air squadrons, would now be used to reinforce CFE in West Germany.

The decision to end the Norwegian role was made somewhat easier by the fact that it did not entail any new spending. Indeed, it represented a potential saving because something would have to have been done to make the CAST role more effective. There will be additional expenditures in maintaining ground forces in West Germany, especially if the troops already there, as well as the new units earmarked for reinforcement, receive new equipment, particularly tanks. Some of this equipment will have to be pre-positioned in Germany, and additional airlift may be required. But there will be no major increase in Canadian forces based in Germany.

The NATO allies will be waiting to see if Canada takes steps to improve its reinforcement abilities for CFE. Given the shift in emphasis in the White Paper from Europe to maritime and North American defence, they may be concerned that Canada will give lower priority to these improvements than to those involving continental air defence and the navy. But there is little they can do about Canada's decision to withdraw from the Norwegian role despite the fact that the northern flank has not decreased in importance. At the same time, it is recognized that Ottawa is still committed to NATO and its strategies.

What the Norwegian decision shows is that Canada has some leeway in determining how it will contribute to the common defence of Europe. The decision to assume the commitment in 1968 was taken somewhat irrespective of allied wishes and developments in the external strategic environment, as was the decision to withdraw twenty years later. In both instances, Canada was not seeking to abandon NATO, but was rather attempting to cope with the cost of maintaining forces dedicated to the defence of Europe. Of course, Canada could escape these problems by withdrawing entirely from NATO, or by not making forces available in peacetime to the allied commands, or by not making any forces available at all. For many reasons, Canada has decided against these options, and this has constrained defence policy making. Yet, as the case of the Norwegian commitment reveals, even with the determinants of alliance participation and past defence decisions, Canada has room to decide what commitments it will assume and how it will posture its forces to fulfil them.

In making the decision on Norway, the Conservative government did not have to be concerned about the domestic policy environment. Apart from the handful of academics and public-interest groups who watch defence decisions on a regular basis, there was little interest in the problem associated with the CAST commitment. Moreover, even among this group there appeared to be a majority that supported dropping Norway in favour of consolidation in Germany.[30] Since the decision to withdraw from Norway did not involve any new expenditure, nor any reduction in current spending (for example at bases in Canada) there was no domestic financial interest that the government had to consider.

As for the peace and disarmament groups, Norway and the problems of the commitment–capability gap were not the focus of their attention. They concentrated on those aspects of the White Paper that in their view drew Canada too close to U.S. strategies and postures. Thus, the government was given no credit for going against Washington on the Norwegian decision. Instead, the consolidation in Europe was buried in the controversy over the general tone of the White Paper and especially over the decision it announced to acquire nuclear-fuelled submarines. In this sense, the Norwegian decision was typical of commitment and posture choices made by Canadian governments: the public will not react one way or the other unless the decision can be linked to Canada–U.S. relations.

Funding and Procurement Decisions

Funding Decisions Once Ottawa has decided on its broad defence policy objectives and on the particular commitments and roles of the CF that will reflect and serve them, it is confronted with the task of giving some tangible expression to the achievement of these goals. In short, it must provide the resources necessary to staff, train, and equip its armed forces. In the abstract this would appear to be a relatively straightforward matter of determining (1) the missions and activities of the military in order of priority and (2) the most cost-effective combination of personnel, training, logistics support, and equipment needed by the CF to carry out their operational requirements in accordance with the objectives and priorities established by the government.

In practice, however, this has proved to be a far from simple task. Except in time of war, federal governments have resisted needs-based funding for the armed forces, partly because they perceived that it would subject them to constant, open-ended requests from the military for more money to achieve (professionally) credible force postures, and partly because they had to satisfy competing budgetary demands from other departments and agencies. As a result, cabinet has tended to provide the forces with amounts it has deemed both appropriate and affordable in a political sense, rather than with amounts deemed necessary by the forces in a military sense.[31]

Since at least the mid-1960s, what the forces have wanted most has been new weapons and equipment. Between 1964 and 1974 the forces were saddled with an overall budget that remained fairly static (or even slightly declining) in terms of real purchasing power—that is, after allowing for price inflation. Thus, the forces were hard pressed to find the money to replace equipment that had been destroyed or that was becoming obsolescent and costly to maintain. This squeeze on DND's capital funds persisted in spite of drastic reductions in military personnel and some cutbacks in CF operational activities during this period.

Part of the problem lay with the manner in which cabinet chose to determine DND's budget levels. Eschewing a needs-based approach, since 1966 cabinet has resorted to a formula-approach to Canadian defence funding. Essentially, this formula approach sought to generate real increases in defence funding through pre-determined percentage increases either in DND's overall budget or in specific components of that budget. In practice, the capital component (equipment, construction, and research and development) was singled out for the greatest percentage increase. By seeking to boost capital spending to about 20-25 percent of total defence expenditures, cabinet and DND hoped to rectify the recognized deficiencies in the CF's equipment inventory.

Unfortunately, the early formula plans fell victim to rapidly rising rates of inflation, sharply escalating costs of modern weapons systems, and steadily increasing costs of staffing, operating, and maintaining Canada's military establishment. As a result, instead of expanding, the capital component continued its downward slide as a percentage of total DND spending. Moreover, through the cumulative effect of years of capital underfunding, each of the service environments had a lengthy and growing list of badly needed equipment replacements, and each was advancing its own funding claims on a beleaguered NDHQ staff. Thus, by late 1974 the forces were facing a re-equipment crisis of major proportions.

In December 1974 cabinet instituted the Defence Structure Review to provide broad policy for defence planners, establish priorities among the CF's competing equipment requirements, and address DND's funding difficulties. Defence Minister James Richardson announced the results of Phases I and II of the DSR in November 1975, as follows: a government reaffirmation of the four main roles of the CF as set out in the 1971 White Paper on Defence; the maintenance of existing manpower levels; a commitment to a substantial equipment modernization and replacement program; and cabinet acceptance of the need to provide more realistic and stable funding for the forces.[32]

With respect to the last point, cabinet had approved an interim-funding formula whereby the POM component of the defence budget would be allowed annual increases sufficient to offset the effect of inflation. To finance the new re-equipment program, the capital portion of DND's budget would be increased annually by 12 percent in real terms (indexed for inflation) for a five-year period beginning in the fiscal year 1977-78. The goal was to stabilize POM expenditures at existing staffing levels, while permitting capital expenditures to rise to about 20 percent of DND's total budget to enable the CF to replace and upgrade their depleted equipment holdings.

Through this differential indexing formula, the government hoped to remedy the major shortcoming of previous formula plans—inadequate compensation for inflation in the capital component of the budget. Provided that successive cabinets honoured the new funding formula, DND would have a more stable and predictable basis for planning and programming to meet the CF's pressing re-equipment needs.

The Canadian Patrol Frigate Procurement Decisions In his announcement, Richardson had indicated that the government would purchase 18 Lockheed LRPA and would begin immediate negotiations to acquire modern tanks either by retrofit (upgrading) or by new acquisitions. While the procurement of the LRPA would enhance MARCOM's ASW and sovereignty-protection capabilities, the MND's announcement left the issue of future ship acquisitions unresolved. In January 1976, however, the CDS, General J.A. Dextraze, announced that DND had begun to examine the detailed requirements for a new fighter aircraft and a ship-replacement program (SRP).[33]

For MARCOM, the funding and SRP announcements were welcome news. Following World War II, the RCN had continued to develop as a specialized ASW force. The Korean War provided the catalyst for a dramatic expansion in the size of the RCN, with the majority of its ships being dedicated to ASW and convoy-escort roles in support of NATO, with some additional capacity for harbour and coastal defence, and Arctic operations.[34] Nevertheless, from its zenith in the late 1950s, the navy waged a steadily losing battle to maintain the size and type of fleet it had acquired as a result of the Korean expansion.

By 1957 mounting personnel costs, combined with increasing operating and maintenance costs, had begun to squeeze the RCN's fleet structure and operations as the navy's budget went into a steady decline. The navy continued to build ASW ships—which reached a postwar high total of 43 in 1964—but had to give up its only icebreaker and its two cruisers in an effort to cut costs. The result was an increasingly ASW-specialized fleet and a navy facing a growing shortage of capital funds.

An in-house naval study in 1961 attempted to reverse the trend toward an exclusively ASW-oriented fleet. The Brock Report emphasized the need for a more versatile, balanced, general-purpose fleet and advocated a "small, cheap, and many" concept for future naval acquisitions. The report was accepted for planning purposes by the navy, the military chiefs of staff, MND Douglas Harkness, and eventually by the cabinet and Treasury Board. On 11 April 1962 Harkness announced the government's approval of the acquisition of eight new, general-purpose frigates along with three British-built, diesel-electric submarines.

Following the change in government in 1963, however, the new Liberal MND, Paul Hellyer, initiated a review of all major defence procurement programs. Following this review, and despite an energetic defence of the navy's aspirations for a broader, multipurpose capability by the Chief of the Naval Staff, Vice-Admiral Rayner, Hellyer cancelled the general-purpose frigate program on cost-effectiveness grounds. Obviously, the navy was feeling the impact of general budgetary pressures on the overall defence budget. But, in addition, Hellyer's 1964 White Paper on Defence made it clear that the government considered ASW to be the primary role of the navy in support of Canada's NATO commitments. In December 1964 the Liberal government announced its intention to acquire four helicopter-carrying destroyer escorts—the DDH-280 program. Despite soaring cost escalation during their construction in Canada, these destroyers were eventually commissioned by 1973 and became the last major warships to enter the fleet.

By 1976 the Canadian navy had been reduced in size to four modern destroyers, 16 aging steam-driven destroyers (plus three on reserve status), three conventionally powered submarines, and three underway replenishment vessels. In addition, sharply rising personnel costs in the early 1970s had squeezed MARCOM's capital expenditures to a mere eight percent in 1975, a postwar low. Clearly, the navy was in desperate need of new ships.

But how many ships and of what type? Following the DSR, naval planners began to consider the appropriate fleet structure required to meet Canada's maritime commitments. The navy regarded inadequate numbers of ships as its most pressing problem. An in-depth study of future warship requirements determined that Canada should continue to participate in collective maritime-defence arrangements "at current levels."[35] Thus, the navy proposed a one-for-one replacement of the existing steam-driven destroyers as they came to the end of their operational life. Given the long lead times in naval ship-procurement programs (seven to ten years from concept to acquisition), the navy believed it had to stake out a firm claim to future defence funds now that its turn had come in the funding queue. In this context, a 20-ship program appeared to be a reasonable request, at least from the navy's standpoint.

The DSR had reaffirmed the basic roles of the CF as set out in the 1971 White Paper, so this was an obvious point of departure for naval planning. According to the White Paper, in the future MARCOM would give a higher priority to surveillance and control tasks for the protection of Canadian national interests, and less emphasis to ASW directed against ballistic missile-carrying submarines. Echoing the 1961 Brock Report, it also stated that "the Government believes Canada's maritime forces must be reoriented with the long term objective of providing a more versatile general purpose capability."[36]

However, if approved, the navy's plan to replace existing destroyers with similar types of ships would mean that MARCOM would continue its traditional ASW roles, largely within a NATO context. A later "Future Ship Study" confirmed that the navy rejected the "small and cheap" idea and preferred to meet the government's sovereignty surveillance and enforcement role "by multiple tasking fully combat capable ships maintained for the more demanding missions" associated with collective defence.[37] These missions required ASW, anti-air warfare (AAW), and surface-to-surface warfare (SSW) capabilities for surface ships of the kind the navy was considering.[38]

In keeping with their service preferences, the navy staffs interpreted the objectives of the 1971 White Paper and the 1975 DSR in such a way that NATO ASW roles and missions would determine both the numbers and types of ships to be included in the navy's ship-replacement program.

DND developed a plan to achieve its replacement program in phases. Earlier navy studies had shown that to attempt to combine the two most demanding and "system-intensive" capabilities of ASW and AAW into a single platform would result in too large and costly a ship. Therefore DND decided to build different classes of the same basic type of ship to deal separately with the ASW and AAW tasks. Because the six existing St. Laurent steam destroyers were nearing the end of their operational lives, DND decided to replace them first with six ASW patrol frigates. These would be followed by another batch of six ASW CPFs, and then a batch of eight AAW frigates. DND also reasoned that phasing the different classes of ships into smaller batches would make the entire SRP more financially manageable for the cabinet.[39] However, this approach would also leave the program vulnerable to political and other pressures as each batch came before cabinet for approval.

For planning purposes, both DND and cabinet accepted the navy's proposal to operate a fleet of 24 fully capable surface ships. On 22 December 1977 the MND, Barney Danson, announced the government's approval-in-principle for DND to proceed with the first phase of a long-term ship-replacement program. Initially, this would involve the acquisition of six ships costing a total of $1.5 billion (in 1977 dollars), with construction of the lead ship to begin in 1981 and be completed by 1985; the rest of the contracts would be awarded by 1983, with all ships phased in by 1989.[40] To this end, cabinet authorized $63 million for a project-definition study for Phase I of the SRP.

An interdepartmental CPF Project Management Office was established in 1978, and, on August 1, issued a request for proposals inviting submissions from suitably qualified contractors for the design and development of six fully supported ships. The government stipulated that the ships had to be built in Canada, but imposed no restrictions on foreign participation. It also reserved the right to consider procurement abroad if the Canadian bidders could not stay within the cabinet's program-cost ceilings. The proposals had to satisfy two main criteria: the enhancement of the long-term viability of Canadian program-management and electronic-systems integration, and maximum participation for Canadian industry. Five companies and consortia responded by January 1979, and in April 1979 the project office recommended two finalists to DND for the funded contract definition stage.

However, the evaluation of the proposals was disrupted by the change in government in June 1979. Although DND's recommendations were forwarded to the new Progressive Conservative cabinet in late summer 1979, they could not be considered until cabinet had reached a final decision on the controversial NFA procurement program, which had also been held up by the transition of government. Further delays were caused by yet another change of government in March 1980, and by an extension granted to three groups to add more Canadian content to their proposals. On 8 December 1980, two finalists were selected: Saint John Shipbuilding and Dry Dock Company Limited (Saint John, New Brunswick) and SCAN Marine (Longueuil, Quebec). After extensive negotiations with both finalists on how they intended to conduct the next phase of the CPF project, in July

1981 the government awarded them contracts totalling $39.4 million to develop detailed proposals for the design, systems integration, construction, tests and trials, and life-cycle support of the ships.

This was a massive and complex undertaking, and in several respects represented a significant departure from other major Canadian defence-procurement programs. From the outset, the government wanted more than warships; it sought "to introduce a new strategy for the procurement of naval vessels and, at the same time, to advance the objective of Canadianization."[41]

To achieve these goals, the project definition process established several conditions for the CPF project. First, unlike the LRPA, NFA, and tank acquisitions, the six ships were to be designed and built in Canada. Second, a Canadian contractor would provide the overall program management. This decision to farm the work out to Canadian industry reflected the government's appreciation that, after such a long hiatus between shipbuilding programs, the navy had effectively lost its ability to design warships and manage their construction. In effect, for the first time, the navy was reduced to the status of a simple customer, albeit one with some monitoring responsibilities.[42] Third, the program was to help establish a Canadian industrial capacity to manage the integration of comparable large-scale projects, especially in the area of electronic-systems integration. Finally, the program was to create large and widespread economic and regional development benefits for Canadian industry, again with a special focus on the enhancement of a Canadian high-technology electronics capability.[43]

Each contractor's "implementation proposals and offers" were submitted on 2 October 1982 and were evaluated by an interdepartmental team that included representatives from the departments of National Defence, Supply and Services, Regional Industrial Expansion, Justice, Manpower, Employment and Immigration, and the Ministry of State for Science and Technology. After lengthy consideration by the project team and cabinet, the government finally awarded the CPF contract to Saint John Shipbuilding and Dry Dock Company on 29 June 1983.

Saint John won the contract partly because it proposed a lower overall cost to the government—a total project target price of $2.584 billion and a total project ceiling price of $3.020 billion (in 1983/84 dollars). (These were later amended to $3.414 billion and $3.850 billion respectively.) In addition,

Saint John proposed a very comprehensive procurement and industrial benefits package.

As part of the Saint John consortium, the U.S.-based Sperry Incorporated agreed to transfer its electronic-systems-integration and systems-management technology, as well as world product mandates in several high-technology fields, to a new Canadian-owned subsidiary, PARAMAX Electronics, which would be located in Montreal. Two other Canadian-owned companies, SED Systems of Saskatoon and Leigh Instruments Limited of Carleton Place, Ontario, would provide other major subsystems.

But perhaps most important, Saint John agreed to split the actual ship construction work while retaining overall management responsibility for the program. Three ships would be built in New Brunswick, while the other three would be built in two different yards in Quebec. This concession not only satisfied the government's stated goal of spreading the CPF industrial benefits across the country, but also satisfied the traditional (albeit unstated) political requirement that Quebec should receive a major share of any major defence procurement contract.

Indeed, from the start, the government had made it clear that it was seeking the maximum possible industrial benefits from the program. To this end, Saint John had agreed that two-thirds of the target-price value of the contract would be supplied by Canadian firms, and that foreign suppliers of the remaining one-third would be required to provide an equivalent value of industrial offset work in Canada. The value of industrial benefits was expected to total $2.42 billion with regional distribution as follows: Atlantic, 26 percent; Quebec, 40 percent; Ontario, 27 percent; and the West, 6.5 percent. These benefits would produce at least 30 000 person-years of work across Canada.

Under the terms of the 1983 contract, construction of the lead ship was to begin in July 1985, and it was to be delivered for operational duties in February 1989. Delivery of all remaining ships was to be completed by March 1992. This was a demanding schedule, and even if met, it would put the CPF program some three years behind the completion date announced by Danson in 1977.

The program soon encountered a number of serious problems that threatened to cause further delays. These problems could in large part be attributed to the fact that the Canadian shipbuilding industry had not received a major naval construction contract in well over a decade. There were simply not enough skilled workers in Canada to undertake such a vast project. The Saint John design team found it difficult to produce the many highly detailed drawings required for the modern "zone construction" techniques developed earlier by American and European shipbuilders. PARAMAX also found itself spending huge amounts of money and time to train Canadian electrical engineers, computer programmers, and combat-systems engineers, rather than hiring Americans to do the work. Management problems and discord at Saint John led to the resignation of its president and the hiring of senior management consultants from a U.S. company, Bath Iron Works, for project planning and design engineering. Later, Saint John's CPF program manager was replaced by a former U.S. shipyard executive.

The new management team regarded the original CPF delivery schedule as virtually impossible to meet and sought to obtain a revised and more realistic one from the government throughout 1985 and 1986. A shipment of corroded steel was discovered early in 1986, and this too threatened to delay the construction program.

But the government's insistence on "Canadianization" may create problems in the CPF program beyond those involved in overcoming the shortage of skilled managers and workers. By splitting the construction contract among three different yards, the government virtually ensured that the same problems would be repeated later at the Quebec yards. Moreover, DND estimated that the split contract would add an extra $58 million to the program's cost. The full potential learning-curve saving of time and money could only be realized if Phases II and III of the SRP went ahead, and the contracts were awarded to the same contractors. Indeed, this was an important rationale for the "Canadianization" approach in the first place.

However, beginning in 1980, and despite repeated assurances from politicians and other government officials that approval of a follow-on program was imminent, the fate of Phase II of the SRP was to remain uncertain for a long time. Indeed, cabinet approval for the procurement of another batch of six CPF-type ships was not announced until 18 December 1987. The reason for the long delay was a familiar one: there were too many demands on too few defence dollars.

During the 1980s, both the Liberal and Conservative parties favoured a continuation of the frigate program. Yet once in power, both refused to approve the required funding. Confronted with rapidly expanding deficits and continuing demands from social and economic development programs, governments in Ottawa had found it difficult to honour consistently their post-1978 pledges to NATO to increase defence spending by at least three percent annually in real terms.

Despite some steady increases in DND's budget, defence planners encountered cash-flow problems in trying to incorporate several large procurement programs into the DSP at the same time; the CF-18 and CPF I programs consumed the major share of the capital funds available. In addition, in order to keep the navy's modest fleet operational, DND had to resort to a number of expensive stopgap measures (the Destroyer Life Extension Program, the Submarine Operational Update Program, and the Tribal Update and Modernization Program). All of this required money, and because no significant infusions of additional capital funds were forthcoming for major new programs, Phase II of SRP had to be deferred.

However, given the run-down state of the Canadian navy, the follow-on program could not be delayed forever. Perrin Beatty's 1987 White Paper acknowledged the deteriorated capabilities of the navy, and promised "a vigorous naval modernization program" to rectify a condition that was truly approaching the stage of "rust-out."[44] As part of this modernization effort, the government would acquire six more CPFs.

The knowledge that the cabinet would be selecting the contractor before the end of the year sparked a flurry of energetic provincial lobbying. Citing the need to promote regional economic development and to alleviate the high unemployment rates in the area, the three Maritime premiers sent a telegram to Prime Minister Mulroney urging that the entire six-ship construction contract be awarded to Saint John Shipbuilding.[45] Daniel Johnson, Quebec's minister of industry, raised the spectre of massive layoffs in the province's shipyards if Quebec did not receive contracts for at least two of the frigates.[46]

In the end, in December 1987 cabinet decided to award the entire six-ship follow-on frigate program to Saint John Shipbuilding. The government reasoned that, as a result of the original CPF contract, Saint John and PARAMAX had established the necessary resources and infrastructure to manage the construction program. Thus it was most economical to concentrate construction at the one yard by way of a relatively simple $2.7 billion amendment to the original contract. MND Beatty claimed that it would cost more than $200 million to split the contract.

With this decision came further changes that appear to have marked the end of the SRP, at least as it was originally conceived in the mid-1970s. While there may ultimately be more frigates built in the next century, Phase III of the SRP, which involved AAW variants of the CPF, has been superseded by the nuclear-powered submarine program announced in the 1987 White Paper. However, it has been reported that the navy is exploring the possibility of expanding the CPF design for SRP II to make room for future equipment changes, including the addition of more vertically launched AAW missiles.[47] While this would likely entail the need for costly design changes, it represents an attempt by the navy to salvage part of the original SRP III mission concept.

The experience of the Canadian Patrol Frigate program demonstrates the influence of, and the intimate interrelationships among, the three environments of Canadian defence decision making. The external environment played its greatest role in establishing the basic CPF requirement. Canada's long-standing commitment to contribute to NATO's maritime collective-defence missions provided the essential rationale for some form of ship-replacement program in the first place. Moreover, Canada's NATO allies supported the program as a necessary, but modest, step in the right direction toward restoring the navy's eroded capabilities. The CPFs would help to counter the growing Soviet submarine threat to NATO's vital SLOCs, especially at a time when the alliance was becoming aware of the need to prepare for a longer conventional war. Finally, the fact that the Canadian navy had become specialized in ASW operations for NATO was a major factor in determining the CPF's design concept.

The CPF case also shows just how important the federal government can be in funding and procurement decision making. Cabinet involvement was high in setting the terms of reference of the CPF procurement program. Many departments other than DND were involved in establishing the objectives of the program and in evaluating the bids. Their influence was clearly reflected in the great importance attached to the "Canadianization" and industrial-benefits aspects of the contract definition process. Cabinet's requirement that the ships be built in Canada rather than purchased abroad, and that the construction work be split among different yards, added to the overall costs and contributed to the delays that ensued. The many changes in government as the result of elections also caused significant disruptions and delays in both phases of the frigate program.

Funding proved to be an intractable problem. The inadequacies of the early funding formulas created a backlog of major defence equipment-acquisition programs all requiring urgent attention. But, given the competing pressures of other social programs, no government was prepared to commit itself to the dramatic increases in defence spending that would be required to accommodate all of DND's re-equipment needs. Instead, the cabinet turned the problem of living within modest financial means over to the military. Through the DSR in 1975, DND had to sort out its own procurement priorities, and the navy's SRP was not at the top of the list.

However, the CPF case showed the extent to which the navy planners could reinterpret cabinet's general policy objectives to suit their service interests. In formulating the design requirement for the CPF, the navy downgraded the sovereignty-protection role in favour of the more demanding ASW mission in support of traditional Canadian maritime collective-defence roles. Nevertheless, this case also reveals the difficulties the military faces in trying to plan and manage large, complicated procurement programs with long lead times in a climate of severe funding constraint. Delays appear to be inevitable. These delays in turn provide the political executive with opportunities to alter the planning basis of the procurement program, sometimes in fundamental ways. The Conservative government's 1987 decision to replace the original SRP III with the SSN program is a case in point.

The domestic environment appears to have exerted the least direct influence on the CPF decisions, although the CPF case may be atypical in this respect. Unlike some major defence procurement decisions (Arrow, Bomarc, and SSN), the CPF decisions were not the subject of great public controversy. Canadian peace groups did not mount campaigns against the frigate program and industrial groups favoured it. Parliamentary involvement was limited, and the 1983 Senate committee's *Report on Canada's Maritime Defence* supported the need for SRP I and II. Both the Liberals and the Progressive Conservatives supported the CPF program, and in its response to the 1987 White Paper, the NDP indicated that it might consider a third batch of six frigates.

Nevertheless, as might be expected in any major defence procurement program, the CPF decisions did generate some provincial squabbling over the distribution of industrial benefits. The decision to divide the construction contract for the first six ships shows just how hard it is for cabinet to ignore the special demands of various regions and industrial groups. But the CPF case also demonstrates how DND's procurement programs can suffer from the shortcomings of Canada's defence industrial base. Yet, as certain regions and industrial sectors become dependent on defence contracts, a domestic constituency is created for a continuing flow of procurement programs. In this respect at least, the predominantly naval orientation of the 1987 White Paper will help to create powerful vested interests in support of the forces' ongoing re-equipment program.

Notes

1. Canada, Department of National Defence, *Defence in the 70s* (Ottawa: Information Canada, 1971), pp. 6, 29–30.

2. John M. Collins, *U.S.–Soviet Military Balance, 1980–1985* (New York: Pergamon-Brassey's, 1985), p. 154. See also Joel J. Sokolsky, "Changing Strategies, Technologies and Organization: The Continuing Debate on NORAD and the Strategic Defense Initiative," *Canadian Journal of Political Science* 19, no. 4 (December 1986): 751–74.

3. John Hamre, "Continental Air Defence, the United States Security Policy and Canada–United States Defence Relations," in *Aerospace Defence: Canada's Future Role?* ed. G.R. Lindsey et al., Wellesley Papers 9 (Toronto: Canadian Institute of International Affairs, 1985), p. 22.

4. Canada, House of Commons, SCEAND, *Canada–U.S. Defence Cooperation and the 1986 Renewal of the NORAD Agreement* (1986), pp. 30–31.

5. Douglas Ross, "American Nuclear Revisionism, Canadian Strategic Interests and the Renewal of NORAD," *Behind the Headlines* 39, no. 6 (April 1982). On trends in U.S. strategy, see Jeffrey Richelson, "PD-59, NSDD-13, and the Reagan Strategic Modernization Program," *Journal of Strategic Studies* 6, no. 2 (June 1983): 125–46. On SDI, see Steven E. Miller and Stephen Van Evera, eds., *The Star Wars Controversy* (Princeton, N.J.: Princeton University Press, 1986).

6. On the earlier ABM debate in the United States, see *Anti-Ballistic Missile: Yes or No?*, A Special Report from the Center for the Study of Democratic Institutions (New York: Hill and Wang, 1968).

7. On U.S. ABM development before SDI, see Steven W. Guerrier, "Looking Back: Strategic Defense and U.S. National Security," in *Perspectives on Strategic Defense*, eds. Steven W. Guerrier, Wayne C. Thompson (Boulder, Colo.: Westview, 1987).

8. *Agreement Between Canada and the United States of America,* Canada Treaty Series 1968, no. 5, p. 2.

9. SCEAND, *Canada-U.S. Defence Cooperation and the 1986 Renewal of NORAD,* p. 20.

10. SCEAND, *Canada-U.S. Defence Cooperation,* p. 62. See also James A. Everard, "Canada and NORAD: The Eroding Agreement," *Journal of the Royal United Services Institute* 127 (1984), p. 21.

11. United States, Department of Defense, *Report to Congress on the Strategic Defense Initiative* (Washington: 1985), p. C-21.

12. United States, Congress, Office of Technology Assessment, *Strategic Defenses: Ballistic Missile Technologies* (Princeton, N.J.: Princeton University Press, 1986), pp. 191-92.

13. David Cox, *Trends in Continental Defence: A Canadian Perspective,* Occasional Papers, no. 2 (Ottawa: Canadian Institute for International Peace and Security, 1986), p. 29.

14. Cox, *Trends in Continental Defence,* pp. 32-34.

15. SCEAND, *Canada-U.S. Defence Cooperation,* p. xi.

16. Canada, Special Joint Committee on Canada's International Relations, *Interim Report Pertaining to Bilateral Trade with the United States and Canada's Participation in Research on the Strategic Defense Initiative* Ottawa, 23 August 1985, p. 118.

17. Canada, House of Commons, SCEAND, *Minutes of Proceedings and Evidence,* Issue no. 52, 6 December 1985, p. 52:6.

18. SCEAND *Canada-U.S. Defence Cooperation,* p. xi.

19. SCEAND, *Minutes of Proceedings and Evidence,* Issue no. 52, 6 December 1985, p. 52:11.

20. On public opinion polls conducted by the Department of External Affairs in 1985, see P.H. Chapin, "The Canadian Public and Foreign Policy," *International Perspectives* (January/February 1986), pp. 14-16.

21. For the strategic situation along the northern flank, see: Johan J. Holst et al., eds., *Deterrence and Defence in the North* (Oslo: Norwegian University Press, 1985); Erling Bjol, "Nordic Security," *Adelphi Papers* 181 (Spring 1983); John C. Ausland, *Nordic Security and the Great Powers* (Boulder, Colo.: Westview, 1986); and Paul M. Cole and Douglas M. Hart, eds., *Northern Europe: Security for the 1990s* (Boulder, Colo.: Westview, 1986).

22. Joseph T. Jockel, *Canada and NATO's Northern Flank* (Toronto: Centre for International and Strategic Studies, York University, 1986), pp. 20-22.

23. Jockel, *Canada and NATO's Northern Flank,* p. 42.

24. Jon L. Lellenberg, "The Military Balance," in *Deterrence and Defence in the North,* eds. Johan J. Holst, et al., p. 61.

25. Ausland, *Nordic Security,* p. 137.

26. R.B. Byers, "Canadian Security and Defence: The Legacy and the Challenges," *Adelphi Papers* 214 (Winter 1986), p. 43. See also Joel J. Sokolsky, "Canadian Defence Policy: Coping with the Gap," in *Canada Among Nations 1986: Talking Trade,* eds. Brian W. Tomlin and Maureen A. Molot (Toronto: James Lorimer, 1987).

27. See Sokolsky, "Canadian Defence Policy: Coping With the Gap," pp. 60-61 and Jockel, *Canada and NATO's Northern Flank,* pp. 26-28.

28. On Brave Lion, see Lieutenant-Colonel G.D. Hunt, "Reinforcing the NATO North Flank: The Canadian Experience," *Canadian Defence Quarterly* 16, no. 4 (April 1987): 31–38.

29. Canada, Department of National Defence, *Challenge and Commitment: A Defence Policy for Canada* (Ottawa: Supply and Services Canada, 1986), p. 61.

30. See, for example, R.B. Byers et al., *Canada and Western Security: The Search for New Options* (Toronto: Atlantic Council of Canada, 1982), pp. 36–37. For an argument in favour of consolidating in Norway, see Joseph T. Jockel and Joel J. Sokolsky, *Canada and Collective Security: Odd Man Out*, The Washington Papers, no. 121 (New York: Praeger, 1986), pp. 80–94.

31. This section on Canadian defence funding is drawn primarily from the following sources: Dan Middlemiss, "Paying for National Defence: The Pitfalls of Formula Funding," *Canadian Defence Quarterly* 12, no. 3 (Winter 1982/83): 24–29; R.B. Byers, "Canadian Security and Defence: The Legacy and the Challenges," *Adelphi Papers* 214 (Winter 1986), pp. 31–34; and R.B. Byers, "Canadian Defence and Defence Procurement: Implications for Economic Policy," in *Selected Problems in Formulating Foreign Economic Policy*, eds. Denis Stairs and Gilbert R. Winham (Toronto: University of Toronto Press, 1985), pp. 140–52.

32. Canada, Parliament, House of Commons, *Debates*, 27 November 1975, pp. 9502–03.

33. General J.A. Dextraze, "A New Era for Canada's Armed Forces," *Statements and Speeches*, no. 76/3, 16 January 1976.

34. For the historical background on the development of the Canadian navy, see Sharon Hobson *The Composition of Canada's Naval Fleet, 1946–85* (Halifax: Centre for Foreign Policy Studies, Dalhousie University, 1986); Danford W. Middlemiss, "Economic Considerations in the Development of the Canadian Navy since 1945," in *The RCN in Transition: Challenge and Response, 1910–1985*, ed. W.A.B. Douglas (Vancouver: University of British Columbia Press, forthcoming); G.M. Dillon, *Canadian Naval Policy since World War II: A Decision-Making Analysis*, Occasional Paper (Halifax: Centre for Foreign Policy Studies, Dalhousie University, October 1972); and articles in James A. Boutilier, ed., *RCN in Retrospect, 1910–1968* (Vancouver: University of British Columbia Press, 1982).

35. Canada, House of Commons, SCEAND, *Minutes of Proceedings and Evidence*, Issue no. 31, Appendix "EAND-20," 19 March 1981, p. 4. In fact, the study had concluded that some 30 ships would be needed to carry out fully Canada's maritime defence tasks in the Atlantic and Pacific in wartime. However, in view of future funding forecasts and the existing level of infrastructure support, the study recommended that "a fleet of 24 fully combat capable surface vessels would realistically meet Canada's collective defence requirements."

36. Canada, Department of National Defence, *Defence in the 70s* (Ottawa: Information Canada, 1971), p. 28.

37. Canada, DND, *Defence in the 70s*, p. 5.

38. Lieutenant Commander R.F. Archer, "The Canadian Patrol Frigate," *Canadian Defence Quarterly* 14, no. 2 (Autumn 1984): 15.

39. Archer, "The Canadian Patrol Frigate," p. 15.

40. Remarks by the Honourable Barney Danson, "Announcement by the Minister of National Defence on the DND Ship Replacement Program," Ottawa, DND, 22 December 1977.

41. Canada, Department of National Defence, "Background Information: Canadian Patrol Frigate Project," Ottawa, 29 June 1983, p. 5.

42. Archer, "The Canadian Patrol Frigate," p. 13

43. Canada, Department of National Defence, "Background Information: Canadian Patrol Frigate Project," p. 5.

44. Canada, Department of National Defence, *Challenge and Commitment: A Defence Policy for Canada*, pp. 45, 51.

45. "N.B. wants frigate contract", *Globe and Mail*, 9 December 1987, p. A9.

46. Sarah Scott, "Shipyards dead without frigate work: Johnson", *The Gazette*, 2 December 1987, p. A5.

47. "Quebec shipyard reorganizing for frigate work", *Financial Post*, 8 February 1988, p. 51. It should be noted that the approved CPFs do possess anti-air self-defence capabilities. However, these ships cannot provide area anti-defence for other vessels.

8

CONCLUSIONS:
DECISIONS AND
DETERMINANTS

Alignment, Alliances, and Strategies: The Fundamental Decisions

Canada, like all nation states, even the superpowers, must shape its defence policy in the context of an anarchic international system where there is no supranational authority to guarantee each country's security and where, therefore, the decisions of other states, both friend and foe, will impose constraints on the choices available. In the nuclear age, for relatively modest middlepowers like Canada, the constraints often seem overwhelming, leaving little, if any, room for choice. The greatest threat to Canadian security is a nuclear war between the superpowers, the catastrophic consequences of which Canada could not hope to escape. This threat would exist regardless of the level of Canadian military spending or the nature of its alliance commitments. In this, though, Canada is not entirely unique. Most of the world, especially the nations of the north, are in a similar situation.

Yet, Canada's strategic outlook is not that of an impotent middlepower that sees itself as caught between two equally threatening giants. Since the beginning of the Cold War, successive Canadian governments have regarded some sort of Soviet aggression, or threat of aggression, as likely to endanger global stability and, perhaps, global peace. This perception, coupled with historical ties, common democratic values, economic interests, and cultural affinity, drew Canada toward alliance with the United States and the West Europeans. To be sure, Ottawa has from time to time been concerned about the threat posed by American actions and overreactions to Soviet activities. But the foreign policy of Canada, and hence its defence policy, has proceeded from the fundamental decision to align with the West. From this decision flowed other decisions. Regarding Europe as the most likely arena for Soviet aggression, and insecurity in Europe as detrimental to global peace, Canada promoted the creation of NATO in 1949. Recognizing U.S. concerns about a Soviet bomber threat and wishing to provide for its own air sovereignty, Canada co-operated with the United States in the integration of North American air defences, eventually leading to the establishment of NORAD in 1958.

In aligning with the United States and in committing itself to two American-dominated international military organizations, Canada implicitly adopted the basic military strategies of the West as the basis of its own defence policy. The cornerstone of those strategies, and hence of Canadian security, was nuclear deterrence, and the means to this end were the strategic nuclear weapons of the United States. With the growth in Soviet strategic nuclear capabilities, the security of the West came to be identified with the maintenance of a secure American second-strike force, making mutual assured destruction the most likely outcome of a nuclear war that began with a Soviet first strike against the West.

During the 1950s Canada directly supported the maintenance of the nuclear deterrent in two ways: by co-operating with the United States in the air defence of North America, especially against a Soviet first strike that might destroy the U.S. retaliatory capability, and by providing airfields for U.S. strategic bombers. With the advent of ICBMs, Canada's importance in both these roles declined as the Soviet bomber threat diminished and as the United States no longer required bases in Canada for its bombers. Although it is now of lesser significance, Canadian participation in NORAD still involves Canada in maintaining the credibility of the American strategic nuclear deterrent insofar as it provides for warning of air and ballistic missile threats.

Not only has Canada recognized the role of nuclear deterrence in the defence of North America, it has supported the extension of the American nuclear guarantee to overseas allies, especially those in Europe. Canada identifies its security with that of Western Europe and has chosen its defence policies accordingly. But in doing so, Canadian governments have based the European part of their defence policy on nuclear weapons as well. This has led to Canadian support for the deployment of tactical and theatre nuclear weapons in Europe. (And, in the 1960s, for U.S.-supplied nuclear warheads for its own air and ground forces.) Such weapons are viewed as deterring not only a Soviet nuclear attack, but also any possible conventional attack. Over the years, Ottawa has thus lent its support to NATO's position of not disavowing the option of the first use of nuclear weapons. Canada has also supported the view that the presence of American nuclear weapons in addition to ground forces in Europe serves to reinforce extended deterrence and assures the Europeans that their security is coupled with that of the United States.

From the mid-1960s, NATO has attempted to base its defence on a broader range of capabilities, especially in conventional forces. Flexible response began as an American initiative and has always been viewed somewhat warily in Europe because of its possible decoupling implications. And whereas the United States tends to see conventional and tactical-theatre nuclear weapons as rungs on an escalation ladder, the Europeans see such weapons, especially the nuclear ones, as fast-moving steps on an escalator, presenting the Soviets with the near-certainty of strategic nuclear war should they attack at any level. The Europeans maintain conventional forces in order to secure the American nuclear guarantee. Therefore, while flexible response may be no more than an agreement to disagree on strategy, it has, nevertheless, resulted in the maintenance of substantial Western conventional forces. Canada, which shares some of the U.S. concern about the credibility of a deterrent posture that rests too heavily on strategic nuclear weapons, yet which also shares some of the European concerns about decoupling, has generally found flexible response to be a satisfactory framework within which to structure allied strategy. It represents the kind of consensus, however ambiguous, that keeps the allies allied.

Given its support for strategic nuclear deterrence and flexible response, there is very little scope for an independent Canadian strategy. And to this extent, defence policy decisions do not involve the selection of alternative strategies for confronting the Soviet Union and its Warsaw Pact allies. Having aligned itself with the West, having formally allied itself through NATO and NORAD with the United States, and having thereby subscribed to certain approaches to national security in the nuclear age, Canada has already made its fundamental strategic decisions.

This does not mean that Canada accepts each and every variation or trend in U.S. strategic thinking. There are, for example, concerns about the Strategic Defense Initiative, and about certain trends in U.S. antisubmarine warfare. Overall, Canada prefers the status quo of MAD and flexible response, upon which there already exists an allied consensus. Indeed, for Canada, the problem with changes in U.S. strategic thinking is that it could demand choices that Ottawa would rather not have to make, such as whether to participate in SDI or whether to support U.S. ASW operations directed against Soviet SSBNs in the Arctic.

Although aligned with the West, Canada has been free to employ its military in activities not directly related to the East-West balance of power. Peacekeeping has been one role that Canada decided to undertake largely on its own initiative. Still, Canada's peacekeeping operations have been consistent with alliance commitments and have had the support of the United States and other allies. Indeed, in some cases, Canada has been selected as a contributor because of its Western alignment. Nevertheless, the level of Canada's contributions makes this activity a unique feature of the country's defence policy. Canada has also used its armed forces for non-military sovereignty-protection purposes and for aid to the civil power. In this regard, Canada does not differ from any other ally.

Alliance commitments have driven defence spending, but, as shown by Canada's involvement in peacekeeping and use of the armed forces for non-military sovereignty purposes, these commitments are not the sole determinants of defence policy decisions.

Posture and Procurement: The Choices

The fundamental decisions about alignment, alliances, and strategies that successive Canadian governments have taken are reflected in the posture of the Canadian armed forces. Canada has generally postured its forces to support its alliances and their strategies. But this does not mean that the actual weapons and deployments of the armed forces are automatically determined by alliance membership or that the level of spending on weapons and deployment is dictated by allies. Choices have been available and decisions have been made in posturing the armed forces.

Canada shares with its allies, including the United States, many of the complexities and uncertainties surrounding weapons choices in the nuclear age. What is needed to give credibility to deterrence and how much is enough? The simple fact is that nobody—not the generals, not the political leaders, and not the academic strategists—can determine with any certainty what mixture and levels of weapons will assure security. Deterrence, after all, is ultimately based on speculations about Soviet behaviour and about the possible consequences if deterrence failed. What would a Soviet-American war be like? At the strategic nuclear level, there is little doubt that the results of such a war would be catastrophic. Yet this leaves open the question of how to maintain the strategic nuclear balance. Below the strategic nuclear level, there is even less certainty, and certainly no agreement, on whether an East-West limited nuclear war or a conventional war is possible. And it is at the conventional level that Canada makes most of its contributions. The NATO allies must posture their forces based on calculations about the outcome of hypothetical battles they hope to avoid by showing the Soviets they are ready to fight them.

To be sure, the West can use the character of Soviet forces and its own strategic objectives to guide force development and procurement. Thus, given the large number of Warsaw Pact tanks, NATO has invested heavily in tanks of its own and in antitank forces. The requirement for forward defence places a premium on maintaining large forces right at the inter-German border, while the need to keep the sea lanes open in the face of large numbers of Soviet attack submarines has made ASW a top NATO maritime priority. For North American defence, the relatively small Soviet bomber force has reduced the need to invest heavily in air defence, and opened up the possibility of shifting NORAD's resources to warning and surveillance against missile attack. The advent of cruise missiles, however, has meant a partial shift back to air defence.

Selecting the right kinds of weapons is only the beginning. Planners must then determine how many to buy and, because resources are limited, the choices and trade-offs involved must be made on the basis, again, of uncertain calculations. How many Soviet tanks must NATO be able to destroy and how fast? Are enough ASW forces to destroy 50 percent of Soviet attack submarines entering the North Atlantic sufficient, or will the remaining 50 percent still pose too great a threat? How many interceptor aircraft should NORAD deploy and how many radars will be required? Does NATO need more airlift for rapid reinforcement and resupply or sealift for sustained combat? And if there is too little of the former will the forces be able to sustain combat operations until the latter is implemented?

Apart from calculations about how much is necessary to deter the Soviets, the Western allies must also posture and fund their forces with a view to intra-alliance politics. The Europeans maintain conventional forces partly to secure the American nuclear guarantee, while the United States deploys ground and air forces in Europe to help solidify its position in Europe. NATO frequently sets spending targets, such as the three percent real-growth goal, which all allies are expected to attain in order to enhance solidarity through equitable burden-sharing. Often the question of "how much is enough" is answered by the minimum that can be agreed on by the maximum number of allies, and this may have no precise relationship to specific weapons systems.

All allies, collectively and individually, face such questions. For Ottawa, "what to buy" and "how much is enough" are particularly difficult questions because of Canada's unique geostrategic situation. Unlike the European allies, it is not directly threatened by Soviet conventional forces. Unlike the United States, it does not supply strategic nuclear and tactical-theatre nuclear forces or vast numbers of ships, aircraft, and tanks. Even if doubled, Canada's armed forces would still only count marginally in the overall balance of power between East and West. It cannot be argued that either Canada or its allies would be significantly less secure if Canada did not contribute to the common defence. Canada's armed forces do have symbolic and political importance insofar as they help sustain allied unity. Yet even on this score, they are less important than the European forces. Politically, it is important to the United States that Canada is aligned with the West and that it co-operates in the defence of North America and Europe. At the same time, it is more important from Washington's perspective for the Europeans to sustain their defence efforts than for Canada to do so, because of the place of Europe in superpower relations. Canada does not gain any additional extension of the nuclear guarantee either to itself or to Europe by its contributions there, while its North American efforts are not crucial for maintaining the credibility of the nuclear deterrent that protects the continent. From Ottawa's viewpoint, allied contributions have secured Canada a seat at the table where its voice will be heard and its influence felt. However, it is almost impossible to correlate specific levels of contributions to collective defence with the actual degree of Canadian influence. All of this, combined with the uncertainties of force posturing in the nuclear age, have made it particularly difficult for Canadian governments to answer the questions of what and how much military equipment to acquire.

Yet the very factors that complicate Canadian defence policy decision making also afford Ottawa some leeway in the conduct of military affairs and allied relations. The Western deterrent posture is comprehensive, involving everything from jeeps and small patrol boats to main battle tanks, aircraft carriers, and intercontinental ballistic missiles. The United States is the only "full-service" ally contributing to nearly every Western military role. Others have had to select the roles they will assume and the forces to fulfil them. Canada has, to be sure, been guided in its choices by what its alliances needed. Thus, in the 1950s Canada contributed to NATO's air and armoured ground forces in Europe and to NATO's ASW posture. In North America, Canada put resources into the creation of an air defence system, building radar stations and deploying interceptors. During the leaner years of the 1960s and 1970s, Canada continued to maintain and to acquire such forces as would be useful to its allies.

Has Canada been constrained in the kinds of forces it has dedicated to collective defence? To a certain extent the answer is yes. As noted, Canada has generally contributed what was useful to NATO and NORAD. Yet, it is unlikely that, with no such constraints, it would have preferred a wholly different set of contributions. For example, Ottawa would not have offered amphibious forces, or a strategic bomber wing, or more aircraft carriers, or even an exclusively submarine ASW force. Other kinds of contributions would have been more expensive. But more important, most of the weapons Canada did decide to contribute could also serve in a sovereignty-protection role. This would include the air and surface ASW forces and the NORAD-dedicated interceptors. In other words, Canada was able to posture its armed forces to meet allied *and* national roles. These forces could also be used for peacekeeping. As the experience of the mid-1960s to early 1970s showed, Ottawa was unwilling to buy armed forces exclusively for national sovereignty or peacekeeping purposes. Thus, it has not been so much a matter of allied commitments constraining choices in the posturing of the armed forces, but that such commitments generated demands for the kinds of modern armed forces that, in the absence of allied roles, would simply not have been as strongly present.

These allied roles remained relatively unchanged throughout the Cold War and on into the 1970s and 1980s. But it was not pressure from Washington or Brussels that constrained the choices available and resulted in this continuity. Rather it was the decisions of previous Canadian governments, reaffirmed again and again, to remain allied and to sustain the same allied roles. Here, again, Canada is not entirely unique. The overall Western military posture has not altered dramatically since the Cold War. Weapons have changed, numbers have fluctuated, but NATO still relies on a triad of strategic nuclear, theatre-tactical nuclear, and conventional forces. Over a quarter of a million U.S. service personnel are still in Europe, and Britain still maintains an army on the Rhine. Western governments have generally tried to maintain the status quo or have implemented only incremental changes as opposed to wholesale and radical alterations. France withdrew from NATO's integrated command structure in the mid-1960s, yet it remained within the alliance, and French forces are still in Germany and coordinate with those of other allies. This consistency in the Western military posture reflects the relative consistency in the perception of the threat, especially in Europe. Soviet conventional forces in Europe, now backed by a nuclear arsenal on par with that of the United States, require the continuation of deterrence.

It has been the case that successive Canadian governments have been constrained by past equipment choices, since that equipment had been dedicated to a specific role. Thus, the attempt by the Trudeau government to drop the heavy-armour role in Europe was complicated by the fact that Canada had carried out that role for over a decade and tanks were necessary on the central front. Similarly, both the Trudeau and Mulroney governments were compelled to improve ASW forces dedicated to NATO and air forces earmarked for NATO and NORAD in order to fulfil previously acquired roles. But in these cases, Canada's choices were constrained as much by its own past decisions as by allied preferences.

The 1987 White Paper continues in this tradition, proposing to close the commitment-capability gap mainly by buying new equipment to replace or add to older systems to do the same job. The proposal to acquire a fleet of nuclear-powered attack submarines does, however, represent something of a challenge for Canada. The Mulroney government has pledged to increase defence spending to acquire the SSNs and to enhance remaining long-standing commitments such as the one to the central front. Where the funds will be found to do all of this is far from clear.

The funding question is particularly important for Canada and its allies, because if there is one area in which Canada has had considerable latitude it is in the proportion of its national wealth that it devotes to defence spending. Within NATO Canada ranks sixth in terms of both absolute defence expenditures and per capita spending. For most of the period since 1971, however, Canadian defence expenditure as a percentage of GDP has hovered around the two percent mark, putting it above only Luxembourg and Iceland (the latter of which does not maintain any armed forces). The NATO Europe average is 3.8 percent. Such figures do not give an exact comparison of each nation's share of the burden of collective defence. In 1985 Greece led NATO countries in terms of the percentage of GDP it devoted to defence, but its armed forces are postured to meet a perceived threat from Turkey, another NATO ally. The United States outspends all of the NATO nations combined, but its forces are tasked to fulfil many non-NATO roles. Canada spends nearly all of its defence budget on collective-defence tasks. Japan, which also depends for its security on the United States, is judged to be contributing even less than Canada, based on its comparative national wealth. Moreover, throughout the West, defence expenditures have declined relative to other government spending. Indeed, U.S. defence-budget growth will not meet the NATO target of an annual three percent real increase in the coming years.

Some in Canada may nevertheless find the country's relative contribution to collective defence embarrassing, even immoral. Certainly the Mulroney government believes the commitment–capability gap must be closed, although its record on defence spending is not much better than that of previous Liberal governments. Others in Canada, especially those in the peace movement, may find even the current level of spending too high. But whatever the view, it cannot be denied that Canada has had the freedom to set its own level of defence spending and that, since the early 1970s, that level has been below what other allies of comparable national wealth have chosen. The ability to make this choice, yet still remain an active participant in Western collective defence, indicates that, while alliance participation has very much determined Canadian military posture, it has not entailed rigid guidelines as to how much Canada spends on its armed forces. Since 1968 Canada has answered the question "how much is enough" by spending *just* enough—just enough to keep its armed forces together and to allow the military to operate alongside allied units undertaking similar roles. The allies have not been altogether happy with this but there is little they can do. Short of asking Canada to leave the Western collective-defence system, a step that would not be in anyone's interests, Canada's allies have almost no real leverage over the size of Ottawa's defence budget. If they did, it can safely be argued that Canada would be spending much more on its military than it currently does.

Making the Decisions

Because Canadian policy makers confront a host of pressures and constraints when making defence policy, the decisions have not been simple or easy to make. As we have attempted to show in this book, defence policy decision making is a complex phenomenon. To be sure, defence is not often at the top of a prime minister's agenda, but when it is, it can prove as difficult and intractable as any other area of governmental activity. Ironically, Canadian governments have found it easier to settle the broader questions of strategy and force posture than the narrower ones of the particular weapon to buy and the amount to pay for it. It has been easier to bring in White Papers than to acquire the weapons necessary to fulfil the tasks outlined in those documents. Acquisition decisions and the year-to-year, month-to-month, and day-to-day running of DND and the armed forces require a continual decision-making process wherein real choices must be made. The making of defence policy does not end with the release of a White Paper; it begins there, and sets in motion a train of subsequent decisions to be made or unmade.

Since 1968 Canada has made a number of significant decisions regarding its force posture and allied roles. Initially, it reduced the size of its European-based forces, but also assumed a new role—the CAST brigade commitment to Norway. The Trudeau government also decided to drop Canada's nuclear roles in Europe and North America. Within NORAD, it was deemed unnecessary to increase forces because of the decline in the bomber threat. All of this was codified in the 1971 White Paper, which also emphasized sovereignty tasks, but retained most allied commitments. At this time, Canada chose to freeze defence spending and reduce the size of the armed forces.

By 1974 it became clear that Canada could not retain its allied commitments (to which were now added non-military sovereignty roles) *and* cut back on defence spending. Thus, the government initiated the Defence Structure Review. Out of the DSR came a new set of decisions, some of which reversed earlier trends, such as the decision to retain the heavy-armoured role in Germany. But the DSR dealt mainly with capital acquisitions. The decisions to cut the forces in Europe and to assume the CAST brigade commitment, but not to invest in air defence, were not reversed. Sovereignty remained the first priority, but it could not serve as a guide for force-posture decisions as long as the allied roles were retained.

The Mulroney government inherited the posture and capital-acquisition program that emerged out of the DSR. For the most part these were NATO-related, and the Conservatives, during their first years in office, made further decisions to bolster Canada's contributions to European defence, adding 1200 troops to CFE, continuing with the frigate program, and acquiring low-level air defences. It was also left to the Mulroney government to conclude the agreement with the United States on the modernization of NORAD's air defences. The 1987 White Paper, like the 1971 White Paper, codified decisions already taken but also pointed to new directions in defence policy and dropped one commitment— the CAST role in Norway, undertaken in 1968. Should the force posture outlined in the White Paper become a reality, the emphasis in Canadian defence policy will shift from NATO Europe to the maritime sphere and to North America.

The shift will not take Canada out of the Western collective-defence system nor even out of NATO and NORAD. Indeed, it is the contention of the Mulroney government that the changes announced in the White Paper will make Canada a better, more reliable ally. While the United States and Europe appear to have their doubts about this latest change in the Canadian posture, there is little they can do to influence Ottawa. As noted above, although Canada's alliances set the context in which defence-posture decisions are made, resulting in an armed force geared almost exclusively to NATO and NORAD roles, the Canadian government has had considerable leeway in selecting the kinds and levels of weapons it purchases and where it deploys them. The various changes since 1968 demonstrate this. It is essential to recognize the external determinants of defence policy decision making, but it is also necessary to acknowledge that these factors do not automatically determine the substantive details of the policy itself.

Thus, Canada has made a number of important decisions regarding force posture. Yet all of these decisions, including the issuing of the White Papers, were made by the political executive and the bureaucracy with little or no parliamentary, interest-group, or public involvement. To be sure, there was intragovernmental discussion, and outside experts were sometimes consulted. But mainly it is DND and DEA who are involved, with differences between them being resolved, and final decisions made, by cabinet. All of this is done in secret, and the results are presented as *faits accomplis* to the public. Changes to previously stated policies, such as those that emerged out of the DSR, are made in a similar fashion. In 1968 the Trudeau government decided to assume the CAST brigade commitment and in 1987 a new government decided to drop it, even though in the summer of 1986 it had authorized a multimillion-dollar CAST forces' exercise in Norway. At first the ground forces in Europe were to be "lightened up," then new tanks were bought. In 1971 Canadians were told that air defence did not require new resources, but by 1980 discussions were underway with the United States to modernize NORAD. The 1987 White Paper called for the acquisition of nuclear-powered submarines at tremendous cost, although outside of DND there was little expectation that this was a viable option.

Some of these decisions have been relatively uncomplicated because they did not involve major expenditures; in fact they were made to reduce spending or to forestall potential increases in spending. The cuts in the European force in 1968 coincided with a general freeze on defence spending, while the assumption of the CAST brigade commitment involved hardly any new expenditures. Dropping CAST in 1987 saved the government the expense involved in making it credible. The renewal of NORAD in 1986 involved no new spending at all beyond that which had been decided a year earlier, when Canada and the United States signed the agreement to modernize air defences. The tough decisions relating to the 1987 White Paper have yet to be made—those that involve locating the funds to support the new posture. And, if the past is any guide, those decisions are going to be exceedingly difficult and complex.

Defence-expenditure decisions, both overall and to do with the acquisition of particular weapons, involve pressures and constraints not ordinarily present in general force-posture decisions. Capital spending decisions bring in a wider range of governmental and non-governmental actors. Compared to the external environment, which has by and large allowed Canada to posture its allied commitments as it wished, the domestic policy-making environment presents governments with relatively less freedom of choice.

The Department of National Defence, like other departments and agencies, must compete for a limited amount of governmental revenue. And it must do so in a political environment in which national security and defence issues are rarely a high priority for the prime minister and his cabinet. This competition must also take place in a political culture in which there are very few votes to be gained by spending more on defence. For while opinion polls have shown that the Canadian public favours increases in defence expenditures, and this in turn has allowed recent Liberal and Conservative governments to give DND more money, governments cannot expect to be rewarded on election day for giving the armed forces more guns. In the choice between "guns and butter," the Canadian public may want some of the former, but they want a good deal more of the latter. Thus, at the highest political level, where decisions and trade-offs must be made between new weapons and new social programs, or even between sustaining the existing level of defence spending and maintaining domestic expenditures, DND often finds itself in a somewhat disadvantaged position.

Defence spending decisions, unlike posture decisions, will draw in cabinet members and bureaucrats from across the government outside DND and DEA. In cabinet's Priorities and Planning Committee and in the Treasury Board, defence spending must be reconciled with other demands. Here, it is not always a question of how much to spend on defence overall, but when to spend it. What priority will submarines have over day-care? What priority will meeting NATO's target of three percent real increases have over reducing the federal deficit?

Once DND has secured its general budget allocation, it must decide how to spend it. For the most part, normal year-to-year and day-to-day expenditures only concern the department itself and do not involve outside agencies. But in the case of the acquisition of major weapons systems, the situation is even more complex than the overall budget allocation. Canada buys few major weapons systems. Since 1968 there have been fewer than half a dozen multibillion-dollar purchases. Yet, when defence budgets are about $11 billion per year and the capital-acquisition portion is roughly $3 billion per year, decisions on purchases become major aspects of defence policy making. And because of the amounts of money involved, defence acquisition decisions, unlike most other aspects of defence policy, tend to become high-profile public policy issues.

The selection of a particular weapons system involves considerations that go beyond military suitability. Can the weapon be bought in Canada or must DND go to foreign sources, and if it must go to a foreign contractor, to what extent will that contractor do work in Canada to create employment and other investment? If the contractor, foreign or Canadian, intends to construct new facilities, where will they be built and what will be the provincial and regional distribution of the benefits? If the foreign contractor is not going to build new facilities in Canada, can it offset a purchase made abroad by placing orders for subcontracts with Canadian firms? All of these questions bring in a host of actors to the decision-making process: potential contractors, subcontractors, the provinces, the municipalities, and individual citizens who stand to benefit or lose from the decision. Members of Parliament, who normally would not be involved in defence policy, will act on behalf of their constituents, provinces, or regions. Other government departments, especially those concerned with trade and industrial policy, become involved as well.

Given the complexity of the process and the potential financial and political impact of major defence acquisition decisions, it is not surprising that the final decision is usually made by the prime minister and cabinet. When this happens, the media focusses attention on defence policy with an intensity not seen even at the release of a White Paper. It may appear to many Canadians that the only kind of defence decision their government makes has to do with how much to spend, where to spend it, and which part of the country will benefit from the expenditure. All else is predetermined by what Canada's allies are doing and, without pressure from Washington or Brussels, cabinet would not even be making these decisions. It might also appear that the government is ignoring the views of peace and disarmament groups in favour of pro-defence organizations or groups that stand to make money from military spending.

As this book has tried to show, there is much more to defence policy making in Canada than deciding how much to spend on the armed forces. Behind any cabinet decision on a weapons acquisition is a history of fundamental choices and decisions by successive Canadian governments on the best way to assure national security in a dangerous and complex international environment. Since the Cold War, Canada has consistently sought its security in co-operation with the United States and the European allies, formalizing that preference for collective defence in NORAD and NATO. Prior decisions about alignment and alliances have determined subsequent force-posture choices, but there has always been a measure of choice available, which Canada has exercised. Allied commitments have not prevented the use of the armed forces for national sovereignty protection or for peacekeeping.

It is because the external environment does not automatically determine all of Canadian defence policy that the governmental and domestic environments are also important in understanding the process and content of defence decision making. The prime minister and his cabinet colleagues dominate the formulation of both foreign and defence policy with very little input from the legislative branch on broad policy questions or on the day-to-day conduct of diplomatic and military affairs. These elected officials are supported by civilian and military bureaucracies that advise on and execute policy largely out of public view. But this closely held process does not extend to major spending or procurement decisions. On these decisions, other governmental and non-governmental actors weigh in and the interplay between the three policy-making environments becomes evident. Allied commitments generate the need for spending decisions that must be made by government yet cannot be made irrespective of competing domestic interests.

The interplay among the three policy-making environments can explain, to a certain extent, why peace and disarmament groups have less influence over defence policy decision making than pro-defence lobbies and the defence industry. In Canada peace groups have tended to lobby for changes in the fundamentals of defence policy, taking as their point of departure the threat of nuclear war itself rather than the threat posed to Canada and its allies by the

Soviet Union. Rather than have their country contribute to a suicidal arms race, these groups call for withdrawal from NATO and NORAD. Because of the large role played by the United States in Canadian defence policy, peace groups are particularly critical of American strategies and plans, such as SDI. Large reductions in strategic nuclear weapons, and even their total elimination, are also advocated. In general, though, peace groups have not been interested in putting forth alternative postures or force-procurement programs for the CF. They have argued that a neutral Canada would not need armed forces of the kind now deployed and the resources could be diverted to more peaceful tasks at home and abroad.

With their growth in numbers and in media coverage, the peace groups cannot be wholly ignored by the government. Under Mulroney, there has been a deliberate effort to give these groups a hearing and financial support. But it is clear from the decisions made by the Conservative government, as well as from its White Paper, that the views of these groups have little or no impact on Canadian defence policy. The fundamental changes they advocate simply do not accord with past and present Canadian governmental views of the nature of the international strategic environment— an environment that Canada cannot change and that therefore requires it to seek its security in concert with like-minded Western nations. To be sure, the federal government is the interpreter of this environment for the public and may appear, in the view of some, to exaggerate the Soviet threat, as in the case of the 1987 White Paper. Nevertheless, public opinion still overwhelmingly favours alignment even as it supports arms-control measures and opposes certain American policies. The government can argue that Canada will have less impact on U.S. policy and arms control if it adopts a neutral posture. Thus, nonalignment and alliance withdrawal are not considered real options for Canada. Ottawa can be fairly confident that the public will continue to support the basics of the Western nuclear and conventional deterrent posture, and hence Canadian participation in NATO and NORAD.

This means that defence policy making concentrates on issues such as posture and procurement, which the peace and disarmament groups reject *a priori*. Because these groups do not suggest alternative postures or weapons acquisitions, Ottawa has no compelling reason to pay serious attention to them. For this reason, as well, the government will necessarily be more open to pro-defence groups who might suggest alternatives. In the governmental and domestic policy-making environment, the defence industry is influential because it involves itself in questions of technology, cost, and the regional distribution of defence spending, which are the most pressing defence issues facing the government on a continuing basis.

In recent years the arguments of some of the peace and disarmament groups have become more germane to the defence policy-making process. Drawing on the resources of institutes such as the Canadian Centre for Arms Control and Disarmament and the Canadian Institute for International Peace and Security, many of these groups have begun to discuss posture and procurement decisions, debate their implications, and propose alternative programs. Thus, during the debate over the renewal of NORAD in 1986, few advocated withdrawal from the joint command and the dismantling of Canada's air-defence forces. Rather, some suggested putting some distance between Canada and SDI and others even favoured augmenting the CF's capabilities in order to reduce dependency on U.S. systems. Some groups have condemned the alleged "cold war" tone of the 1987 White Paper, yet, like the federal NDP, they have also advanced reasoned alternative posture and procurement proposals involving considerable sums of money. Ironically, the more that non-governmental actors and groups accept the fundamental Western alignment of Canada, and perhaps even NATO if not also NORAD involvement, the more difficult it will be for the government to ignore them in the decision-making process. This will undoubtedly complicate the conduct of Canada's military affairs.

The new interest and sophistication of many Canadian interest groups with regard to their country's defence policy indicate that the public's traditional scepticism is being gradually replaced by an appreciation that Canadian defence policy is not set in Washington or Brussels but in Ottawa. There is a greater understanding that, while the existing policies (and their constraints) are to a large extent the result of past decisions, Canada has the ability to make changes. This is a welcome shift in public attitude, because the coming years are likely to be ones in which many difficult choices will have to be made.

It is too soon to determine what the fate of the entire package of proposals contained in the 1987 White Paper will be. Much will depend on the electoral fortunes of the Mulroney government. It is not certain whether the Conservatives, even if re-elected, will be able to carry through with their full defence program given the financial constraints they already face. They may have to decide to alter or reduce planned capability improvements, or to re-examine certain commitments. A new Liberal or NDP government in Ottawa will have to decide whether to proceed on the basis of the existing White Paper or to begin the review process all over again. Depending on how far the Conservatives have gone with their program, this review might encounter projects too far advanced and entrenched to reverse easily. The public mood will also be a factor. Canadian governments are rarely rewarded for innovative changes in defence policy, and the next federal government, whatever its political stripe, will undoubtedly find the domestic policy agenda full of contentious issues.

The external policy-making environment holds even fewer certainties. While Canadian security will continue to depend on nuclear and conventional deterrence, the weapons and strategies that preserve the East–West balance may change as a result of both arms control and force modernization. The technologies and strategies of North American and European defence are in flux. Whether the current easing of Soviet–American tensions will last is also unknown. Superpower relations have tended to vacillate, with calls for renewed allied commitments accompanying the downturns. Yet the future of trans-Atlantic relations in the wake of the INF Treaty and current trends in U.S. foreign and defence policy is difficult to predict. NATO may survive, but with the United States playing a somewhat lesser role. What Canada's position would be in this situation, whether it would entail more or less emphasis on European defence, is equally unclear.

In sum, a host of new and old constraints arising out of all three policy-making environments will confront future Canadian governments as they formulate defence policy into the next century. As in the past, all three environments will influence decision making simultaneously, although the relative importance of each will vary according to the nature of the decision under consideration. But while each environment will impose definite limits on policy, the need and the ability to make defence policy choices will remain. For to govern is to choose, and despite all the readily apparent constraints, Canada's defence policies have been of Canada's own choosing, commensurate with its sovereignty and independence. Only if Canadians and their governments refuse to recognize the need to decide, if they become too sceptical of their ability to make policy, will the choices no longer be available. If this should happen, then indeed, Canada's sovereignty and independence, as well as its security, will be diminished.

Selected Bibliography

Books, Monographs, and Occasional Papers

Bland, Douglas. *The Administration of Defence Policy in Canada 1947 to 1985.* Kingston: Ronald P. Frye & Company, 1987.

Bland, Douglas, L. *Controlling the Defence Policy Process in Canada: White Papers on Defence and Bureaucratic Politics in the Department of National Defence.* Occasional Paper. Kingston: Centre for International Relations, Queen's University, March 1988.

Bland, Lieutenant Colonel Douglas L. *Institutionalizing Ambiguity: The Management Review Group and the Reshaping of the Defence Policy Process in Canada.* Occasional Paper. Kingston: Centre for International Relations, Queen's University, July 1986.

Boutilier, James A., ed. *RCN in Restrospect, 1910–1968.* Vancouver: University of British Columbia Press, 1983.

Brewin, Andrew. *Stand on Guard: The Search for a Canadian Defence Policy.* Toronto: McClelland and Stewart, 1965.

Business Council on National Issues. *Canada's Defence Policy: Capabilities Versus Commitments. A Position Paper of the Business Council on National Issues.* Ottawa, September 1984.

Byers, R.B., and Gray, Colin S. *Canadian Military Professionalism: The Search for Identity.* Wellesley Papers 2. Toronto: Canadian Institute of International Affairs, 1973.

Byers, R.B.; Hamre, John; and Lindsey, G.R. *Aerospace Defence: Canada's Future Role?* Wellesley Papers 9. Toronto: Canadian Institute of International Affairs, 1985.

Byers, R.B., and Slack, Michael, eds. *Canada and Peacekeeping: Prospects for the Future.* Toronto: York Research Programme in Strategic Studies, 1984.

Cox, David. *Canada and NORAD, 1958–1978: A Cautionary Retrospective.* Aurora Papers 1. Ottawa: The Canadian Centre for Arms Control and Disarmament, 1985.

Cox, David. *Trends in Continental Defence: A Canadian Perspective.* Occasional Papers, no. 2. Ottawa: Canadian Institute for International Peace and Security, December 1986.

Crane, Brian. *An Introduction to Canadian Defence Policy.* Toronto: Canadian Institute of International Affairs, 1964.

Cuthbertson, Brian. *Canadian Military Independence in the Age of the Superpowers.* Toronto: Fitzhenry & Whiteside, 1977.

Diefenbaker, John G. *One Canada: Memoirs of the Right Honourable John G. Diefenbaker.* Vol. 3, *The Tumultuous Years, 1962-1967.* Toronto: Macmillan, 1977.

Dillon, G.M. *Canadian Naval Policy since World War II: A Decision-Making Analysis.* Occasional Paper. Halifax: Centre for Foreign Policy Studies, Dalhousie University, October 1972.

Douglas, W.A.B., ed. *The RCN in Transition: Challenge and Response 1910-1985.* Vancouver: University of British Columbia Press, forthcoming.

Dow, James. *The Arrow.* Toronto: James Lorimer & Co., 1979.

Eayrs, James. *In Defence of Canada.* Vol. 3, *Peacemaking and Deterrence.* Toronto: University of Toronto Press, 1972.

Eayrs, James. *In Defence of Canada.* Vol. 4, *Growing Up Allied.* Toronto: University of Toronto Press, 1980.

Eustace, Marilyn. *Canada's Commitment to Europe.* Vol. I. *The European Force 1964-1971.* National Security Series, no. 1/79. Kingston, Centre for International Relations, Queen's University, 1979.

Granatstein, J.L. *A Man of Influence: Norman A. Robertson and Canadian Statecraft, 1929-68.* Ottawa: Deneau Publishers, 1981.

Granatstein, J.L. *Canada 1957-1967: The Years of Uncertainty and Innovation.* Toronto: McClelland and Stewart, 1986.

Gray, Colin S. *Canadian Defence Priorities: A Question of Relevance.* Toronto: Clarke, Irwin, 1972.

Griffiths, Franklyn. *A Northern Foreign Policy.* Wellesley Papers 7. Toronto: Canadian Institute of International Affairs, 1979.

Haglund, David G. *Soviet Air-Launched Cruise Missiles and the Geopolitics of North American Air Defence: The Canadian North in Changing Perspective.* Occasional Paper, no 16. Kingston: Centre for International Relations, Queen's University, April 1987.

Haglund, David G., ed. *Canada's Defence Industrial Base: The Political Economy of Preparedness and Procurement.* Kingston: Ronald P. Frye & Company, 1988.

Haydon, Commander Peter T. *The Strategic Importance of the Arctic: Understanding the Military Issues.* Strategic Issues Paper, no 1/87. Ottawa: Directorate of Strategic Policy Planning, Department of National Defence, March 1987.

Hobson, Sharon. *The Composition of Canada's Naval Fleet, 1946-85.* Halifax: Centre for Foreign Policy Studies, Dalhousie University, 1986.

Holmes, John W. *The Shaping of Peace: Canada and the Search for World Order 1943-1957.* 2 vols. Toronto: University of Toronto Press, 1979, 1982.

Holmes, John W., ed. *No Other Way: Canada and International Security Institutions.* Toronto: Centre for International Studies, University of Toronto, 1986.

Ing, Stanley, and Olson, Theodore. *Seeking Common Ground on the Defence of Canada: A Colloquy between Peace Activists and Strategic Analysts.* Occasional Paper, no. 1. Downsview: York Research Programme in Strategic Studies, 15 July 1983.

Jockel, Joseph T. *Canada and NATO's Northern Flank.* Toronto: Centre for International and Strategic Studies, York University, 1986.

Jockel, Joseph T. *No Boundaries Upstairs: Canada, the United States and the Origins of North American Air Defence, 1945-1958.* Vancouver: University of British Columbia Press, 1987.

Jockel, Joseph T., and Sokolsky, Joel J. *Canada and Collective Security: Odd Man Out.* The Washington Papers, no. 121. New York: Praeger, 1986.

Kronenberg, Vernon J. *All Together Now: The Organization of the Department of National Defence in Canada, 1964-1972.* Wellesley Papers 2. Toronto: Canadian Institute of International Affairs, 1973.

Lindsey, George R. *The Strategic Defence of North America.* Toronto: Canadian Institute of Strategic Studies, 1986.

Lyon, Peyton V. *Canada in World Affairs, 1961-1963.* Toronto: Oxford University Press, 1968.

MacDonald, Brian, ed. *Parliament and Defence Policy: Preparedness or Procrastination?* Toronto: Canadian Institute of Strategic Studies, 1982.

MacDonald, Brian, ed. *Guns and Butter: Defence and the Canadian Economy.* Toronto: Canadian Institute of Strategic Studies, 1984.

MacDonald, Brian, ed. *High Tech and the High Seas.* Toronto: Canadian Institute of Strategic Studies, 1985.

Massey, Hector J. *The Canadian Military: A Profile.* Toronto: Copp Clark, 1972.

McLin, Jon B. *Canada's Changing Defense Policy, 1957-1963: The Problems of a Middle Power in Alliance.* Baltimore: Johns Hopkins Press, 1967.

Morton, Desmond. *A Military History of Canada.* Edmonton: Hurtig Publishers, 1985.

Munton, Don, ed. *Groups and Governments in Canadian Foreign Policy.* Proceedings. Toronto: Canadian Institute of International Affairs, 1985.

Nossal, Kim Richard. *The Politics of Canadian Foreign Policy.* Scarborough: Prentice-Hall Canada Inc., 1985.

Regehr, Ernie. *Making a Killing: Canada's Arms Industry.* Toronto: McClelland and Stewart, 1975.

Regehr, Ernie. *Arms Canada: The Deadly Business of Military Exports.* Toronto: James Lorimer & Co., 1987.

Regehr, Ernie, and Rosenblum, Simon, eds. *Canada and the Nuclear Arms Race.* Toronto: James Lorimer & Co., 1983.

Reid, Escott. *Time of Fear and Hope: The Making of the North Atlantic Treaty, 1947–1949.* Toronto: McClelland and Stewart, 1977.

Robertson, William Scot. *Canada's Commitment to NATO's Northern Flank: The Northern Base Option.* ORAE Extra-Mural Paper no. 27. Ottawa: Operational Research and Analysis Establishment, DND, December 1983.

Rosenblum, Simon. *Misguided Missiles: Canada, the Cruise and Star Wars.* Toronto: James Lorimer & Co., 1985.

Rosenbluth, Gideon. *The Canadian Economy and Disarmament.* Toronto: McClelland and Stewart, 1967; Carleton Library, 1978.

Ross, Douglas A. *Coping with "Star Wars": Issues for Canada and the Alliance.* Aurora Papers 2. Ottawa: Canadian Centre for Arms Control and Disarmament, 1985.

Sigler, John H., ed. *International Peacekeeping in the Eighties: Global Outlook and Canadian Priorities.* Carleton International Proceedings. Ottawa: Norman Paterson School of International Affairs, Carleton University, Fall 1982.

Stairs, Denis. *The Diplomacy of Constraint: Canada, the Korean War, and the United States.* Toronto: University of Toronto Press, 1974.

Stewart, Larry. *Canada's European Force 1971–1980: A Defence Policy in Transition.* National Security Series, no. 5/80. Kingston: Centre for International Relations, Queen's University, 1980.

Taras, David, ed. *Parliament and Canadian Foreign Policy.* Toronto: Canadian Institute of International Affairs, 1985.

Taylor, Alastair; Cox, David; and Granatstein, J.L. *Peacekeeping: International Challenge and Canadian Response.* Toronto: Canadian Institute of International Affairs, 1968.

Thordarson, Bruce. *Trudeau and Foreign Policy: A Study in Decision-Making.* Toronto: Oxford University Press, 1972.

Tucker, Michael. *Canadian Foreign Policy: Contemporary Issues and Themes.* Toronto: McGraw-Hill Ryerson, 1980.

Warnock, John W. *Partner to Behemoth: The Military Policy of a Satellite Canada.* Toronto: New Press, 1970.

Willett, T.C. *A Heritage at Risk.* Boulder, Colo.: Westview Press, 1987.

Yost, W.J. *Industrial Mobilization in Canada.* Ottawa: Conference of Defence Associations, 1983.

Articles

Allan, Lt.-Col. J.H. "The Future of Peacekeeping for Canada." *Canadian Defence Quarterly* 8, no. 1 (Summer 1978): 30–36.

Atkinson, Michael M., and Nossal, Kim Richard. "Bureaucratic Politics and the New Fighter Aircraft Decisions." *Canadian Public Administration* 24, no. 4 (Winter 1981): 531–62.

Beaton, Leonard. "The Canadian White Paper on Defence." *International Journal* 19, no. 3 (Summer 1964): 364–70.

Belzile, Lt.-Gen. C.H. "Concentration and Deployment—The Canadian Air–Sea Transportable Brigade Group." *NATO's Sixteen Nations* 30, no. 1 (1985). Special Issue.

Blais, Hon. Jean-Jacques. "The 1984 Defence Budget: Goals, Priorities, and the Allotment of Funds." *Canadian Defence Quarterly* 14, no. 1 (Summer 1984): 8–12.

Bland, Lt.-Col. Douglas. "A Conceptual Approach to Defence Policy." *Canadian Defence Quarterly* 14, no. 4 (Spring 1985): 23–29.

Burke, David P. "Hellyer and Landymore: The Unification of the Canadian Armed Forces and an Admiral's Revolt." *American Review of Canadian Studies* 8, no. 2 (Autumn 1978): 3–27.

Byers, R.B. "Canadian Civil–Military Relations and Reorganization of the Armed Forces: Whither Civilian Control?" In *The Canadian Military: A Profile,* edited by H.J. Massey. (Toronto: Copp Clark, 1972): 197–229.

Byers, R.B. "Perceptions of Parliamentary Surveillance of the Executive: The Case of Canadian Defence Policy." *Canadian Journal of Political Science* 5, no. 2 (June 1972): 234–50.

Byers, R.B. "Structural Changes and the Policy Process in the Department of National Defence: Military Perceptions." *Canadian Public Administration* 16, no. 2 (Summer 1973): 220–42.

Byers, R.B. "The Canadian Military and the Use of Force: End of an Era?" *International Journal* 30, no. 2 (Spring 1975): 284–98.

Byers, R.B. "Defence and Foreign Policy in the 1970s: The Demise of the Trudeau Doctrine." *International Journal* 33, no. 2 (Spring 1978): 312–38.

Byers, R.B. "Canadian Maritime Policy and Force Structure Requirements." *Canadian Defence Quarterly* 12, no. 4 (Spring 1983): 9–16.

Byers, R.B. "Canada's Defence Review: Strategic Doctrine and Military Commitments." *Canadian Defence Quarterly* 14, no. 4 (Spring 1985): 23–29.

Byers, R.B. "Canadian Defence and Defence Procurement: Implications for Economic Policy." In *Selected Problems in Formulating Foreign Economic Policy,* research co-ordinators Denis Stairs and Gilbert R. Winham, Toronto: University of Toronto Press, 1985.

Byers, R.B. "Canadian Security and Defence: The Legacy and the Challenges." *Adelphi Papers* 214 (Winter 1986).

Cameron, A. Keith. "The Royal Canadian Navy and the Unification Crisis." In *RCN in Restrospect, 1910–1968,* edited by James A. Boutilier. (Vancouver: University of British Columbia Press, 1983), 334–42.

Canadian Centre for Arms Control and Disarmament. *Canadian Perspectives on the Strategic Defence Initiative.* Issue Brief no. 3. Ottawa, July 1985.

Canadian Institute of International Affairs. "Defence in the 70s: Comments on the White Paper." *Behind the Headlines* 30, nos. 7–8 (October 1970).

Canadian Institute of International Affairs. "Challenge and Commitment: Comments on the Defence White Paper." *Behind the Headlines* 45, no. 1 (September 1987).

Canby, Steven L., and Smith, Jean Edward. "Canada's Role in NATO: The Laggard Who Can Rescue The Alliance." *Strategic Review* 13, no. 3 (Summer 1985): 47–59.

Cotton, Charles A. "A Canadian Military Ethos." *Canadian Defence Quarterly* 12, no. 3 (Winter 1982/83): 10–17.

Cox, David. "Canadian–American Military Relations: Some Present Trends and Future Possibilities." *International Journal* 36, no. 1 (Winter 1980/81): 91–116.

Crickard, Rear-Admiral F.W. (Ret'd). "An Anti-Submarine Warfare Capability in the Arctic a National Requirement." *Canadian Defence Quarterly* 16, no. 4 (Spring 1987): 24–30.

Crickard, Rear-Admiral F. (Ret'd). "The Canadian Navy—New Directions." *Naval Forces,* no. 2 (1987), pp. 78–87.

Crickard, Rear-Admiral F.W. (Ret'd). "Nuclear-Fuelled Submarines: The Strategic Rationale." *Canadian Defence Quarterly* 17, no. 3 (Winter 1987/88): 17–23.

Critchley, W. Harriet. "Does Doctrine Precede Weaponry?" *International Journal* 33, no. 3 (Summer 1978): 524–56.

Critchley, W. Harriet. "Polar Deployment of Soviet Submarines." *International Journal* 39, no. 4 (Autumn 1984): 828–65.

Critchley, W. Harriet. "The Arctic." *International Journal* 42, no. 4 (Autumn 1987): 769–88.

Cronin, Sister Maureen. "A Case of Hornets: The Controversial CF-18A." *American Review of Canadian Studies* 12, no. 3 (Fall 1982): 17–28.

D'Aquino, Thomas. "Paying the Bill: Canada's Share of the NATO Requirement." In *Guns and Butter: Defence and the Canadian Economy*, edited by Brian Macdonald. Toronto: Canadian Institute of Strategic Studies, 1984.

Davis, Mathwin S. "It Has All Happened Before: The RCN, Nuclear Propulsion and Submarines—1958–68." *Canadian Defence Quarterly* 17, no. 2 (Autumn 1987): 34–41.

Dobell, W.M. "Defence Procurement Contracts and Industrial Offset Packages." *International Perspectives* (January/February 1981), pp. 14–18.

Dobell, W.M. "Parliament's Role in Choosing the New Fighter Aircraft." *International Perspectives* (September/October 1981), pp. 10–13.

Douglas, W.A.B. "Why Does Canada Have Armed Forces?" *International Journal* 30, no. 2 (Spring 1975): 259–83.

Eayrs, James. "The Military Policies of Contemporary Canada: Principles, Problems, Precepts, Prospects." In *Contemporary Canada*, edited by R.H. Leach. Toronto: University of Toronto Press, 1968.

Fairweather, R. Gordon L. "The Role of Parliament in the Review and Planning of Canadian National Defence and External Affairs." In *Secrecy and Foreign Policy*, edited by Thomas M. Franck and Edward Weisband. Toronto: Oxford University Press, 1974.

Foulkes, General Charles. "The Complications of Continental Defence." In *Neighbours Taken for Granted*, edited by L.T. Merchant. Toronto: Burns and MacEachern, 1966.

Gellner, John. "Strategic Analysis in Canada." *International Journal* 33, no. 3 (Summer 1978): 493–505.

Gellner, John. "The Defence of Canada: Requirements, Capabilities, and the National Will." *Behind the Headlines* 42, no. 3 (April 1985).

Gray, Colin S. "The Need for Independent Canadian Strategic Thought." *Canadian Defence Quarterly* 1, no. 1 (Summer 1971): 6–21.

Halstead, John. "Canada's Security in the 1980s: Options and Pitfalls." *Behind the Headlines* 41, no. 1 (September 1983).

Head, Richard G. "The Weapons Acquisition Process: Alternative National Strategies." In *Comparative Defence Policy*, edited by F.B. Horton et al. Baltimore: Johns Hopkins University Press, 1974.

Hochban, Major T.J. "North American Air Defence Modernization." *Canadian Defence Quarterly* 15, no. 3 (Winter 1985/86): 13–17.

Jockel, J.T. "Canada's Other Commitment: The Defence of Norway." *International Perspectives* (January/February 1980), pp. 21–24.

LeBlanc, James and Charters, David. "Peacekeeping and Internal Security: Canadian Army Adaptation to Low-Intensity Operations." In *Armies in Low-Intensity Conflict: A Comparative Study of Institutional Adaptation to New Forms of Warfare*, edited by David Charters and Maurice Tugwell. ORAE Extra-Mural Paper no. 38. Ottawa: Operational Research and Analysis Establishment, Department of National Defence, December 1985.

Legault, Albert. "Canada and the United States: The Defense Dimension." In *Canada and the United States: Enduring Friendship, Persistent Stress*, edited by Charles F. Doran and John H. Sigler. Englewood Cliffs, N.J.: Prentice-Hall, 1985.

Legault, Albert. "Les processus décisionnels en matière de politique de défense." *International Journal* 42, no. 4 (Autumn 1987): 645–74.

Lentner, Howard H. "Foreign Policy Decision Making: The Case of Canada and Nuclear Weapons." *World Politics* 29, no. 1 (October 1976): 29–66.

Loomis, Maj. Gen. D.G. "Managing the Defence Services Program." *Canadian Defence Quarterly* 7, no. 4 (Spring 1978): 26–36.

Manson, Brig. Gen. P.D. "Managing the New Fighter Aircraft Program." *Canadian Defence Quarterly* 7, no. 4 (Spring 1978): 8–15.

Marshall, C.J. "Canada's Forces Take Stock in Defence Structure Review." *International Perspectives* (January/February, 1976), pp. 26–30.

McCaffrey, Jerry. "Canada's Envelope Budgeting System." *American Review of Canadian Studies* 14, no. 1 (Spring 1984): 45–62.

Merritt, C.C.I. "The True Requirements of Canadian Defence: A Critique of the White Paper 1971." *Canadian Defence Quarterly* 1, no. 3 (Winter 1971/72).

Middlemiss, Dan. "Defence Policy and Canadian Industrial Development." *Industrial Preparedness and National Security.* (Toronto: Canadian Institute of Strategic Studies, Fall Seminar, 1980), Vols. 1–7, 6–11.

Middlemiss, Danford W. "Department of National Defence". In *Spending Tax Dollars: Federal Expenditures, 1980–1981,* edited by G. Bruce Doern. Ottawa: School of Public Administration, Carleton University, 1980.

Middlemiss, Danford W. "Economic Defence Co-operation with the United States, 1940–63." In *An Acceptance of Paradox: Essays on Canadian Diplomacy in Honour of John W. Holmes,* edited by Kim Richard Nossal. Toronto: Canadian Institute of International Affairs, 1982.

Middlemiss, Dan. "Paying for National Defence: The Pitfalls of Formula Funding." *Canadian Defence Quarterly* 12, no. 3 (Winter 1982/83): 24–29.

Middlemiss, Dan. "Canada and Defence Industrial Preparedness: A Return to Basics?" *International Journal* 42, no. 4 (Autumn 1987): 707–730.

Middlemiss, Dan. "Economic Considerations in the Development of the Canadian Navy since 1945." In *The RCN in Transition: Challenge and Response 1910–1985,* edited by W.A.B. Douglas. Vancouver: University of British Columbia Press, forthcoming.

Morton, Desmond. "Defending the Indefensible: Some Historical Perspectives on Canadian Defence 1867–1987." *International Journal* 42, no. 4 (Autumn 1987): 627–44.

Munton, Don. "Public Opinion and the Media in Canada from Cold War to Détente to New Cold War." *International Journal* 39, no. 1 (Winter 1983/84): 171–213.

Nixon, C.R. "Management of Restraint in the Department of National Defence." In *The Politics and Management of Restraint in Government,* edited by Peter Ancoin. Montreal: Institute for Research on Public Policy, 1981.

Orvik, Nils. "The Threat: Problems of Analysis." *International Journal* 26, no. 4 (Autumn 1971): 675–85.

Orvik, Nils. "Choices and Directions in Canadian Defence Policy—Part 2: A New Defence Posture with a Northern Orientation." *Canadian Defence Quarterly* 10, no. 1 (Summer 1980): 8–13.

Orvik, Nils. "Canadian Security and 'Defence against help'." *International Perspectives* (May/June 1983), pp. 3–7.

Pattee, R.P. and Thomas, Paul G. "The Senate and Defence Policy: Subcommittee Report on Canada's Maritime Defence." In *Parliament and Canadian Foreign Policy,* edited by David Taras. Toronto: Canadian Institute of International Affairs, 1985.

Pearse, Charles R. "Industrial Preparedness—Indispensable Requirement of National Security." *Canadian Defence Quarterly* 13, no. 2 (Autumn 1983): 24–30.

Preston, Adrian. "The Profession of Arms in Postwar Canada, 1945–1970: Political Authority as a Military Problem." *World Politics* 23, no. 2 (January 1971): 189–214.

Regehr, Ernie. "The Utilization of Resources for Military Purposes in Canada and the Impact on Canadian Industrialization and Defence Procurement." *Industrial Preparedness and National Security.* (Toronto: Canadian Institute of Strategic Studies, Fall Seminar, 1980), Vols. 1–7, 14–19.

Regehr, Ernie. "Canada and the U.S. Nuclear Arsenal." In *Canada and the Nuclear Arms Race,* edited by Ernie Regehr and Simon Rosenblum. Toronto: James Lorimer & Co., 1983.

Regehr, Ernie and Rosenblum, Simon. "The Canadian Peace Movement." In *Canada and the Nuclear Arms Race,* edited by Ernie Regehr and Simon Rosenblum. Toronto: James Lorimer & Co., 1983.

Ross, Douglas A. "American Nuclear Revisionism, Canadian Strategic Interests, and the Renewal of NORAD." *Behind the Headlines* 39, no. 6 (1982).

Rossetto, L. "A Final Look at the 1971 White Paper on Defence." *Queen's Quarterly* 84, no. 1 (Spring 1977): 61–74.

Russell, Col. W.N. "The Making of Canadian Defence Policy." *Canadian Defence Quarterly* 12, no. 4 (Spring 1983): 18–24.

Russell, Col. Neil. "Defence Capabilities and Capital Equipment Planning." In *Guns and Butter: Defence and the Canadian Economy,* edited by Brian MacDonald. Toronto: Canadian Institute of Strategic Studies, 1984.

Russell, Col. W.N. "The Management of Canada's Defence Resources." *Canadian Defence Quarterly* 13, no. 4 (Spring 1984): 17–22.

Shadwick, Martin "Canadian Defence Policy." *International Perspectives* (September/October 1983), pp. 7–10.

Shadwick, Martin. "Canadian Air Defence." *International Perspectives* (March/April 1985), pp. 11–15.

Shadwick, Martin. "Canada's Commitments to NATO: The Need for Rationalization." *Canadian Defence Quarterly* 15, no. 1 (Summer 1985): 22–27.

Sheltus, J.A. "The Militia: A Critical View of the Total Force Concept and P26." *Canadian Defence Quarterly* 8, no. 3 (Winter 1978/79): 22–30.

Simpson, Capt. Suzanne. "Women in 'Men's Jobs'." *Canadian Defence Quarterly* 10, no. 2 (Autumn 1980): 32–35.

Sokolsky, Joel J. "Trends in United States Strategy and the 1987 White Paper on Defence." *International Journal* 42, no. 4 (Autumn 1987): 675–706.

Sokolsky, Joel J. "Canada and the NATO Maritime Alliance." *Conflict Quarterly* 4, no. 2 (Spring 1984): 5–28.

Sokolsky, Joel J. "Canada's Maritime Forces: Strategic Assumptions, Commitments, Priorities." *Canadian Defence Quarterly* 15, no. 3 (Winter 1985/86): 24–30.

Sokolsky, Joel J. "Changing Strategies, Technologies and Organization: The Continuing Debate on NORAD and the Strategic Defense Initiative." *Canadian Journal of Political Science* 19, no. 4 (December 1986): 751–74.

Sokolsky, Joel J. "Canadian Defence Policy: Coping with the Gap." In *Canada Among Nations 1986: Talking Trade*, edited by Brian W. Tomlin and Maureen Appel Molot. Toronto: James Lorimer & Co., 1987.

Sokolsky, Joel J. and Jockel, Joseph T. "Canada: The Not So Faithful Ally." *Washington Quarterly* 7, no. 4 (Fall 1984): 149–69.

Stairs, Denis. "The Military as an Instrument of Canadian Foreign Policy." In *The Canadian Military: A Profile*, edited by Hector J. Massey. Toronto: Copp Clark, 1972.

Sutherland, R.J. "Canada's Long Term Strategic Situation." *International Journal* 17, no. 3 (Summer 1962): 199–223.

Swanson, Roger, F. "The United States as a National Security Threat to Canada." *Behind the Headlines* 29, nos. 5–6 (July 1970): 9–16.

Swanson, Roger F. "An Analytical Assessment of the United States–Canadian Defense Issue-Area." *International Organization* 28, no. 4 (Autumn 1974): 781–802.

Treddenick, John M. "Regional Impacts of Defence Spending." *Guns and Butter: Defence and the Canadian Economy*, edited by Brian MacDonald. Toronto: Canadian Institute of Strategic Studies, 1984.

Treddenick, John M. "The Arms Race and Military Keynesianism." *Canadian Public Policy* 11, no. 1 (March 1985): 77–92.

Tucker, Michael. "Conventional Weapons & Wisdoms: A NATO Dilemma for Canada." *International Perspectives* (January/February 1984) pp. 3–6.

Wang, Erik B. "Sovereignty and Canada–U.S. Co-operation in North American Defence." In *Canadian Perspectives on International Law and Organization*, edited by R. St. J.

Macdonald et al. Toronto: University of Toronto Press, 1974.

Willett, Terry C. "Social Control and the Military in Canada." *Power and Change in Canada*, edited by Richard J. Ossenberg. Toronto: McClelland and Stewart, 1980.

Willett, T.C. "A Sociologist Looks at the Militia." *Canadian Defence Quarterly* 10, no. 2 (Autumn 1980): 36–40.

Williams, D. Colwyn. "International Peacekeeping: Canada's Role." In *Canadian Perspectives on International Law and Organization*, edited by R. St. J. Macdonald et al. Toronto: University of Toronto Press, 1974.

Documents and Reports

Canada. Auditor General. *Report of the Auditor General of Canada to the House of Commons Fiscal Year Ended 31 March 1987.* Ottawa: Supply and Services Canada, 1987.

Canada. Department of External Affairs. *Competitiveness and Security: Directions for Canada's International Relations.* Ottawa: Supply and Services Canada, 1985.

Canada. Department of External Affairs. *Canada's International Relations: Response of the Government of Canada to the Report of the Special Joint Committee of the Senate and the House of Commons.* Ottawa: Supply and Services Canada, 1986.

Canada. Department of National Defence. *White Paper on Defence.* Ottawa: Queen's Printer, 1964.

Canada. Department of National Defence. *Defence in the 70s.* White Paper on Defence. Ottawa: Information Canada, 1971.

Canada. Department of National Defence. Task Force on Review of Unification of the Canadian Forces. *Final Report.* Ottawa, 15 March 1980.

Canada. Department of National Defence. Review Group on the Report of the Task Force on Unification of the Canadian Forces. *Report.* Ottawa: Chief of the Defence Staff, 31 August 1980.

Canada. Department of National Defence. " 'North of 60'— The Canadian Military in the Arctic." *Backgrounder,* October 1985.

Canada. Department of National Defence. "Women in the Canadian Forces." *Backgrounder,* July 1986.

Canada. Department of National Defence. *Challenge and Commitment: A Defence Policy for Canada.* Ottawa: Supply and Services Canada, June 1987.

Canada. House of Commons. Standing Committee on External Affairs and National Defence. *Eighth Report of the Standing Committee on External Affairs and National Defence Respecting United Nations and Peacekeeping.* Ottawa: Queen's Printer, 1970.

Canada. House of Commons. Standing Committee on External Affairs and National Defence. *Tenth Report to the House on Maritime Forces.* 12 February 1970.

Canada. House of Commons. Standing Committee on External Affairs and National Defence. *Seventh Report to the House on Armed Forces Reserves, "Action for Reserves."* 16 December 1981.

Canada. House of Commons. Standing Committee on External Affairs and National Defence. *Fourth Report: Canada–U.S. Defence Cooperation and the 1986 Renewal of the NORAD Agreement.* 14 February 1986.

Canada. Senate. Special Committee on National Defence. *Canada's Territorial Air Defence.* Ottawa: Supply and Services Canada, January 1985.

Canada. Senate. Special Committee on National Defence. *Military Air Transport.* Ottawa: Supply and Services Canada, February 1986.

Canada. Senate. Standing Committee on Foreign Affairs. Subcommittee on National Defence. *Manpower in Canada's Armed Forces.* Ottawa: Supply and Services Canada, January 1982.

Canada. Senate. Standing Committee on Foreign Affairs. Subcommittee on National Defence. *Canada's Maritime Defence.* Ottawa: Supply and Services Canada, May 1983.

Canada. Special Joint Committee of the Senate and House of Commons on Canada's International Relations. *Independence and Internationalism.* Ottawa: Supply and Services Canada, 1986.

New Democratic Party of Canada. *Canadian Sovereignty, Security and Defence: A New Democratic Response to the Defence White Paper.* Ottawa, July 1987.

New Democratic Party of Canada. International Affairs Committee. *Canada's Stake in Common Security.* Ottawa, 16 April 1988.

Weinberger, Caspar W. *Report on Allied Contributions to the Common Defense.* Washington, D.C.: Report to United States Congress by the Secretary of Defense, April 1987.

INDEX